TipTop

Teacher's Book 4

Shelagh Rixon

PHOENIX
ELT

incorporating
PRENTICE HALL MACMILLAN

New York   London   Toronto   Sydney   Tokyo   Singapore

Published 1996 by
Phoenix ELT
Campus 400, Spring Way
Maylands Avenue, Hemel Hempstead
Hertfordshire, HP2 7EZ
A division of Prentice Hall International

First Published 1993 by Macmillan Publishers Limited

Music on cassette by Richard Vranch
Produced by AMR

Printed in Hong Kong

A catalogue record for this book is available from the British Library

ISBN 0-13-406042-3

6   5   4   3

1999   98   97   96

CONTENTS

1 THE APPROACH

Tiptop 4 is a continuation of the series of books that is being used in many countries. This level is aimed at children in the 10/11/12 year old age-band (according to the age at which they started English).

It maintains its concern with integrating English with other school subjects and with real-life topics shown in *Tiptop* Levels 1 to 3, and this concern is perhaps more developed at this stage. It is intended for three sorts of situations:

A State schools in which English is 'a subject' and there are opportunities to link English lessons with work done in other parts of the school timetable. *Tiptop 4* offers opportunities for teachers to develop work, through English, in science, history, literature, art, music, maths and social and ethical studies if they wish to. If they do not have such needs or opportunities, it is hoped that the students will still enjoy the rich informational and imaginative content of the lessons.

B Private language schools, when the young students are already studying English in their regular school. Here it may offer a different approach to that of the regular school, and hopefully will supplement and enrich the work the students are already doing in the 'parallel' system.

C Private language schools in those (rare) countries in which English is not part of the regular school curriculum for 10 and 11 year-olds. Here, I hope that its broadly educational approach will still be of some benefit and interest.

In all three situations, I hope that my main aim – to show young learners that English is a 'living' language which they can use now or in the near future to satisfy their curiosity about other countries and other people – will be achieved. The main story is based in Britain, and the reason for this is that in many countries culture and language teaching are seen as two sides of a coin. By setting the main story in Britain, I have tried to offer interesting information about **one** of the places in which English is used, while keeping an international perspective. There is information about many other countries too (see the section on page 9 on **Cultural Information**).

The 10 to 12 age group

In many countries, the age of 10 or 11 marks a 'break' – a transition from one type of school to another, and often a change from a more experiential form of learning to a more formal one.

In other places, schooling is continuous up to the age of about 14 or 15, but there is still often a transition to the more formal modes of learning at the age of 10 or 11.

I have tried to cater for the two types of situation in the following ways:

1.1 A NEW SCHOOL OR A NEW CLASS
Where the school is new, the class companions and the teacher will be new. I have started the book with some 'getting to know you' activities in Unit 1, to help everyone settle down in the new situation. Perhaps the *Tiptop* series itself will be new to some students. I have kept most of the main characters from the previous levels, for the benefit of 'old' users, but have taken care to 'fill in' the background of each character at the beginning of the book, so that every student knows the context.
If students have been using another coursebook before this one, I, and you, the teacher, cannot control or predict what they already 'know'. *Tiptop* has always been rather ambitious in its hopes for children's achievements, and I have had reports that say my ambitions were on the whole achieved, sometimes to the teacher's surprise. However, language items covered in the first three levels are very extensively recycled in Level 4 – there are relatively few new structures. The emphasis is on broadening and extending **use** of that language in many different contexts, and on strengthening language **skills.** That, coupled with the fact that Units 1 and 2 are a sort of 'revision' section of language items that could reasonably be expected to be familiar, will perhaps help newcomers to the book to orientate themselves, and 'catch up', if necessary.

1.2 THE INTRODUCTION OF MORE FORMAL LEARNING **ALONGSIDE** 'LEARNING BY DOING'
I have tried to cater for the need for the more formal approach to learning that is often demanded at this stage, but without sacrificing my major principle: that this should not mean depriving learners of other 'routes to success'. Even many adult language learners do better with large input and experience of the language, and many chances to practise and experiment, and they do not readily take to formal explanations of rules and their application. This applies even more so to children of 10 to 12, some of whom may reach the age of abstract thought and ability to deal with rules and terminology much later than some of their companions. I have tried to make the transition to this more formal way of operating gentle, and I have not given up the other sorts of activity that rely on experience and experiment. See the section on **Grammar teaching**, page 5, for more details.

2 ACTIVITY AND EXERCISE TYPES

Tiptop 4 contains many of the activity types that will be familiar to users of the first three levels. I have kept the activity headings constant and in the same style as for the first three books, since these seemed to be useful 'signals' to students and teachers about what was supposed to happen next.

Here are some of the familiar headings:

READ AND FIND.   SAY A RHYME.
LISTEN AND FIND.   LISTEN AND REPEAT.
LOOK AND FIND.   SPEAK.
SING A SONG.   THINK AND ANSWER.

There are, however, many new activities. I have tried to introduce these gradually so that students do not suffer confusion about what to do. Many of these activities are about the **processes** of making a first attempt, helping each other in pairs or groups, and trying and trying again to produce their best efforts. This applies especially to writing, since writing – both guided and free writing – is one of the major objectives of the book. For detailed information about **skills-based** activities, see pages 10 and 11. The Lesson-by-Lesson Teaching Notes (pages 14 to 133) will be very explicit to help new teachers to see exactly what is intended, and whenever a new activity type is introduced in the book, it will be very carefully explained.

Naturally, I intend the activity headings and Lesson-by-Lesson Teacher's Notes to be a guide and a support, not a strait-jacket. Teachers in different situations may want to develop some activities more, to de-emphasise others, and to insert activities or even whole lessons of their own. The role of a Teacher's Book is to make clear the author's basic intentions for the use of the Student's Book, to provide any information a teacher might need, and to leave the rest to the teacher's own imagination and interests.

For example, I have received many letters from teachers saying things like: *I developed Topic X (e.g. rainforests and the environment) much more than you did in the book.* (This topic was in Level 3) or *I made a memory card game to help my students remember Past and Present forms of verbs.* (This was suggested in both Levels 2 and 3, but this teacher thought of it earlier.) My answer has always been, *Great. That's exactly what I had hoped.* A textbook should provide a framework, interesting topics and a usable language syllabus, but it should also provide plenty of 'openings' for teachers to follow the particular interests or needs of a class, and to use their own professional expertise, to add or adapt or re-focus.

3 LANGUAGE CONTENT

3.1 Grammar teaching

In the first two levels of *Tiptop*, I tried to teach mostly by example and analogy, since I felt that this was more appropriate to very young learners. Only in some cases did I encourage overt discussion of the forms of the language itself. In Levels 2 and 3 (mostly the Workbooks), I started to give a few 'rules' and to use simple grammatical terms such as **singular** and **plural**, **verb** and **adjective** and **Past** and **Present Perfect tenses**. This was to help focus on aspects of English that do need conscious attention by the learner – I see this sort of *metalanguage* as a useful 'short cut' to clear up doubt, once students have reached a stage in which abstract reasoning is within their capacity, or is developing. At Level 4, I had two considerations in mind:

A My belief is that at this stage, many students are more equipped mentally to 'talk about' language, rather than just use it and generalise (rightly or wrongly) from patterns they have internalised.

B The fact that, at this stage, whether or not all students are ready for it, the educational system in many countries demands that they start 'talking about' language, and using terms such as **verb, noun, adjective** in discussion of how language works (including their native language). For this reason, I have introduced such grammar terms, and some simple rules or 'recipes' for use both in the Student's Book, and more extensively in the Workbook. I believe that this is actively helpful to some students. Other students will still learn best by unconscious analogy and generalisation from many examples, so I have tried to provide adequate input and examples of this type, and the continued use of 'substitution tables' in the text of both the Student's Book and Workbook is an attempt to cater for these needs. Please analyse your students and do not impose a particular learning mode.

The educational system in your country may say that an 'educated' person must be able to 'talk about language rules' as well as 'use' a language. I do not disagree, but this is perhaps mostly for the 'high flyers'. I would be happy if every student were able to 'use' the language with some confidence, and this certainly needs experience of it in use, experimentation and encouragement to try to be 'fluent' as well as 'accurate', even if fluency means a few grammatical slips. I hope that *Tiptop 4* provides enough input and information of both types to feed and help all types of learner.

Overt GRAMMAR TERMS such as **Past tense, noun, adjective, pronoun, adverb,** are introduced in the Student's Book, some with helpful colour coding to help students identify them in exercises:

NOUNS are in red. ADJECTIVES are in green.
VERBS are in blue.

3.2 Structures

See the Grammar Summary (page 135) and the Lesson-by-Lesson Notes for detailed information about new and recycled language. Much of the work of *Tiptop 4* is concerned with reactivating and recycling structures that have already been met by Level 3, and on making 'knowledge about' grammar rules more overt than in Levels 1 to 3.

Some major grammar foci are as follows:

Comparison of adjectives – with *-er* and *-est* and with *more* and *most* (introduced and heavily practised in Levels 2 and 3, but consolidated here).

Adverbs (first introduced in Level 3 and extended here).

Relative clauses: *Find someone who ... A vet is someone who looks after sick animals. A book that/which I like ... The picture/person I like most is ...*

The use of *will* for 'neutral' FUTURE REFERENCE: *Today is Monday, so tomorrow will be Tuesday*, and in PROMISES: *I will come to visit you. That's a promise!* The contractions *'ll* and *won't* and the contexts in which they can be used.

Uses of other means of FUTURE REFERENCE (introduced in Level 3, and consolidated here):

I'm visiting Mexico next year (definite plans)
I'm going to be sick (intention or urgent warning)

The use of *that* in simple indirect speech: *I think that he is very rude.* This is alternated with the omitted *that: I think he is very rude*, and students are given wide experience of both forms, which are equally frequent in most discourse.

Passive sentences in Present and Past, building on the Past Passive learned as a 'formula' but not analysed in Level 3 in the Inventions lessons: *The bicycle was invented in 1815.* An additional focal point at this level is *by: ... The dogs are examined **by** a vet.*

The Second Conditional: *If I was in a spaceship, I would be very excited/frightened.* **First Conditional:** *if* sentences have been used since Level 1, so the concepts behind *if* should be well understood. A policy decision was to use the simpler (and more common in everyday use) *if I was ...* rather than the very formal and academic *if I were ...* form, which 'breaks' the general rule of, *put the 'if' verb into the Simple Past.*

(**The Third Conditional** will be covered in Levels 5 and 6.)

Should in advice and moral reasoning: *Scientists shouldn't be superstitious; I think (that) you should tell your friend about the problem.*

Possessive adjectives and pronouns recycled from Levels 1 to 3.

Present Perfect as a means of talking about the recent past: *I've finished* and about life experiences, *I've never had a dream about flying* (but with no overt treatment of the *for* and *since* structures). Overt treatment of this will be reserved for Levels 5 and 6.

3.3 Vocabulary

The vocabulary list for this book is long, but if you compare it with the Consolidated Vocabulary List for the first three levels (Teacher's Book 3) you will see that it is relatively unexpanded, and that many 'new' words are related to words already learned. I have always believed in the virtue of presenting a wide vocabulary to students, on the following bases:

3.3.1 CORE VOCABULARY
There is a 'core' vocabulary that I would hope every student (of whatever ability or stage of development) will be able to use with confidence, both receptively (for understanding when reading or listening) and productively (for speech or writing). I have been careful to recycle such words very often throughout the course, so that constant practice is 'built in' to the material presented in the books. Such words concern, e.g. self, family, animals, classroom and home furniture, rooms, clothes, school subjects, colours, numbers, places, times, months and days and useful adjectives.

3.3.2 SPECIAL INTEREST VOCABULARY
There are words which are going to appeal to particular students according to their interests. I hope that there will be many of these words for most students, but they will differ from student to student, and you may find them used in their personal writing or speech. If other students are puzzled when they hear them, ask the students in question to explain or even to translate so as not to block communication. (Animal fans will retain animal names far beyond the cat, dog, horse, etc. core 'list', others may not.)

You may also decide, yourself, to focus on some of these 'special interest' words because they are very relevant to a particular emphasis you want to give to your teaching. For example, if you want to look at literature, you will want to emphasise the words: *character, story, poem, poet, writer, creative, play, acting, actor, rhyme, publish*, etc. All these words are in Level 4, but you may wish to bring them together to create a lesson of your own. If students are fascinated by recycling and the environment, you can bring together the 'rubbish and pollution' words in the book and create a lesson supplementary to Unit 5, Lesson 5, which provides a good starting point for project work. If they are less fascinated by this subject, just teach the lesson, which brings together the 'core' words that every student at this stage might be expected to know.

3.3.3 'PERIPHERAL' WORDS JUST USED ONCE OR TWICE

I have, throughout the course, introduced 'peripheral' words, which may appear in only one or two lessons. Often they are there as a challenge for the students to work out their meaning from the context as a way of developing **guessing skills**. If some students remember and use them, all the better, but I hope that all students will continue to use **guessing from context** as a strategy, even if they don't later remember or use the word that was the focus of the activity. A very early example, from Level 1, was *absurd* in the silly song about animals. It rhymed with *bird* and it is similar to words in many languages with Latin roots related to some words in English. It was a 'fun' word, but I did not expect all learners to relate to it and use it for evermore. Some will, some won't. In Level 4, *fossil* is a focal word, but *ammonite* (a type of fossil) is not, except for those students who know all about fossils and thus enjoy the word. The same is true of *jet* (not the aeroplane but a type of black fossil wood from which jewellery is made in Whitby – we get the simile *as black as jet*, and the phrase *jet-black* from it).

3.3.4 PERIPHERAL WORDS FROM PREVIOUS LEVELS WHICH ARE REACTIVATED

Level 4 'reactivates' and makes focal many words from previous levels that were 'peripheral' or 'ephemeral' at those stages, e.g. *claw* is prominent in the Level 4 dinosaur work, but it was not essential in Level 3, where it was met in the Workbook. *Skeleton* appeared in Level 2 when Mark won a skeleton of a cobra as a prize in the museum competition. It was 'peripheral' then, but becomes focal in Level 4. In turn, some new words in Level 4 are 'peripheral' or 'ephemeral' at this stage but they will be reactivated in Levels 5 and 6.

3.3.5 STRATEGIES FOR LEARNING VOCABULARY

Level 3 encouraged the creation of Word Books, into which students put words in arrangements that helped them personally – alphabetically, grammatically, in 'families' or subjects, e.g. Animals. I hope that users of Level 3 followed the advice to use this idea. In Level 4, the advice is repeated, in a more sophisticated way, and guidance is given in both Student's and Workbook. This creation of personal study-aids is a very important factor in 'Learning how to learn', and will play an important part in your students' development towards being independent learners. They will be even more appreciative of the input you provide, because they know how to make the best use of it.

4 THEMES AND STORYLINE OF *TIPTOP 4*

4.1 Themes

The major organising principle of all the *Tiptop* series is the language. I have always believed that starting from language objectives and then finding interesting ways of illustrating them is the most accessible approach for most teachers and students. In this way, similar structures are grouped together and the learning load is made lighter. However, students at Level 4 stage are familiar with a lot of English, both lexically and structurally speaking, and there is scope to be as imaginative and ambitious as possible in **how** that language is put to use. A broadly thematic approach seemed appropriate at this level. Each unit has a major theme and within that, topics related to the theme are explored in the individual lessons. The topic of each lesson should be clear from the lesson titles in the Student's Book.

The overall **unit** themes are not stated in the Student's Book, or the Contents Page. This was mainly to keep the layout of the book clear and simple from the student's point of view. The themes are listed below and you can use this information in two ways:

A Tell the students the theme at the beginning of the unit. It is often connected with work on the **Young Ideas** magazine; see page 8 for more information on this.

B Do not reveal the theme until the students are near the end of the unit, and then ask them if they can see any themes for themselves. They may guess the theme stated here, or they may find other valid connections between the lessons, in which case accept them and praise their efforts.

Units and themes

1 Back to school. New friends/old friends. Getting to know new people in the class.
2 Setting up ideas for a magazine (the **Young Ideas** ones in the story, and the ideas for the students' own class magazine)
3 Crazes and fashions/likes and dislikes
4 Places
5 Collections and displays
6 Friendship
7 Beliefs and superstitions
8 Cooperation/helping each other
9 Problems and solutions
10 Ambitions (including jobs)

Many topics are recycled and treated in different ways within this general framework. Dinosaurs, monsters, animals, art, famous people, new technology and inventions, places to go, will be found in several different places in the book.

4.2 Storyline and characters

The overall dramatic framework of *Tiptop 4* is the creation of a new magazine by the characters already familiar from Level 3. After the success of the 'Children for Charity' book project of Level 3, Mrs Wine, the Director of the 'World Help' charity, decides to publish a regular magazine, and asks

Mark, Angela, their schoolfriends and teachers to help once more. Their discussions of good features to include and their attempts to make the magazine as attractive and interesting as possible form the framework of much of the book. There is a small amount of plot-development. Mark makes a new friend (Paul from Whitby) through his contacts with him about Paul's articles and photos for the magazine. They write to each other and phone each other throughout the book, and in the next to last lesson, Mark finally manages to visit his new friend and meet him face to face.

Regretfully, Count Horror and Boris the Cat, are absent from the book. (For 'fans' there are a few mentions of the fact that they are away on another World Tour.) The reason is that, though they have proved very popular with children so far, at this age it was time to drop the pure fantasy characters and adopt a more 'grown up' storyline.

In addition to the 'human' characters already familiar from Level 3, some other human characters come in as contributors to the magazine. Paul from Whitby and Susan from Coventry are the main British characters, but children from other countries regularly send in ideas and articles. Pilar from Spain, Giorgio from Italy, Emilia from Bulgaria, and Zoltan from Hungary are but a few.

4.3 The class magazine

It is strongly advised that you and your class take up the suggestion to make your own class magazine, using **Young Ideas** as a starting point for thought and imagination. The magazine need not be elaborate, and it need not come out every month – once a term or even once a school year might be enough. It need not even be duplicated and distributed, though this would be ideal. Parents and students alike would feel very satisfied to see such a product of your work. If you have not got the facilities to produce something that *looks* like a magazine, consider having a 'notice-board' magazine – a display on a classroom or corridor wall – all showing contributions from all the students. Many compromises like this are possible.

The important thing – as well as a satisfying product – is the processes that the students go through. Even with a simple notice-board magazine they will still have to agree on topics, find or make visual illustrations, pay attention to the layout – the 'look' as well as the content of what they contribute. They will thus be getting extra practice in the sorts of editing and correcting skills that are presented in *Tiptop 4*, as part of **writing skills** (see page 11), as well as in the sorts of decisions that Jim and Mrs Wine make about making the items look attractive and clear in the published **Young Ideas** magazine. This extra practice will have more meaning to your students since it will concern their own creative efforts.

You may, at first, decide to use some of the regular **Young Ideas** features as a model. The **'You tell us'** feature with its short quotes from children giving their opinions on different subjects is very suitable, for example. Later, the students may wish to create their own types of feature, more and different puzzles, for example, or perhaps a Jokes Section, and to choose their own topics for longer articles. It is important for everyone to have a part to play – do not let the 'best' students dominate. Some students, whose English is less good, may have excellent ideas for things that they really want to contribute. Their first efforts may be full of mistakes (so may those of the 'best' students, too!) but that should be seen as an opportunity to seek and give help. Do not correct everything yourself (though you may have the final editorial/checking role). See if students can help each other. Give credit for 'editing' work so that advanced students who help weaker ones feel that their skill and cooperation is being recognised and that they are not being exploited. Every student should have a role and the work done should be listed with names on the inside page of a duplicated magazine, or on an 'honours' panel on a wall display. Here are some possible roles and the skills they may reflect:

Editor (probably better if this is you, the teacher, so that you have the chance to have the final word on disputes, conflicts of interest, and on what is or isn't 'correct')

Special reporters (any students who contribute a section or an article)

Art editors (students who may be good at drawing, and can help with illustrations for someone else's article)

Photo editor and **photographers** (students who find good photos in magazines or take their own photos)

Layout editor (a good role for students with a 'good eye' for arrangement on a page or on a noticeboard. Weaker students who can copy or design decorative headings or labels for a board, should be given this simpler task, yet dignified title!)

Then special credit for organising special features:

e.g. **Jokes Page edited by...**

If you are lucky enough to have access to word processors or typewriters and **even** can persuade someone to type some of the articles for a duplicated magazine, don't forget to give him or her a credit and special thanks, e.g. *Special thanks to Mark's mother, Mrs Green, for her help with typing and layout.*

Finding and agreeing on a good title for your magazine is another important part of the process. In Unit 2, Lesson 2, Mark organised a 'vote' which ended up with the choice of **Young Ideas** as the title of the magazine. If your class really cannot think of a better idea, this title would do for your magazine, too, but it would be much better to organise your own survey of ideas and a vote for a good title that is different.

Emphasise the editing and correcting processes which are introduced gradually in *Tiptop 4* when you arrive at the relevant parts of the book. Re-experiencing them (once they have been practised in the **Young Ideas** context) with their **own** material will make things so much more immediate to your students. They will then see the point that in the real world people do take a pride in producing things which are as good and as pleasurable to other people as possible, and that things don't often come out perfectly at the first try – even if they are native speakers of the language. Mistakes at the first try are not a disaster, it just means that they must think again, seek help where necessary, and above all **experiment.** This is a far cry from the less optimistic attitude to 'homework' and 'exercises' that unfortunately many schoolchildren develop. A piece of writing can too often be seen as a 'test' and a 'chore', to be done once only so that some stern judge can count the mistakes and condemn them! The dramatic framework of a magazine which has editors, not stern 'correctors', is an attempt to break this attitude, and to encourage the idea of 'first drafts', then improvements after discussion. (See the section on **Writing Skills**, page 11, for more details.)

For school systems where Information Technology is part of the curriculum, perhaps the magazine idea offers chances for cooperation with the teachers of this subject. Students who are learning to use word processors or computers could practise their new skills in helping to produce the class magazine in print-out form. This is a common practice in British Primary schools (up to age 10) and Secondary schools, where Information Technology is part of the new National Curriculum. Unit 8, Lessons 1 and 2, look at Information Technology in British schools, and the situation there, in a semi-humorous way. (The teachers are scared and not very confident, but the students are experts, and they teach the teachers!) If this reflects your situation, build these lessons in across your curriculum. If your school system does not include Information Technology, treat these lessons simply as Cultural Information about Britain, and do not feel that you need to develop them more.

5 CULTURAL INFORMATION

Many school systems demand that there is deliberate attention to the Culture or Civilisation behind the language being taught. Throughout the *Tiptop* series, I have tried to provide Culture Teaching which is at the students' level and which perhaps reflects or adds to their own experience as *children* in an international community, rather than the sorts of things that are more appropriate for adult learners.

It's OK, perhaps for adults, to learn all the details of the British Constitution, but I would not think that this would excite 10 to 12 year olds, though recognising the shape of the Parliament building and knowing the name of the clock 'Big Ben', and knowing who is our current Prime Minister, might be legitimate goals at this stage.

Great emphasis in *Tiptop 4* has been placed on necessary and fundamental **facts,** e.g. what the map of Britain looks like, where some important places are, the four different countries that make up the United Kingdom, the many languages that are used in Britain, typical, personal names for people and for animals, what children learn at school, what people eat in Britain.

However, equal emphasis has been placed on what I call **International child culture,** that is things that children all over the world may have in common (whether they know it or not). Many international games – such as 'noughts and crosses' (Level 3) and 'paper, scissors, stone' (Level 2) – have been used. Stories which are known in many countries were used (particularly Level 2). Popular subjects, such as dinosaurs, were used throughout the first three levels and are much developed in Level 4. Jokes which may be translatable – or not – were used in Level 3 to reflect British children's extreme love of word-play, and there are some more very British jokes in Level 4.

These strands are continued in Level 4. The 'Facts about Britain' items are there – geography, food, travel, famous places, famous people, but I have tried to get off the 'beaten track' of lessons about very well-known places such as Oxford or Cambridge, or London, and have looked at some more unusual but still interesting places – Whitby with its connections with Dracula and fossils and jewellery and fishing, Coventry as an industrial town with an important place in the history of bicycle and car manufacture (as well as the famous Lady Godiva legend). London is there, but with emphasis on the Battersea Dogs' Home and the Natural History Museum. (Britain is a famously caring culture as regards animals, but there are also many people who are cruel or neglectful to their animal friends.)

Teachers who wish to supplement these lessons with information about more 'conventional' places, should of course do so. My feeling is that most teachers have this sort of information at their fingertips and it does not need me to supply input. I hope you will appreciate my more unusual choices as a source of fresh ideas about Britain.

I have tried to introduce some literary ideas in Level 4 – not often 'high literature', but the sort of books and stories that are internationally known (*Dracula* and *Frankenstein, Treasure Island, The Lost World, Sherlock Holmes*) and often the subjects of film or TV interpretations. I am also interested in where creative people get their ideas from, and it so happens that both Bram Stoker and Mary Shelley dreamed the first 'draft' of their horror stories. Unit 7, which also concerns beliefs and superstitions, looks at the mystery of creativity, and how dreams helped these creators. The influence of places is also important – Bram Stoker was so impressed by the Gothic magnificence of Whitby Abbey, that this inspired him to start the story of *Dracula*. Lord Byron (present when Mary Shelley got the idea for *Frankenstein*) is mentioned as a famous poet, but in the humorous 'pets' context with the famous story of his keeping a bear as a pet when he was at Cambridge University. I feel that this sort of anecdotal and 'familiar' introduction to famous literary figures will perhaps provide a good and motivating background knowledge for those students who will later go on to study 'literature' seriously at school. It is important for students to see creative people as human beings, who had starting points for their creativity, and not just as abstract figures on a pedestal.

Interest in the media is also important. *Dracula* and *Frankenstein*'s monster are members of a family of famous horror film monsters, known and liked by most children. *Godzilla*, the dinosaur film monster, links with the more serious sections of the books about 'real' dinosaurs.

Whitby is a focus because it is a small town, unusual in most language textbooks, but it has many cultural connections – as an important place in the history of Religion (The Synod of Whitby) as a famous holiday resort (excellent fish and chips!), as the inspiration for Bram Stoker's *Dracula*, as a place full of fossils which is world-famous amongst scientists, as a place where a particular form of jewellery was (and is) made – black jet jewellery is collected all over the world. It was also the home of a very famous photographer very important in the history of photography worldwide – Frank Meadow Sutcliffe. His photos – of up to a century old – are beautiful in their own right, show why Whitby is such an evocative place, and allow young enthusiasts for photography to find out more about the history of this art-form. This is another area where you might create your own lesson, bringing together all the 'photography' vocabulary that Levels 1 to 4 have included: e.g. *develop, negative, print, album, photo, photographer, camera, film*. Many cities and towns have regular photography exhibitions, and the British Council has a travelling exhibition of Sutcliffe's photos which you may find in your town one day.

The dramatic device of the **Young Ideas** magazine also allows teachers to look with students at children's magazines, newspapers and comics, nationally or internationally. My main inspiration for this idea was the *Young Telegraph,* a Saturday Supplement to the British *Daily Telegraph* newspaper. The supplement is included free with the Saturday

newspaper in most countries where the *Daily Telegraph* is sold. It's probably expensive, if you buy it in your country, but it's worth buying just one copy to keep you up to date with *child culture* internationally. You can also join the Y.T.Club for about £6 sterling and get a fabulous folder of jokes, secret codes, puzzles, a diary and a dictionary, for your classroom. I joined it, and have had much inspiration for keeping in touch with what appeals to children. The address to write to is:
Young Telegraph Club,
PO Box 20,
Wetherby,
Yorkshire LS23 7EB

Tiptop 4 contains a 'cast of characters' of general historic and international interest. This cast includes places and buildings as well as people – the Taj Mahal, the Great Wall of China, the Eiffel Tower, Julius Caesar, Helen Sharman – the first British astronaut, Mr Havel from the Czech Republic, Luciano Pavarotti, the great Italian tenor – the Barcelona architect, Gaudi.

Beyond this, there is an attempt to look at general contemporary *child culture*. Dinosaurs are popular, so are baseball caps and trainer shoes in many countries. Children collect things and have 'crazes'. In the body of the Student's Book, I have been careful not to emphasise very expensive 'crazes' such as Nintendo or Sega computer games that require a high parental income to support, but the teacher has the freedom to look at crazes that are relevant to the particular class. Find out what is 'in' or 'out' and get your students to tell you about it.

The theme of International Contacts through penfriend schemes, is continued from Level 3. The information about penfriend agencies given in Teacher's Book 3, is repeated in this Teacher's Book on page 134. Setting up a penfriend scheme in your school could bring many benefits, as could the more ambitious idea of exchanging 'magazine items' or sending **'You tell us'** questionnaires to classes in schools in another country via computer-mail. The 'other' country need not be one in which English is the native language. English could serve as a 'lingua franca' between students for whom it is a second or foreign language – just as it does in the adult world.

6 SKILLS DEVELOPMENT

6.1 Reading

The passages to read in *Tiptop 4* are longer and more complex than those in the previous levels. Most passages have pre-reading questions, which aim to make students **predict** or guess possible content, or to look quickly at the passage to find specially important information. This will help them to cope better with new language items and to build up a 'mental framework' which will make the comprehension of the passage much more accessible to them.

Most passages also have **detailed reading** questions, to be done later, during a second or third careful and slower reading of the passage, which will make them go back and look for particular information.

Follow the order of activities suggested, but if you wish to add new **pre-reading** or **detailed reading** questions, please do.

Most passages contain carefully built-in **focal grammar points**. Overt attention is drawn to these structures in the Workbook. If you wish to do more work on the structures in a particular passage, please do so, but do it **after** a satisfactory level of comprehension has been reached. All students, young or older, learn grammar better if they have first grasped the **meaning** of a piece of new language. And please do not regard the passages as mere **containers** or **exemplifications** of new grammar or vocabulary. They were also written to communicate new ideas and new information, which I hope the students will be interested in and enjoy.

6.2 Listening

Most listening passages have a **prediction** or **expectation** phase, built into the accompanying exercises, to be done before the students hear the cassette. (This is similar to the pre-reading questions for the reading passages.) This will help students to get an idea of what sort of information they have to find before they listen. This strategy of prediction is vital to a better understanding the first time of listening. Repeat and replay the cassettes as often as necessary. Many of the words of the tapescript are given in the Workbook activities, so look to see what support is given in the Workbook. The emphasis in all listening activities in the Student's Book is on *finding information*, rather than collecting structures and words. Workbook activities often concentrate more on the exact words, and encourage students to listen again to help them, so many listening-linked Workbook activities should be carried out in class. The tapescript will be found on pages 144 to 164 and can be used by teachers for reference to the exact words used.

6.3 Speaking

Most speaking activities have a 'Language model table' to help all students to say **something,** but there is scope for free-er speech too. Often, there is scope (in the Student's Book or Workbook) for a Class Survey, which will involve speaking. Most Class Surveys can be carried out in two different ways, and each will suit different types of teaching situation.

The simplest is a question from the teacher, then 'Hands up' and a count of responses. This allows the teacher to remain in full control of the whole class, (e.g. for Unit 7, Lesson 1.) *How many people were born under the sign of Aries? Hands up!* Then ask each student to say his or her exact date of birth, so that each person says something.

If your students are trained to work in groups or to move around the class without disruption, you could do the survey in a more interesting and interactive way. Give out a list of all the students in the class, and then let them move around and ask each other when they were born and what sign they were born under, and collect their own numbers for each sign.

In both cases, there is an **outcome** – a chart which shows how many people were born under each sign (and this chart, of course, links with maths work – the production of bar charts).

6.4 Writing

6.4.1 PROCESS OR PRODUCT?

Writing something that is **correct** in its language, and also **well organised** in what is said, is not easy, even for native speakers of any language. This should be recognised, particularly by teachers of young learners of English as a Foreign or a Second Language. Do not expect your learners to be able to do easily what native speakers of the same age still cannot do! I have always felt strongly about this, and my feelings were reinforced by a brilliant chapter by a Polish teacher in the book mentioned below.

Machura L, in Kennedy and Jarvis (Eds) *Ideas and issues in Primary ELT;* 'British School English and Foreign Learners' English – two different worlds?

If you cannot find this book, I summarise what she said:

Her Polish speaking daughter (at the time learning in a British State School) was actually better (because of the careful training her English teacher-mother had given her) at many aspects of English **spelling** and **grammar** than many British children of the same age. All the British children needed help with this. Her daughter needed some help, too, of course, but she was in many ways better than native speaker children of the same age.

This reinforced my idea that teachers should think of training **writing skills** in two ways:

Product
Yes, we want a good **product** (something that makes sense, is well organised, *and* has the minimum of grammatical, vocabulary, spelling and punctuation errors).

Process
But, we should allow time for this **product** to be achieved. This is done by a good **process** before their work is considered to be *final*. The first attempt is likely to have many things wrong with it. This is not the student's fault. They are learners, not experts, so they need help. Give them time to think. Let their friends help them. Look at the interim work yourself, as an *editor*, not a *judge*. Give them ideas about improvements.

This is all the **process** of making their writing better. I can say, as a University teacher, that even highly educated, native-speaker adults benefit from this 'step-by-step' helping **process** approach. Of course, the native-speakers' language is mostly correct, but their organisation and focusing of information can often be improved. Discussion, and sympathetic suggestions, during the **process,** help them to achieve better results.

Try to do the same when you see something less than perfect from your young learners.

6.4.2 WRITING ACTIVITIES IN *TIPTOP* 4

In *Tiptop 4*, many writing activities have a **model** to help students to do their best for a first 'try', so that we can hope for something that is nearly or completely correct. But there are also many **check with a friend** activities that allow students to change their responses if a friend or teacher finds a mistake. Try to encourage the attitude that a **bad** 'first try' can always be improved, and that students can help one another to do better. You can also help in the first stages, as well as being the final 'judge' and 'helper', but please try to act as an 'editor' rather than as a 'stern judge' and try to help every student to produce the best work that he or she can, before you 'mark' it. The philosophy of *Tiptop 4* is that writing well is difficult, even for native speakers, and that *everyone* needs suggestions and help.

7 WORKBOOK

Some countries already use the Workbooks for *Tiptop* Levels 1 to 3 extensively, but some countries do not use them at all. However, the Lesson-by-Lesson Notes which follow also include ideas about Workbook use (in class or for homework) to assist teachers with information about the options for using it for support and further work. I think that, on the whole, the use of the Level 4 Workbook enriches and deepens students' work greatly, in class or at home. It contains much of the extra Cultural Information that many countries wish for, and most of the overt treatment of grammar items, as well as the more 'puzzle-type' and 'fun-type' activities which I felt to be a little less essential (though still very desirable) for 'mainstream' work in many classes, at this age of learning. It is also quite possible to use *Tiptop 4* **without** the Workbook. It has been deliberately designed so as *not* to be indispensable to respect the economic conditions of some students.

8 FURTHER INFORMATION

Useful books to read

Brumfit et al (Eds) Teaching *English to Children from Practice to Principle*, Nelson/Collins, 1981

Halliwell, S. *Teaching English in the Primary Classroom*, Longman, 1992

Kennedy, C. and Jarvis, J. (Eds) *Ideas and Issues in Primary ELT*, Nelson, 1991

Useful journals

The English Teaching Journal (ELTJ) published by Oxford University Press, has an increasing number of articles about Young Learners. You can find it in your local British Council office, or subscribe to it directly. The address to write to is:
Journal Subscriptions Department,
Oxford University Press,
Pinkhill House,
Southfield Road,
Eynsham,
Oxford OX8 1JJ

Jet (Junior English Teaching) is published by Mary Glasgow Publications and is dedicated entirely to ideas and issues concerning the teaching of Young Learners. You can find it in your local British Council office, or subscribe to it directly. The address to write to is:
Mary Glasgow Publications,
Avenue House,
131-133 Holland Park Avenue,
London W11 4VT

Modern English Teacher (MET) is published by Macmillan, and has many articles about Young Learners. You can find it in your local British Council office, or subscribe to it directly. The address to write to is:
Macmillan Publishers Ltd
Houndmills
BASINGSTOKE
Hants RG21 2XS

Practical English Teacher (PET) is published by Mary Glasgow Publications and has many articles about ideas and issues concerning the teaching of Young Learners. You can find it in your local British Council office, or subscribe to it directly. The address to write to is:
Mary Glasgow Publications,
Avenue House,
131-133 Holland Park Avenue,
London W11 4VT

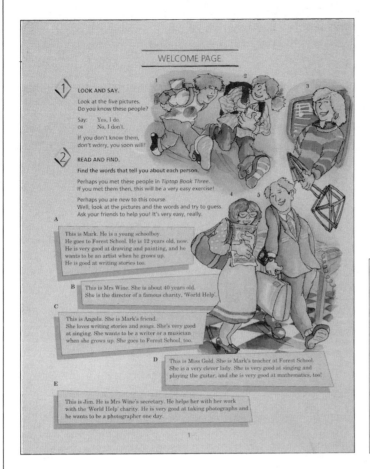

REVISION:	
KEY VOCABULARY	artist, director, musician, photographer, schoolboy, secretary, teacher, writer
KEY GRAMMAR POINTS	*Do you know ...?* *Yes, I do/No, I don't;* *He/She is ...;* *He/She is good at ....;*
SKILLS	Building up an idea of the important people in this book

The main purpose of this page is to introduce new users of *Tiptop* to the main characters and situations and to remind 'old' users of the same. The language used is designed to be well within the capacity of any student who is in his or her fourth year of learning. Encourage students to answer orally to the questions in Exercise 1, and to do the reading and matching task in Exercise 2 using the information contained in the pictures to help them. They can collect and revise the vocabulary items connected with jobs and ambitions. The focus is not, however, on the **language items** on the page so much as in the information contained on the page.

Once the students are happy that they 'know' the five main characters, the rest of the work in the book will have more context for them. If you wish, and you are working with a class of 'old' users of *Tiptop*, you can in this lesson recapitulate what happened last year, though this is covered in Unit 1, Lesson 1. Students may ask, *Where are Boris the Cat and Count Horror?* The answer is that they are away on holiday again and do not appear in this book in person. (Boris fans can see him on the cover of the book in Unit 1, Lesson 1!) However if students wish to, they can imagine the adventures of Count Horror and Boris, draw pictures and send letters from them to their human friends. We feel that it is time to 'drop' the purely fantasy characters from the teaching materials in *Tiptop*, Level Four.

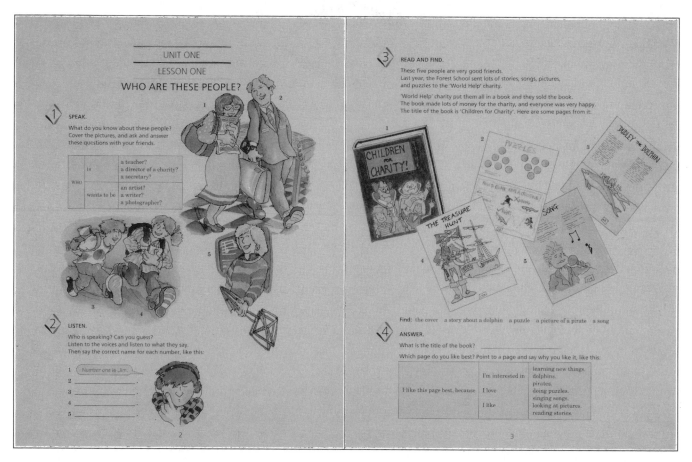

KEY VOCABULARY	(**Revised** from *Tiptop 3*) artist, charity, cover, director, page, photographer, picture, puzzle, secretary, story, teacher, title, writer
KEY GRAMMAR POINTS	(**Revised** from *Tiptop 3*) *Who* in questions: *I like ...... best because...; I'm interested in ...; I love/like ...*
SKILLS	Talking about the parts of a book cover, title, pages, subjects in a book, being aware that personal preferences will be taken seriously in this course

UNIT 1

LESSON 1   WHO ARE THESE PEOPLE?

The aim of this lesson is to establish the characters in the book and to revise a few simple structures. Even students who have not followed *Tiptop* before should already know most of the language used.

1 SPEAK.

Students try to remember (either from the Welcome Page for students new to the course, or from their memories of *Tiptop 3*) who is who. Start by saying the number of each picture, then *Who is this?* to elicit the names. Then ask the questions in the substitution box, e.g. *Who is a teacher?*, *Who wants to be a photographer?* Short answers like *Miss Gold* or *Miss Gold is* or *Jim does* are acceptable and are often the most natural. Then students can cover the pictures as per the instructions in the book, and ask each other the same questions. They can do it round the class or in pairs. Round the class is the 'safest', and best for a group of children, who do not know each other or the course very well.

2 ▭ LISTEN.

Students write the numbers 1-5 in their exercise books, then listen to the voices and the information on the cassette. They take notes opposite each number. They can write abbreviations of the names, e.g. M=Mark. Let them compare notes and see if they have the same answers. Rewind and play the cassette again, stopping it after each 'speech' to elicit answers like *Number one is Jim* or *That's Jim.*

3 READ AND FIND.

Read the paragraph to establish or recall the story for all students. The language of the paragraph is very easy and is not intended to be a comprehension challenge.
Let the students look at the five pictures and think

about them. Help any 'new' students who need it. Then talk about the pictures. For students who know *Tiptop 3*, ask questions like: *Who wrote about the dolphin? Do you remember?* (Angela). *Did you like the Treasure Hunt puzzle?* For others, ask questions from the book like: *Find a puzzle; Find the cover of the book.* Add questions of your own like: *Find a picture with a pop star in it* (answer number 5).

4 ANSWER.

Ask the question from the book: *What is the title of the book?* (Children for Charity). Then let them look again at the pictures and decide which pages they like best (only four pages, picture 1 is the cover). Each student prepares a sentence, using the substitution table, and points to it and tells the person next to him or her the 'verdict'. Then ask individuals from the whole class to tell you their answers. For this, encourage them to say first: *My page is number 2* (or the Puzzle Page), then *I like this page best because .....* .
You could count the 'votes' for each page to find the most popular one.
This might be a good moment to collect ideas informally (in English or the native language) from the students about what they like doing in general. There will be more formal activity about this in Unit 1, Lesson 5 and Unit 1, Lesson 6.

WORKBOOK

All of the Workbook activities for this lesson can be done after the Student's Book lesson, for consolidation in class or for homework. In later lessons there are opportunities to use the Workbook in a more integrated way, but at the beginning of a school year, the simple 'Student's Book then Workbook' sequence seems the most encouraging and least confusing.

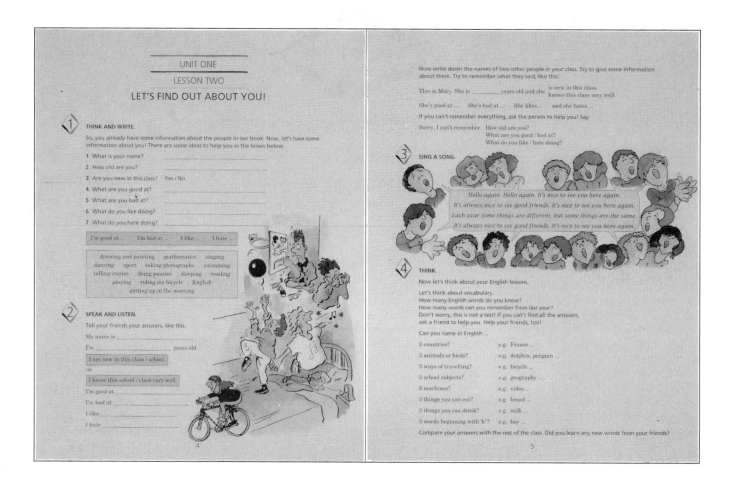

UNIT ONE

LESSON TWO

LET'S FIND OUT ABOUT YOU!

1 THINK AND WRITE.

So, you already have some information about the people in our book. Now, let's have some information about you! There are some ideas to help you in the boxes below.

1 What is your name? _____

2 How old are you? _____

3 Are you new in this class? Yes / No.

4 What are you good at? _____

5 What are you bad at? _____

6 What do you like doing? _____

7 What do you hate doing? _____

| I'm good at ... | I'm bad at ... | I like ... | I hate ... |

drawing and painting   mathematics   singing
dancing   sport   taking photographs   swimming
telling stories   doing puzzles   sleeping   reading
playing   riding my bicycle   English
getting up in the morning

2 SPEAK AND LISTEN.

Tell your friends your answers, like this:

My name is _____

I'm _____ years old.

I am new in this class / school.

or

I know this school / class very well.

I'm good at _____

I'm bad at _____

I like _____

I hate _____

4

Now write down the names of two other people in your class. Try to give some information about them. Try to remember what they said, like this:

This is Mary. She is _____ years old and she is new in this class. / knows this class very well.

She's good at ...   She's bad at ...   She likes ...   and she hates ...

If you can't remember everything, ask the person to help you! Say:

Sorry, I can't remember.   How old are you?
What are you good / bad at?
What do you like / hate doing?

3 SING A SONG.

Hello again. Hello again. It's nice to see you here again.
It's always nice to see good friends. It's nice to see you here again.
Each year some things are different, but some things are the same.
It's always nice to see good friends. It's nice to see you here again.

4 THINK.

Now let's think about your English lessons.

Let's think about vocabulary.
How many English words do you know?
How many words can you remember from last year?
Don't worry, this is not a test! If you can't find all the answers,
ask a friend to help you. Help your friends, too!

Can you name in English ...

3 countries?   e.g. France ...

3 animals or birds?   e.g. dolphin, penguin ...

3 ways of travelling?   e.g. bicycle ...

3 school subjects?   e.g. geography ...

3 machines?   e.g. video ...

3 things you can eat?   e.g. bread ...

3 things you can drink?   e.g. milk ...

3 words beginning with 'b'?   e.g. boy ...

Compare your answers with the rest of the class. Did you learn any new words from your friends?

5

KEY VOCABULARY	Vocabulary linked to activities, sports, school subjects, daily activities (**revised** from *Tiptop 1* and *2*)
KEY GRAMMAR POINTS	*Wh-* questions linked with personal information; *be + good/bad at something*
SKILLS	Grouping vocabulary items according to 'word families'; Sharing knowledge with the other pupils

LESSON 2   LET'S FIND OUT ABOUT YOU!

1 THINK AND WRITE.

These personal 'getting to know you' *Wh-* questions should be familiar to all students, whatever course they have been following. They have a double purpose. Firstly, they are an 'easy' and reassuringly familiar set of questions for children in a new class. Secondly, they will fulfil the real communicative purpose of letting a new class get to know each other. The list of activities that they are good or bad at is for revision of words from the first three levels of *Tiptop*. The exercise is for writing, to allow students to 'prepare' answers with minimum stress for the following SPEAK AND LISTEN.

2 ☷ SPEAK AND LISTEN.

Start by having some individual pupils tell their answers to Exercise 1 to the whole class under your supervision. In this way, you can help and correct any serious slips that you think might become general. Then have the students speak to each other in pairs or groups of three, exchanging the information orally (**not** looking at each other's books!) Warn them that they must listen carefully because they will be required to talk about one of the people they have been with.
Ask individual students (different ones from before) to tell the whole class about one of 'their' people. Do not worry if they forget some of the information, but encourage the person who is being described to help if appealed to with the *Sorry I can't remember...* sentence on page 5 of the book. Do not ask everybody in the class, but make sure that at least six individuals speak.

3 SING A SONG.

The song is a reprise of the 'Hello' song from *Tiptop 3*. It is there to provide a relaxing interlude after the speaking and before the quite tough THINK which follows in Exercise 4 (as well as to recycle some of the 'friends' and 'back at school' language).

4 THINK.

This activity will give you the chance to find out informally how much your class already knows (or remembers) from previous years of English. If most people find answers with ease and quickly, you should have few problems. If there is a difficulty for some students, you will need to take account of it in future teaching, and try to balance the levels in your class. It also provides a gentle introduction for the students of two very important procedures and principles in *Tiptop*: **a)** the usefulness of thinking of words in 'families' such as are suggested in the activity, and **b)** the usefulness of sharing information and knowledge with classmates. This should **not** be thought of as 'cheating', but as cooperative learning. You may have to work hard to instil this attitude into all students, but it is worth it for the greater amount of learning that it brings about and for the healthier relationships in class that it promotes.

WORKBOOK

Exercise 1, recycles the personal information language of the Student's Book and can be done in class or for homework. Exercise 2 shows how the short sentences can be built into a personal communication such as a pen-friend letter, and the questions that follow make sure that the students read Angela's letter for the information it contains. In Exercise 3, students use the letter in a different way, this time as a language model for their own attempt at a penfriend letter. It is suggested that Exercise 3 should be checked thoroughly in class, at the beginning of the next lesson if it has been set for homework. Do **not** just collect the Workbooks and 'mark' the letters. Spend time in class, talking about the letters and even allowing the pupils to look at each other's work and to suggest corrections if they find any mistakes. Forming the habit of this method of working is worth starting early, since, when the students come to edit each other's articles for the class magazine, this will be the best way to work.

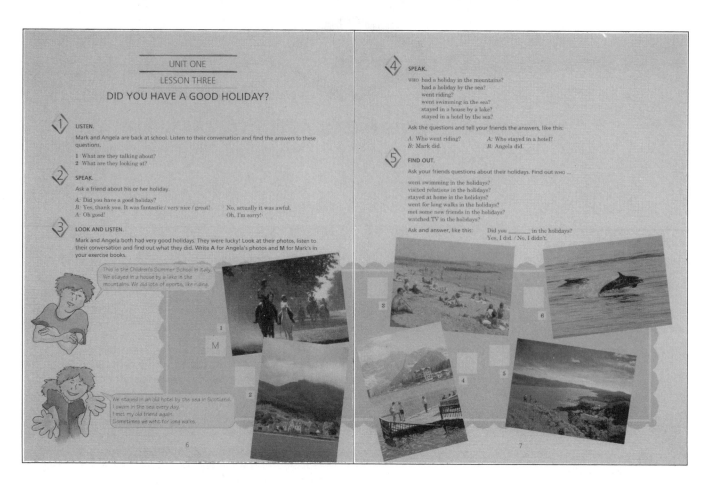

KEY VOCABULARY	(revised): awful, great, holiday, hotel, lake, mountains, nice, riding, sport, stay (*verb*), swimming, walking (new): course (*noun*), expert
KEY GRAMMAR POINTS	Past tense questions and answers (revised): *Did you have a good holiday?* *Yes I did/No I didn't* *It was awful/fantastic* Wh-questions and short answers in the Past tense: *Who had a good holiday?* *Mark did.* Name + apostrophe + s (revised) for recognition
SKILLS	Listening to descriptions and matching them with pictures; Asking questions and listening carefully to friends' answers to get specific information

LESSON 3   DID YOU HAVE A GOOD HOLIDAY?

1 ⊙⊙ LISTEN.

Read the introduction to set the scene. Read the two questions BEFORE the students listen so that they know what information they must find. Play the cassette, and collect the answers orally. Play the cassette again with pauses if necessary if some students have had difficulty.

2 SPEAK.

Students use the language model in the book to practise the short conversation in pairs. Demonstrate how to do this by first taking the part of A yourself and asking a confident student to reply. Respond with *Oh good!* or *Oh I'm sorry!* according to the answer. Ask another student to be A and ask you about your holiday. Then ask two students to demonstrate. Then let the class work in pairs, while you circulate to give help.

3 ⊙⊙ LOOK AND LISTEN.

Look at the six photos and ask some general questions e.g. *What can you see in photo no.1?* Then draw attention to Mark's and Angela's speech bubbles on the left, and ask the students if they can guess which photos are Mark's and which are Angela's. Then say that they can check their guesses by listening to the cassette. If students can write in the Student's Book, they can answer by writing 'M' or 'A' next to the photos. If not, ask pupils to write two columns (A and M) in their exercise books and write the photo numbers under them as they listen. Play the cassette once, then ask, *Have you got all the answers?* Let the students compare answers, and see if they agree with each other. If they do not agree or if some people do not have all the answers, say *Don't worry! Listen again!* and play the cassette again. Collect the answers orally by saying e.g. *Photo 2. Is that Mark's or Angela's?* or *The photo with the dolphins. Is that Mark's or Angela's?*

4 SPEAK.

This activity builds on the information collected in Exercise 3. To demonstrate, ask one or two questions of individuals to elicit the short answers modelled in the book e.g. *Mark did.* Then let them practise the mini dialogues in pairs. If wished, some pairs can 'act out' the dialogues that they have just made up.

5 FIND OUT.

This activity allows the students to use the language practised in Exercise 4 in a controlled but communicative way, talking about their own holidays. The FIND OUT WHO .... activity requires them to find names within the class of people who did the different things. Start in pairs. Probably they will not be talking to someone who did all the things, so when the pairs have 'finished' change round the pairs so that each student meets a new person. Of course at this stage they should concentrate on the questions that they have not yet found a name for. Change the pairs again and see if anyone is able to find a name for each activity. Collect the results orally by saying e.g. *Who went swimming in the holidays?* and collecting answers from round the class e.g. student no.1 *Peter went swimming,* student no. 2 *And Margaret and Paul went swimming, too.* If wished you can make a bar chart from the results showing the numbers of students who did each thing.

WORKBOOK

The Workbook extends the theme of holidays, and gives a Language Awareness practice building on the use of the French 'loan word' souvenir. Exercise 1 could be introduced and discussed in class, and the rest of it can be done in class or for homework.
In Exercise 1, find out if the word 'souvenir' is used in the student's own language, then ask them to think of three words that they use that come from different languages (easy examples could be 'Pizza' or 'football').
In Exercise 2, students guess the 'holiday places' by looking at the very 'typical' souvenirs. Their attention will be on the puzzle, but meanwhile they will be revising the Past tense 'went' and some place names.
Exercise 3 is a reminder. Students have already practised postcard writing in *Tiptop 2* and *3*.
They use Mark's postcard as a model to help them.

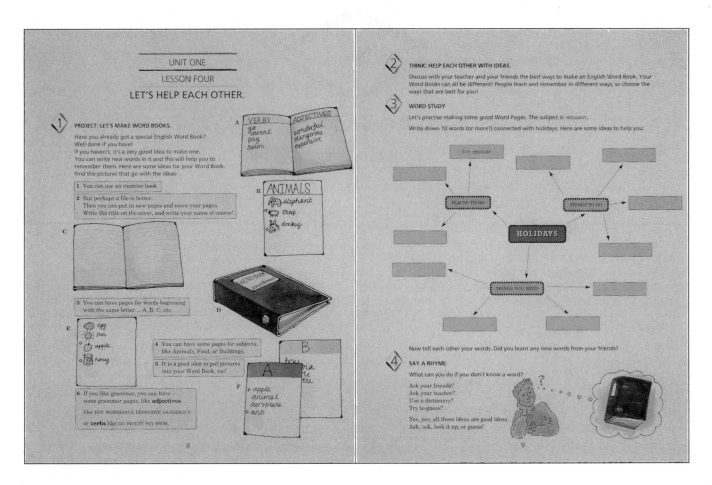

KEY VOCABULARY	file, seaside – recycling of all the 'holiday' words, Unit 1, Lesson 3
KEY GRAMMAR POINTS	Revision of grammar terms: adjectives, verbs
SKILLS	Approaches to keeping a Word Book or file; Consideration of own favoured ways of organising words to help memorise them; Using a 'spider-chart' to generate ideas; Sharing words and ideas with friends

LESSON 4   LET'S HELP EACH OTHER.

1 PROJECT: LET'S MAKE WORD BOOKS.

This lesson reminds students who followed the advice in *Tiptop*, Level 3 about Word Books to continue to add to them, and suggests strongly that students without them should make one immediately! Allowing students to make and organise their own Word Books in a way which suits each individual is an important but simple first step on the way to greater autonomy and independent learning.

Let the students read the ideas in the boxes and try to match them with the pictures. Students who may not write or draw in the Student's Book should write the numbers and the letters in their exercise books. Check answers.

2 THINK: HELP EACH OTHER WITH IDEAS.

Let the students read the ideas in Exercise 1 again for the **information**, and tell you which ideas they like best.

You can spend the time at the end of the lesson, or now if you prefer, acting on the suggestions and starting the different types of Word Book.

3 WORD STUDY

This activity practises a technique which is very useful for collecting families of words in a Word Book, (**or** for generating ideas for topics to write about, at a later stage in the course). The model is given only once, here in the Student's Book, but do not forget it. You can use it often for board-work, or for brain-storming about a topic (e.g. the Dinosaur lesson in Unit 9, Lesson 4 is a good topic to use it with). The idea is that you put your core or focal idea or word in the centre, and then draw branches from it to collect sub-topics – or words connected with it. These in turn generate more words or sub-topics. To take the example here, HOLIDAYS is the central theme (and Unit 1, Lesson 3 has given many ideas and words connected with holidays). Three ideas branch off from this: places to go, things to do, and things you need. (There could be more, e.g. ways of travelling there, and students may add their own extra boxes in their exercise books.) Under these headings, new words will be suggested, e.g. *the seaside, the mountains* under 'Places to go' – or *money* under 'Things you need'.

Show students how the diagram works on the board, collect a few suggestions for words from students, then let them re-draw the diagram in their exercise books, adding as many ideas and words as they can.

Let them compare and discuss their diagrams with a partner, or in small groups. This stage is **very** important, as helping to establish the procedures of comparison, discussion and cooperation which are central to this coursebook.

Have a 'round-up' discussion, collecting words suggested by the class and adding them to the diagram you started on the board.

4 SAY A RHYME.

The rhyme gives advice which encourages students to cooperate, ask for help or use reference or guessing for context skills. It is a very good idea to memorise at least the last two lines yourself, and say them – in a light-hearted way – every time a student gets 'stuck' on a word in future lessons. Try to make it a 'slogan' of this course!

WORKBOOK

The Workbook activities can be done in class, after the Student's Book work as part of the process of setting up a good personalised Workbook. They can also be studied at home and checked through in class.

Exercise 1 reminds students of English alphabetical order, and asks them to reflect on their own alphabet which may be very similar to or completely different from the English one.

Exercise 2 gives very detailed ideas for students to match up. This activity needs follow-up discussion in class, even if it is prepared for homework.

Exercise 3 challenges students to organise a list of words in different ways, to allow them to discover more about how vocabulary items can be grouped and thought about. This activity can be done at home, but students will profit from comparisons of results and discussion in class.

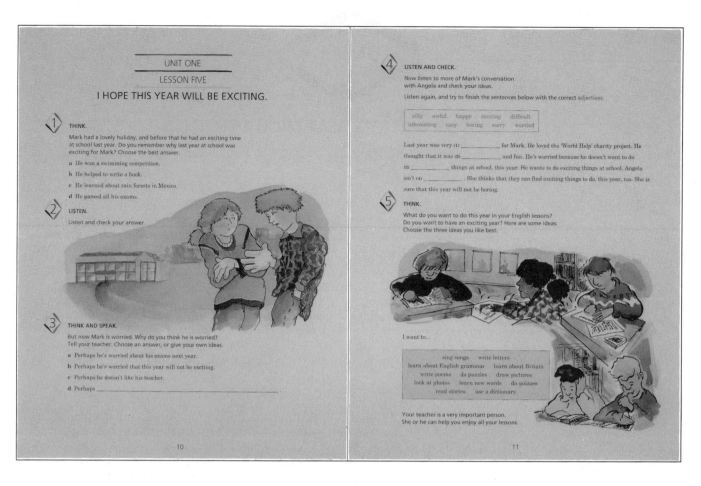

UNIT ONE

LESSON FIVE

I HOPE THIS YEAR WILL BE EXCITING.

1 THINK.

Mark had a lovely holiday, and before that he had an exciting time at school last year. Do you remember why last year at school was exciting for Mark? Choose the best answer.

a He won a swimming competition.

b He helped to write a book.

c He learned about rain forests in Mexico.

d He passed all his exams.

2 LISTEN.

Listen and check your answer.

3 THINK AND SPEAK.

But now Mark is worried. Why do you think he is worried? Tell your teacher. Choose an answer, or give your own ideas.

a Perhaps he's worried about his exams next year.

b Perhaps he's worried that this year will not be exciting.

c Perhaps he doesn't like his teacher.

d Perhaps _____

4 LISTEN AND CHECK.

Now listen to more of Mark's conversation with Angela and check your ideas.

Listen again, and try to finish the sentences below with the correct adjectives.

| silly | awful | happy | exciting | difficult |
| interesting | easy | boring | sorry | worried |

Last year was very (1) _____ for Mark. He loved the 'World Help' charity project. He thought that it was (2) _____ and fun. He's worried because he doesn't want to do (3) _____ things at school, this year. He wants to do exciting things at school. Angela isn't (4) _____ . She thinks that they can find exciting things to do, this year, too. She is sure that this year will not be boring.

5 THINK.

What do you want to do this year in your English lessons? Do you want to have an exciting year? Here are some ideas: Choose the three ideas you like best.

I want to...

sing songs   write letters
learn about English grammar   learn about Britain
write poems   do puzzles   draw pictures
look at photos   learn new words   do quizzes
read stories   use a dictionary

Your teacher is a very important person. She or he can help you enjoy all your lessons.

10

11

KEY VOCABULARY	exam, glad, pass (exam), quiz (**revised**): competition, perhaps Adjectives: awful, boring, difficult, easy, exciting, happy, interesting, silly, sorry, worried
KEY GRAMMAR POINTS	*I hope* / *I'm worried* } (*that*) + future *-ing* and *-ed* adjectives
SKILLS	Thinking about the ways in which each individual learns best; Discussing the emphases that the class would enjoy and benefit most from

LESSON 5   I HOPE THIS YEAR WILL BE EXCITING.

1 THINK.

This activity encourages students to think about the story-line of Level 3, and how it might connect with Level 4's future story-line. Even students new to *Tiptop* can answer, since they were given a summary in Unit 1, Lesson 1. The correct answer is of course (**b**) *He helped to write a book (Children for Charity)*. See if students can remember the title from Unit 1, Lesson 1. The four questions also give passive revision of four Past tense forms.

2 ⬚ LISTEN.

The listening passage confirms the answer in Exercise 1, but also establishes the new situation – Mark is worried about next year at school. The reason is not given on the cassette at this stage.

3 THINK AND SPEAK.

Students have to speculate about why Mark is worried. The correct answer is (**b**). Quick students will pick up the implications from Exercises 1 and 2, but allow others to choose, or invent an answer for (**d**). *Perhaps* is revised passively in these speculations, and will be re-used extensively in the rest of the course.

4 ⬚ LISTEN AND CHECK.

Tell the students that the first time they listen, they must find the correct answer for Exercise 3. Play the cassette once and check that everyone now agrees that the answer is (**b**).
Now tell them to listen again. The words in the book are not the words that Mark says – they are a **summary** of the situation (in the third person). They have to find the correct information and fill in the words in the passage. Students who may not write in their Student's Book should copy the passage, or just the numbers 1-4, in their exercise books, before they listen. Let them look at the 10 green adjectives in the box. Remind them that only four of these adjectives will 'fit' the information required. Give them time to look and predict the correct adjectives **before** they listen. Then play the cassette. Correct answers are: **1** exciting, **2** interesting, **3** boring, **4** worried. Collect answers from the class and play the cassette again (with pauses at appropriate points) to confirm right answers, or to show why they must be changed where incorrect. Read the completed passage aloud to the students.

5 THINK.

Some of the discussion will be best done in the native language to allow for all opinions to be clearly expressed. Obviously, if you and your students are following a textbook (this one!) closely, you cannot change the basic outline. But you **can** agree to focus on particular aspects. For example, if your students want to learn more about Britain (though there is a lot of cultural information in the rest of the course) you will know that you must do a lot of extra homework yourself. If they want to write letters, do try to contact the Penfriend Associations listed on page 134. If they want to draw as well as write, the class magazine idea will give them scope. If they want to read stories, investigate the many excellent simplified readers series that exist. (The story of 'Dracula' (Count Horror's first cousin!)) exists in many simplified readers series and the outline of this story is given later in *Tiptop*, Level 4, so you could link the work there. The idea is NOT for the students to 'take over' the course, but to feel that you are interested in helping them work in the most interesting way for them.

WORKBOOK

Exercise 1 reminds students of the Word Book, and of the grammar term 'adjective'. They can draw lines between the 'opposite' pairs. (Work on this will be developed later in the Workbook.)
In the Student's Book, students had to summarise Mark's fears about next year. Now, in Exercise 2, for students who like to 'hear' all the words of the cassette, here are the exact words of Mark's and Angela's conversation. You can do this in class using the cassette to give ideas, or students can use the box to suggest words for homework and check their answers by hearing the cassette again in the next lesson.
Exercise 3 looks at pairs of adjectives connected to verbs. First, students sort them into two lists. Then, they look at the meanings of the *-ed, -ing* endings and try to choose the correct words for the contexts. The first eight sentences contain *-ed* words, and the next eight sentences contain *-ing* words. (Each sentence number in each group corresponds with the 'root' verb in the other, e.g. first group *interested*, second group *interesting*.
This activity can be done in class, or prepared for homework, but, in either case, needs checking and discussion in class.

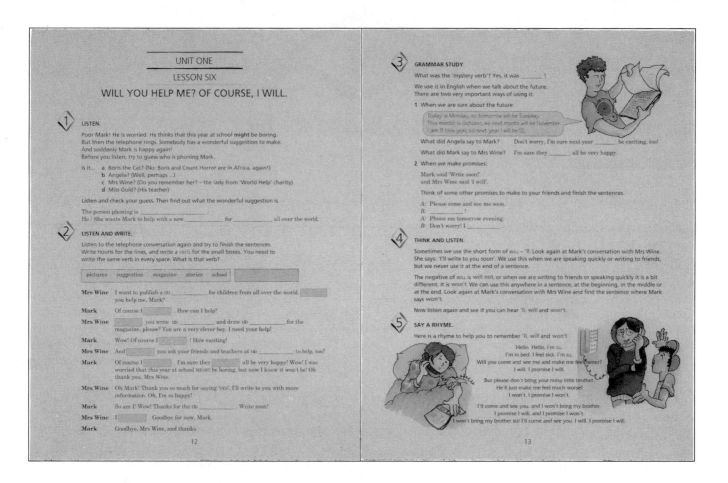

UNIT ONE

LESSON SIX

WILL YOU HELP ME? OF COURSE, I WILL.

1 LISTEN.

Poor Mark! He is worried. He thinks that this year at school **might** be boring.
But then the telephone rings. Somebody has a wonderful suggestion to make.
And suddenly Mark is happy again!
Before you listen, try to guess who is phoning Mark.

Is it... a Boris the Cat? (No. Boris and Count Horror are in Africa, again!)
 b Angela? (Well, perhaps ...)
 c Mrs Wine? (Do you remember her? – the lady from 'World Help' charity)
 d Miss Gold? (His teacher)

Listen and check your guess. Then find out what the wonderful suggestion is.

The person phoning is _____
He / She wants Mark to help with a new _____ for _____ all over the world.

2 LISTEN AND WRITE.

Listen to the telephone conversation again and try to finish the sentences.
Write nouns for the lines, and write a verb for the small boxes. You need to
write the same verb in every space. What is that verb?

| pictures | suggestion | magazine | stories | school | |

Mrs Wine I want to publish a (1) _____ for children from all over the world. ☐ you help me, Mark?

Mark Of course I ☐ . How can I help?

Mrs Wine ☐ you write (2) _____ and draw (3) _____ for the magazine, please? You are a very clever boy. I need your help!

Mark Wow! Of course I ☐ ! How exciting!

Mrs Wine And ☐ you ask your friends and teachers at (4) _____ to help, too?

Mark Of course I ☐ . I'm sure they ☐ all be very happy! Wow! I was worried that this year at school MIGHT be boring, but now I know it won't be! Oh thank you, Mrs Wine.

Mrs Wine Oh Mark! Thank you so much for saying 'YES'. I'll write to you with more information. Oh, I'm so happy!

Mark So am I! Wow! Thanks for the (5) _____ . Write soon!

Mrs Wine I ☐ . Goodbye for now, Mark.

Mark Goodbye, Mrs Wine, and thanks.

12

3 GRAMMAR STUDY

What was the 'mystery verb'? Yes, it was _____ !
We use it in English when we talk about the future.
There are two very important ways of using it:

1 When we are sure about the future:

> Today is Monday, so tomorrow will be Tuesday.
> This month is October, so next month will be November.
> I am 11 this year, so next year I will be 12.

What did Angela say to Mark? Don't worry, I'm sure next year _____ be exciting, too!

What did Mark say to Mrs Wine? I'm sure they _____ all be very happy.

2 When we make promises:

Mark said 'Write soon!'
and Mrs Wine said 'I will'.

Think of some other promises to make to your friends and finish the sentences.

A: Please come and see me soon.
B: _____ !
A: Phone me tomorrow evening.
B: Don't worry! I _____ .

4 THINK AND LISTEN.

Sometimes we use the short form of WILL – 'll. Look again at Mark's conversation with Mrs Wine.
She says: 'I'll write to you soon'. We use this when we are speaking quickly or writing to friends,
but we never use it at the end of a sentence.

The negative of WILL is will not, or when we are writing to friends or speaking quickly it is a bit
different. It is won't. We can use this anywhere in a sentence, at the beginning, in the middle or
at the end. Look again at Mark's conversation with Mrs Wine and find the sentence where Mark
says won't.

Now listen again and see if you can hear 'll, will and won't.

5 SAY A RHYME.

Here is a rhyme to help you to remember 'll, will and won't.

> Hello. Hello. I'm ill.
> I'm in bed. I feel sick. I'm ill.
> Will you come and see me and make me feel better?
> I will. I promise I will.
>
> But please don't bring your noisy little brother.
> He'll just make me feel much worse!
> I won't. I promise I won't.
>
> I'll come and see you, and I won't bring my brother.
> I promise I will, and I promise I won't.
> I won't bring my brother BUT I'll come and see you. I will. I promise I will.

13

KEY VOCABULARY	conversation, ill, magazine, penfriend, publish
KEY GRAMMAR POINTS	*Will/won't* for 'neutral' future reference (**revised**); *will/won't* for promises; *Might* for future possibility (passive understanding)
SKILLS	Dealing with the formal grammar rules about *will/won't* and the contraction *'ll*; Listening to hear the grammar-markers for *the will/won't/'ll* future

LESSON 6   WILL YOU HELP ME? OF COURSE, I WILL.

1 ▭ LISTEN.

This lesson picks up on the situation in Unit 1, Lesson 5. Mark thinks that the next school year *will possibly/perhaps* (= *might*) be boring. Read the introduction and explain the word *might*.
Establish that the students will hear a telephone conversation. Let them look at the four questions **(a)-(d) before** they listen.
(a) is eliminated immediately, but tells Boris fans where he and Count Horror are at the moment!
Let them make guesses, for answers to questions **(b)-(d)**, and try to fill in (or re-write and complete in their exercise books) the sentences below. Play the cassette once through for them to collect the information.

Answers: The person phoning is *Mrs Wine*. She wants Mark to help with a new *magazine* for *children* all over the world.

2 ▭ LISTEN AND WRITE.

The same cassette extract is used once more, but this time with a strong grammar focus. If you think it will be easier for students, establish again the difference between a **noun** and a **verb**, and say that the next time they must listen only for the **nouns** listed in the yellow box (numbered 1-5).

Answers: **1** magazine, **2** stories, **3** pictures, **4** school, **5** suggestion

Then, say that they must listen for the 'mystery verb', shown by a blue/grey box in the Student's Book. In all cases on the cassette the verb is in the form *will*. Then, let the students copy out the whole conversation or just write the noun numbers **(1)-(5)** and the **verb word** in their exercise books. Play the cassette again, for them to listen and follow the words.

3 GRAMMAR STUDY

Establish that the 'mystery verb' was *will* (they have met it extensively in Level 3, and also in the previous lesson).

Go through the grammar explanation, adding your own examples and help (in the native language, if necessary). The two uses focused upon are **neutral future (1)** and **promises (2)**. The Workbook, Exercises 1, 2 and 3, offer support for this, and these activities can be done in the lesson or after it, as you prefer.

4 ▭ THINK AND LISTEN.

The explanation, here, focuses upon the short form *'ll*, and the contracted negative *won't*. Students are invited to look back at Student's Book, Exercise 2 to find examples printed in the book, and to listen again to the cassette to 'hear' the different instances of both forms.

5 ▭ SAY A RHYME.

The rhyme gives good examples in context, of the forms *will*, *won't* and *'ll* used in both **neutral future** and **promise senses.** Let the students listen to it on cassette, following in their Student's Books. Then rewind and play the cassette again, asking them to speak with the cassette (**NB** the adjective *ill* looks very much like the pronoun + verb *I'll*. This is a deliberate 'visual joke' which quick students may notice. Do not labour the point, however, if no-one notices!) Later Workbook lessons will look at correct insertion of the apostrophe.

WORKBOOK

As mentioned above, the three Workbook activities can be integrated with the lesson to support the work there, or they can be done after the Student's Book work for consolidation. Exercise 2 is perhaps best done with cassette-support in class, though students can prepare their answers for homework and check them by listening to the cassette again in the following lesson.
Exercise 3 can be done in class, or for homework, but needs checking and discussion in class.

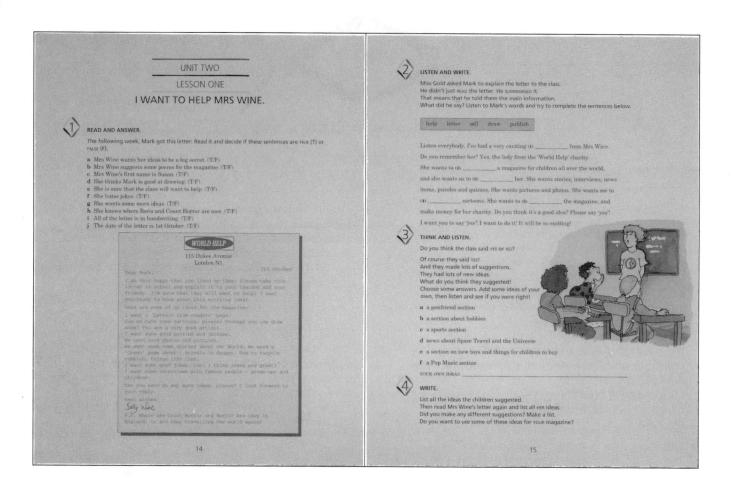

UNIT TWO

LESSON ONE

I WANT TO HELP MRS WINE.

1 READ AND ANSWER.

The following week, Mark got this letter. Read it and decide if these sentences are TRUE (T) or FALSE (F).

a Mrs Wine wants her ideas to be a big secret. (T/F)
b Mrs Wine suggests some poems for the magazine. (T/F)
c Mrs Wine's first name is Susan. (T/F)
d She thinks Mark is good at drawing. (T/F)
e She is sure that the class will want to help. (T/F)
f She hates jokes. (T/F)
g She wants some more ideas. (T/F)
h She knows where Boris and Count Horror are now. (T/F)
i All of the letter is in handwriting. (T/F)
j The date of the letter is 1st October. (T/F)

WORLD HELP

115 Dukes Avenue
London N1
3rd October

Dear Mark,

I am very happy that you liked my ideas. Please take this letter to school and explain it to your teacher and your friends. I'm sure that they will want to help! I want everybody to know about this exciting idea!

Here are some of my ideas for the magazine:

I want a 'Letters from readers' page.
Can we have some cartoons, please? Perhaps you can draw some? You are a very good artist!
I want some good puzzles and quizzes.
We need good photos and pictures.
We want some news stories about our World. We need a 'Green' page about - Animals in danger, How to recycle rubbish, things like that.
I want some good jokes, too! I think jokes are great!
I want some interviews with famous people - grown-ups and children.

Can you send me any more ideas, please? I look forward to your reply.

Best wishes,
Sally Wine

P.S. Where are Count Horror and Boris? Are they in England, or are they travelling the world again?

14

2 LISTEN AND WRITE.

Miss Gold asked Mark to explain the letter to the class.
He didn't just READ the letter. He SUMMARISED it.
That means that he told them the main information.
What did he say? Listen to Mark's words and try to complete the sentences below.

| help | letter | sell | draw | publish |

Listen everybody. I've had a very exciting (1) _____ from Mrs Wine.

Do you remember her? Yes, the lady from the 'World Help' charity.

She wants to (2) _____ a magazine for children all over the world,

and she wants us to (3) _____ her. She wants stories, interviews, news

items, puzzles and quizzes. She wants pictures and photos. She wants me to

(4) _____ cartoons. She wants to (5) _____ the magazine, and

make money for her charity. Do you think it's a good idea? Please say 'yes'!

I want you to say 'yes'! I want to do it! It will be so exciting!

3 THINK AND LISTEN.

Do you think the class said YES or NO?

Of course they said YES!
And they made lots of suggestions.
They had lots of new ideas.
What do you think they suggested!
Choose some answers. Add some ideas of your
own, then listen and see if you were right!

a a penfriend section
b a section about hobbies
c a sports section
d news about Space Travel and the Universe
e a section on new toys and things for children to buy
f a Pop Music section

YOUR OWN IDEAS _____

4 WRITE.

List all the ideas the children suggested.
Then read Mrs Wine's letter again and list all HER ideas.
Did you make any different suggestions? Make a list.
Do you want to use some of these ideas for YOUR magazine?

15

KEY VOCABULARY	cartoon, interview, joke, news item, pop music, recycle (*verb*), reply (*noun*), section, summarise, universe
KEY GRAMMAR POINTS	*want to* + verb (**revised**): *I want to help Mrs Wine.* *want to* + noun/pronoun + verb: *Mrs Wine wants me to draw cartoons.*
SKILLS	Predicting information before a listening passage; Selective listening to discover items from a list that are mentioned or not mentioned; Summarising information

LESSON 1   I WANT TO HELP MRS WINE.

1 READ AND ANSWER.

Check that the students understand the procedure for a true/false activity (extensively practised in Level 3, but here for the first time in Level 4). Use question (**a**) as an example. Then read questions (**b**) to (**j**) and ask them to read the letter by themselves and decide on their answers. They can then compare answers in pairs, and if they disagree, they can go back to the passage to support or modify their own answers. Collect answers orally, asking students to read out the parts of the letter that support their answers.
(**NB** Mrs. Wine asks where Boris the Cat and Count Horror are. Establish that they are travelling the world again!)

2 ⊙⊙ LISTEN AND WRITE.

In Lesson 1, Unit 5, students summarised Mark's worries. Now they listen to him summarising Mrs Wine's letter in Exercise 1. Before they listen, let them read the gapped summary and begin to guess some of the answers. Then they listen to confirm or change their answers. Pupils who may not write in the Student's Book should first write the numbers 1 to 5 (referring to the gaps in the passage) in their exercise books, and then write the words as they hear them. A secondary aim of this exercise is to let students see some words as they hear them, to help them to 'match up' in their aural and visual memories the way words sound when spoken naturally and the way they look in the written form.

3 ⊙⊙ THINK AND LISTEN.

The students know that Mark's class said 'Yes' to Mrs Wine's idea about a magazine. Let them look at the list of possible ideas for what to put in the magazine, and then add any ideas of their own. Then they listen to the cassette and tick all the ideas from the list that were mentioned (not all of them are). They should also listen for any 'new' ideas not seen on the list, but mentioned on the cassette.

4 WRITE.

This is the place where the idea that your students should make a magazine of their own is first suggested. (See Introduction for ideas about the different forms this could take.) Let them choose the ideas for this magazine that they really like. It can of course be built up from the ideas in Exercises 1 and 3 but new ideas should also be welcomed.

WORKBOOK

Exercise 1 is a word-classification activity that encourages students to see that vocabulary items can be looked at and collected in many different ways. It can be started in class and finished for homework, but results need discussing in class. Its aim is to support students in the compilation of their own Word Books.
Exercise 2 focuses on and gives controlled practice in the 'want to' structures seen in the Student's Book. You may want to prepare it, and give extra explanation, in class, then it could be done in class or for homework.
Exercise 3 is 'just for fun' but has a serious Language Awareness point, too. It builds on the jokes work from Level 3, which is about words which are ambiguous because of their similar sounds.

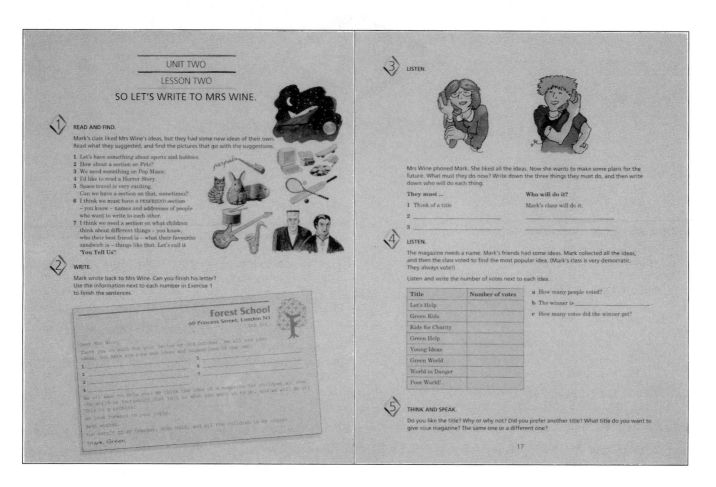

UNIT TWO

LESSON TWO

SO LET'S WRITE TO MRS WINE.

1 READ AND FIND.

Mark's class liked Mrs Wine's ideas, but they had some new ideas of their own.
Read what they suggested, and find the pictures that go with the suggestions.

1 Let's have something about sports and hobbies.
2 How about a section on Pets?
3 We need something on Pop Music.
4 I'd like to read a Horror Story.
5 Space travel is very exciting.
  Can we have a section on that, sometimes?
6 I think we must have a PENFRIEND section
  – you know – names and addresses of people
  who want to write to each other.
7 I think we need a section on what children
  think about different things – you know,
  who their best friend is – what their favourite
  sandwich is – things like that. Let's call it
  'You Tell Us'!

2 WRITE.

Mark wrote back to Mrs Wine. Can you finish his letter?
Use the information next to each number in Exercise 1
to finish the sentences.

Forest School
69 Princess Street, London N1

3 LISTEN.

Mrs Wine phoned Mark. She liked all the ideas. Now she wants to make some plans for the future. What must they do now? Write down the three things they must do, and then write down who will do each thing.

They must ...	Who will do it?
1 Think of a title	Mark's class will do it.
2	
3	

4 LISTEN.

The magazine needs a name. Mark's friends had some ideas. Mark collected all the ideas, and then the class voted to find the most popular idea. (Mark's class is very democratic. They always vote!)

Listen and write the number of votes next to each idea.

Title	Number of votes
Let's Help	
Green Kids	
Kids for Charity	
Green Help	
Young Ideas	
Green World	
World in Danger	
Poor World!	

a How many people voted?
b The winner is
c How many votes did the winner get?

5 THINK AND SPEAK.

Do you like the title? Why or why not? Did you prefer another title? What title do you want to give your magazine? The same one or a different one?

17

KEY VOCABULARY	democratic, each other, kid, look forward to, on behalf of, vote (*verb* and *noun*)
KEY GRAMMAR POINTS	Expressions concerned with suggestions: *Let's .... How about ...* + noun + *-ing* *We must ... We need ... Will* (**revised**) *How many?* (**revised**)
SKILLS	Revision of layout and conventions of a semi-formal letter; Listening for detail; Going through a democratic decision-making process to arrive at title for the class's own magazine

LESSON 2 SO LET'S WRITE TO MRS WINE.

1 READ AND FIND.

Students point to the pictures which illustrate each suggestion. To revise the Function Making Suggestions, ask the students to change the sentences and make suggestions in a different way. e.g. using *Let's ...* instead of *How about ...?*

2 WRITE.

Students transfer the suggestions from Exercise 1 to the letter just listing the main words, e.g. **1** Sports and Hobbies. They can copy this part of the letter in their exercise books, or more interestingly, write their own versions of the letter, by changing some of the expressions slightly, e.g. *We all love ...* to, *We all like your ideas very much.*

3 ⌑ LISTEN.

Look at the introductory sentences to 'set the scene'. Let them try to guess the three things that new publishers of a magazine must do, using their knowledge of the world, but the answers to the 'Who will do it?' section need to wait until the students listen to the cassette.

Play the cassette once, encouraging them to try to write down as much as they can the first time, but saying that they will have a second or even a third chance if they need it. Let them compare their answers together without your intervention at this stage. Let them understand that comparing answers like this is NOT 'cheating' but is intended to alert them to a possible mistake if answers do not agree. Play the cassette again once or twice, making it clear that you expect everyone to try to get all the answers.

Collect answers orally. You can do this as a sort of drill, like this: Teacher: *What must they do first?* Student: *They must think of a title.* Teacher: *Who will do it?* Student: *Mark's class (will).* Teacher: *And then?* Student: *They must ....*

4 ⌑ LISTEN.

The context for this activity has been set in Exercise 3. Look at the grey and yellow table and establish that it contains all the suggestions for a good title. Ask round the class, *Which title do YOU like best?* Then ask: *Which title do you think Mark's class chose?* Then they listen and find the answer. They also need to write down the number of votes each title got. They can copy the table and write their answers in their exercise books. Check answers orally, practising *How many ...?* by asking e.g. *How many people voted for Green Kids?*

5 THINK AND SPEAK.

The students should go through the same steps as Mark's class did in Exercises 1 to 3 in order to suggest, discuss and vote on titles. The Workbook activities give support for this process.

WORKBOOK

Exercise 1 invites each student to think of his or her own idea for a title. This can be set as a simple homework task. Exercise 2 needs to be done in class. Students ask each other about their ideas and 'collect' all the title ideas in the box provided. You can ask round the class for each idea, or with a smaller or well-disciplined class, students can move from group to group and find out. Elicit the titles again and write them all in a list on the board. Exercise 3 is the voting. You can do this in two ways: **a** Ask each student to write his or her choice on a small slip of paper, then collect them, and count them, or **b** Ask for a show of hands for each title. Write the results on the board. Encourage students to be fair and sensible and not just vote for their own original idea, if they think another idea is better! Students summarise the results by filling in the table in their Workbooks. Exercise 4 is suitable for relaxing classwork while you count the ballot-papers from Exercise 3, or it can be set for homework. The 'mystery word' is Magazine.

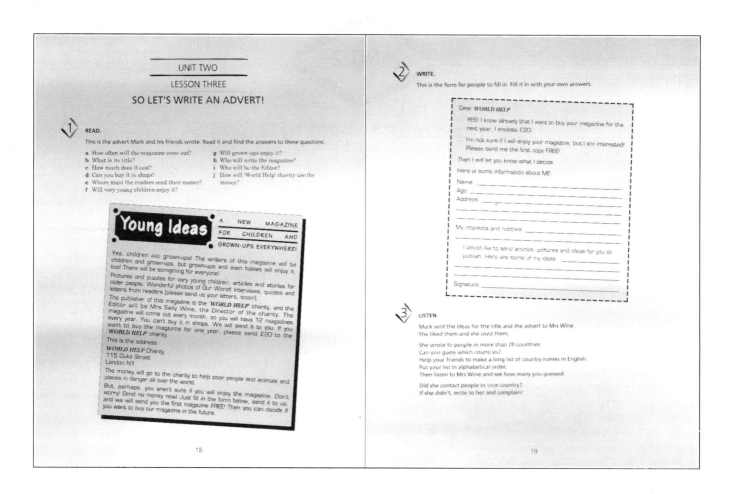

KEY VOCABULARY	advert, alphabetical order, article, come out (= be published), complain, editor, enclose, free (= gratis, no money is charged), future, grown up, money, pound, prepare, signature **revision** of country names: (see tapescript for full list)
KEY GRAMMAR POINTS	*will* for future use (**revised** and consolidated) *would like* (**revised** and consolidated)
SKILLS	Scanning a text quickly to find required information; Completing a form with personal information; Cooperating to build up a long list (countries); Putting a list into alphabetical order; Listening to find out if items from a list are or are not mentioned; Writing a short letter of complaint (optional)

1 READ.

The advertisement text should first be used for training the students in scanning quickly before they read a passage more slowly at their own pace. Gradually more demanding practice in this is given throughout the course.

Read the first question (**a**), and ask the students to look quickly at the passage to find the answer. Make it a light-hearted competition, *Hands up when you have found the answer!* to encourage rapid reading. Do not ask for the answer immediately from the first pupil who puts his or her hand up, but wait until more than half the class have their hands up, saying *Come on!* to encourage all to try. Then this time you can 'reward' the first pupil by asking for the answer. Do the same for questions (**b**) to (**j**), but do not always ask the 'first' pupil, or the others may get discouraged and give up.

LESSON 3   SO LET'S WRITE AN ADVERT!

By now, students should be familiar with the contents of the advert, so they should be able to read it by themselves without much difficulty. Let them do this, and ask you for any extra help they want. It is important to follow scanning activities with a chance to read more slowly at one's own pace, since students need to become aware of the value of reading in different ways according to the needs of the situation. Do not allow them unlimited time for this reading by themselves. Set a realistic time limit in each case. A realistic time for this advert would be no more than two and a half minutes, probably less. To estimate the time-limits for future passages, time yourself reading them, and then multiply the time by two or three according to the capacities of your class.

2 WRITE.

Let the students read through the form. Make sure that they understand that it is connected with the advert in Exercise 1 and sent to possible readers with the advert. Ask them to fill in the details about themselves. If students may not write in the Student's Book, they can write the main headings and their information in their exercise books, while you move around the class to help and check. Ask them to pay particular attention to the IDEAS section. Collect ideas from this section orally.

3 ⬚⬚ LISTEN.

Before students listen to the cassette, ask them to make their own lists of countries individually, at least ten for each person. Then let them work with one or two other students to make a longer combined list of all the countries they thought of. They should then put this list into alphabetical order. Collect all the countries on the board in the right order by asking e.g. *Who has some countries beginning with 'A'/'B' etc?* Tell them that they will now hear a conversation between Mark and Mrs Wine. Mrs Wine tells Mark all the countries she has contacted. Their task is to listen and try to remember (or take notes on) all the countries Mrs Wine mentions. Play the cassette once only. The country names on the cassette are in alphabetical order to make your board work easier. Then point on the board to the list of countries suggested originally by the students and ask e.g. *Did Mrs Wine write to people in France/this country?* to elicit the answers *Yes*, or *No*. Then ask if Mrs Wine mentioned any countries which are NOT

on the board. If students do not agree in all their answers (and they probably will not) say, *Listen again, and find out if you are right!* Students will pay special attention to names over which they did not agree. Then play the cassette with pauses and tick all the countries mentioned and add any 'extra' ones to the list on the board.

If the students' own country is not mentioned on the cassette, adopt the light-hearted suggestion of writing a note to Mrs Wine to complain! This is optional, so do not spend a long time on it. Build up the letter on the board using students' suggestions. Here is a possible model:

school address
date

Dear Mrs Wine,

My class heard about your new magazine **Young Ideas**, but you haven't written to anybody in (name of country) about it. Please don't forget us! Please send details to our school.

Best wishes,

(name of class)

WORKBOOK

Exercise 1 can be done wholly in class or the first part can be thought about and prepared in class and then finished for homework, with class follow up later. You could extend the procedure to include a class vote like that in Unit 2, Lesson 2 if you wish. In Exercise 2 further discussion is needed in class to agree on a policy for the class magazine. This is a REAL discussion and the results should be acted upon, so make sure that the decisions are realistic and practical. Students then design their own draft adverts for the magazine using the layout ideas on page 19 to help them. (This part can be done for homework.)

In Exercise 3 students compare their ideas and try to combine the best to make poster-sized adverts for the magazine to be displayed in the school. The class may agree on just one design and wording, or separate groups may produce variants which can be used for different posters.

Exercise 4 consolidates the names of countries. This activity can be used as a 'time-filler' in class (in this lesson or a later one) if some students have finished their work more quickly than others, or it can be done for homework.

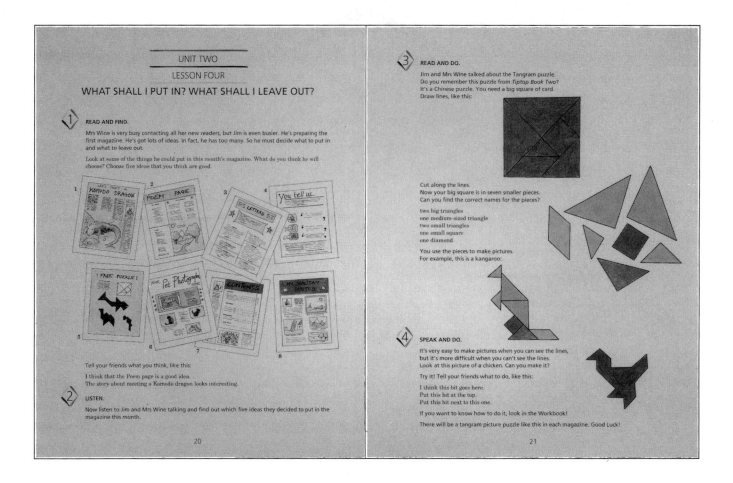

UNIT TWO

LESSON FOUR

WHAT SHALL I PUT IN? WHAT SHALL I LEAVE OUT?

1 READ AND FIND.

Mrs Wine is very busy contacting all her new readers, but Jim is even busier. He's preparing the first magazine. He's got lots of ideas. In fact, he has too many. So he must decide what to put in and what to leave out.

Look at some of the things he could put in this month's magazine. What do you think he will choose? Choose five ideas that you think are good.

Tell your friends what you think, like this:

I think that the Poem page is a good idea.
The story about meeting a Komodo dragon looks interesting.

2 LISTEN.

Now listen to Jim and Mrs Wine talking and find out which five ideas they decided to put in the magazine this month.

20

3 READ AND DO.

Jim and Mrs Wine talked about the Tangram puzzle. Do you remember this puzzle from *Tiptop Book Two*? It's a Chinese puzzle. You need a big square of card. Draw lines, like this:

Cut along the lines.
Now your big square is in seven smaller pieces.
Can you find the correct names for the pieces?

two big triangles
one medium-sized triangle
two small triangles
one small square
one diamond

You use the pieces to make pictures.
For example, this is a kangaroo:

4 SPEAK AND DO.

It's very easy to make pictures when you can see the lines, but it's more difficult when you can't see the lines. Look at this picture of a chicken. Can you make it?

Try it! Tell your friends what to do, like this:

I think this bit goes here.
Put this bit at the top.
Put this bit next to this one.

If you want to know how to do it, look in the Workbook!

There will be a tangram picture puzzle like this in each magazine. Good Luck!

21

KEY VOCABULARY	certainly, contents page, leave out, medium-sized, poetry, revision of shape words: triangle, square, diamond
KEY GRAMMAR POINTS	*I think that ...*; Expressions of location (**revised**): *at the top/bottom, next to*
SKILLS	Exercising personal taste in choice of magazine features; Listening to confirm or reject previous guesses; Spatial awareness in making and playing with a tangram; Identifying a 'mystery' animal by reading a description, which starts very general and then becomes more and more specific

LESSON 4   WHAT SHALL I PUT IN? WHAT SHALL I LEAVE OUT?

Try to bring some card or paper to the lesson for the students to make tangrams from.

1 READ AND FIND.

Set the scene by reading the introduction. We are looking at different ideas for the magazine with Jim. He will choose only five out of the eight pages for this month. Let the students look at the eight ideas and make comments about them using the language model suggestions at the end of Exercise 1. Then ask them to guess privately which five ideas they think he will choose. (**NB** Emphasise that this is just a guess – there are no prizes for guessing all the ideas correctly!) The point of guessing is so that they will have some key words in the forefront of their minds, and these will help them to recognise key information when they listen in Exercise 2. It may also help students if you refer to the title of the lesson and pick out the key verbs, *leave out* and *put in*. See if anyone can explain them in context, e.g. *If Jim leaves out the story about the Komodo dragon, he doesn't choose it for the magazine – he doesn't put it in.*

2 🔘 LISTEN.

Students listen to the conversation between Mrs Wine and Jim and identify the five ideas chosen. Let them take notes, and then compare their notes with a friend. Play the cassette again for them to confirm or change their first answers. Then elicit ideas orally, like this, *What did Jim put in?* or *Did he put in the Komodo dragon story, or did he leave it out?* Play the cassette again with pauses to check each answer if there is any remaining difficulty.

3 READ AND DO.

The tangram was first met in *Tiptop*, Level 2. Please try to make it with your class, since the physical involvement with following the instructions will give them valuable revision of the different shape words met in *Tiptop*, Levels 2 and 3. Let them make the kangaroo. Talk about the position of the pieces, like this, e.g. *One small triangle is the head. It is at the top. The tail is the diamond. It is at the bottom. The body is made of the two big triangles.*

4 SPEAK AND DO.

The 'chicken' puzzle is more difficult. There are no lines to show which piece goes where. Let the students experiment. Move around the class and help, talking about the arrangement of the pieces, using the language suggested in the language model in the book. (The solution to the puzzle and the description of the position of the pieces will be found in the Workbook.)

WORKBOOK

These activities can be done in class as follow-up to the Student's Book lesson, or they can be tried for homework.
Exercise 1 provides a summary of the choices Jim made, and gives practice in the use of the verbs *put in* and *leave out*. Exercise 2 gives the solution to the 'chicken' puzzle and provides instructions for making it, for the students to complete, using the picture to help them. This revises and consolidates 'shape' and 'position' language. Exercise 3 is an extract from the Komodo Dragon story, but this is not obvious until the students have read past the first two sentences. Students have to use 'clue' words like *green* and *grey* and *scales*. They choose the appropriate picture from the three possibilities and write in the title to the article. (Remind students who followed *Tiptop*, Level 3 about the Komodo dragon story that appeared there.)

UNIT TWO

LESSON FIVE

LET'S MAKE THE COVER REALLY ATTRACTIVE!

READ AND THINK.

So now Jim has decided what to put into the first magazine.
Now he must design a really good cover.

What do you think is important about a magazine cover?
Here are some ideas. Choose the two most important for you.
You can add your own ideas, too.

> It must be very colourful.
> It must be clear.
> The title of the magazine must be easy to see.
> The names of some important sections must be on the cover.
> There must be some pictures of things in the magazine on the cover.
>
> My own ideas _____

Tell your friends your answers.

LOOK, THINK AND SPEAK.

Look at these five possible covers.

Which one has the title a at the top?
　　　　　　　　　　　　b at the bottom?
　　　　　　　　　　　　c in the middle?
　　　　　　　　　　　　d down the left side?
　　　　　　　　　　　　e diagonally, from corner to corner?

Which cover do you think is the best?

Tell your friends, like this:

I think number _____ is the best, because it is the clearest.
　　　　　　　　　　　　　　　　　　　　　　　most colourful.
　　　　　　　　　　　　　　　　　　　　　　　most interesting.

LISTEN.

Now listen to Jim and Mrs Wine and find out which cover they chose.
Do you agree with them?

23

KEY VOCABULARY	attractive, bottom, clear, colourful, corner, cover, diagonally, left, middle, right, side, title, top
KEY GRAMMAR POINTS	Language of location and position: *At the top/bottom; in the middle; diagonally* (from corner to corner); (**revised** from Level 3) *Let's ......* (**revised**)
SKILLS	Identifying positions; Personal taste about visual impact of different designs

LESSON 5   LET'S MAKE THE COVER REALLY ATTRACTIVE!

If possible, bring in some magazines for students to look at the covers and express their opinions about how they look.

1 READ AND THINK.

Ask students for their opinions about a good magazine cover. Use any magazines you have been able to bring in to illustrate the meanings of words like 'clear' and 'colourful'. Let them discuss their opinions.

2 LOOK, THINK AND SPEAK.

Students look at the five covers and identify the position of the title on each one. They can write the numbers of the pictures and of the sentences in their exercise books.

Then they decide for themselves which cover design is the best. Then they compare their ideas with a partner, using the language model in the book. Put the numbers 1 to 5 on the board, and elicit opinions around the class from each student, putting a tick next to each number according to the 'votes' given. Find, in this way, the most popular cover design.

3 🔲 LISTEN.

Tell the students that they will now hear about the design that Mrs Wine and Jim chose. Perhaps it will be the same one as the class chose, or perhaps it will be different. Play the cassette for them to find out (it's number 2). See if the class agrees or disagrees. (There is no right answer, to some degree it is a matter of taste.)

WORKBOOK

The Workbook activities follow on logically from those of the Student's Book. They can all be done in class or for homework, but Exercises 2 and 3 need discussion in class, and the designs for a cover by individual students need to be looked at together, in class, in order that the students can write a letter in Exercise 4 to the designer of the cover they like best. This letter can be finished for homework, but discussed later.

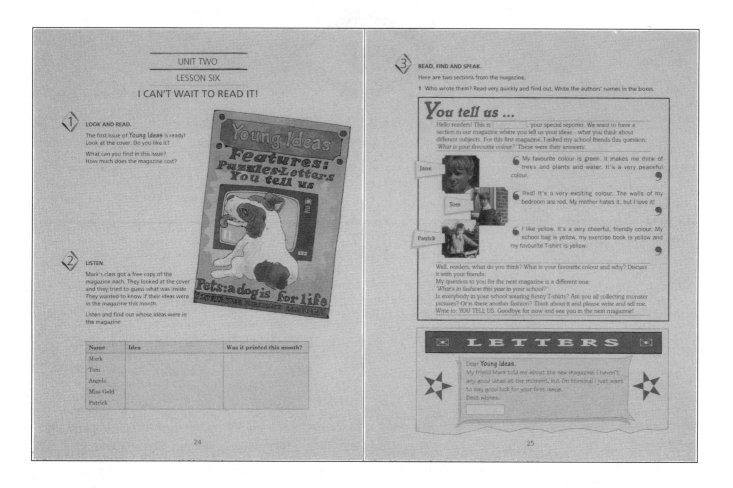

KEY VOCABULARY	cheerful, fashion, feature, issue, peaceful, print (*verb*), reader, reporter
KEY GRAMMAR POINTS	No new structures; *Do you like it?* (**revised**)
SKILLS	Listening to collect the important information in a passage; Expressing (and justifying) personal taste (favourite colours)

LESSON 6   I CAN'T WAIT TO READ IT!

1 LOOK AND READ.

The first question *Do you like it?* about the cover, is intended to draw strong reactions, for and against, for the students, since the colours are deliberately very bright (some would say clashing).

Take a note of who likes it and who does not. Then ask students to look and tell you what is in the magazine (the features) – and the price (remember readers must pay for a year, so an acceptable answer is *Twenty pounds per year – that's 12 magazines*).

2 [⊙⊙] LISTEN.

Read the introduction with the students and make sure that they understand the situation; the five people are looking in the new magazine to see if their ideas are in it this month. Look at the chart with the students and check that they know what to do. (They can copy the chart in their exercise books and write their answers there.) See if they remember the ideas that some of the people had before they listen, since this will help them. A good class can probably put some answers in both columns the first time they hear the cassette. A less confident class should be encouraged to listen for the ideas alone the first time they hear it, then to listen again and write *Yes* or *No* in the second column. There are several 'traps' on the cassette.

After the students have collected all the answers they can individually, let them compare answers with a friend to see if they agree. Then play the cassette again, pausing it at the end of each person's 'section' and eliciting answers. Say, *What was Miss Gold's idea? Is it in the magazine this month?* Try to give the students the idea that this is **not** a test. You are giving them, by pre-listening preparation, several chances to hear the cassette, and the chance to help each other, every possible opportunity to get most of the answers right, and to **learn** as they try and try again.

3 READ, FIND AND SPEAK.

The first task is very easy if the students got the answers to Exercise 2. They simply have to recognise Mark's **'You tell us'** idea and Patrick's letter, and supply the two names. Then, go back and look at Mark's **'You tell us'**. This format appears frequently in the Student's Book, and provides an excellent starting-point for students to give their own opinions on the topics included. Let the students read it again and then ask orally, *Who likes red/green/yellow?* Then *Why?*

Do an oral Class Survey. First elicit the names of all the colours that students know, and write them on the board. Go round the class asking, *What's your favourite colour?* or indicating that a student should say, e.g. *I like..... best* or *My favourite colour is..... .* For each vote put a tick next to the appropriate colour name. Then ask the students to total the votes and find the most popular colour. If wished, and if this links with work in maths lessons, the students could draw a 'bar chart' showing the number of votes for each colour (colouring the bars in the appropriate colours). They could also write sentences like, *In our class nobody likes grey* or *Most people like blue.*

WORKBOOK

Exercises 1 and 2 provide the model for a similar **'You tell us'** class magazine feature, but extending the idea to colours which students do **not** like. Students can try these at home, but you will need to look at answers for Exercise 2 and give help and advice.

Exercise 3 allows for the exercise of personal taste. Students colour the pictures of clothes to show colours that they think look nice or awful together. This can be done at home, but the comparison of ideas with friends' ideas needs to be done in class.

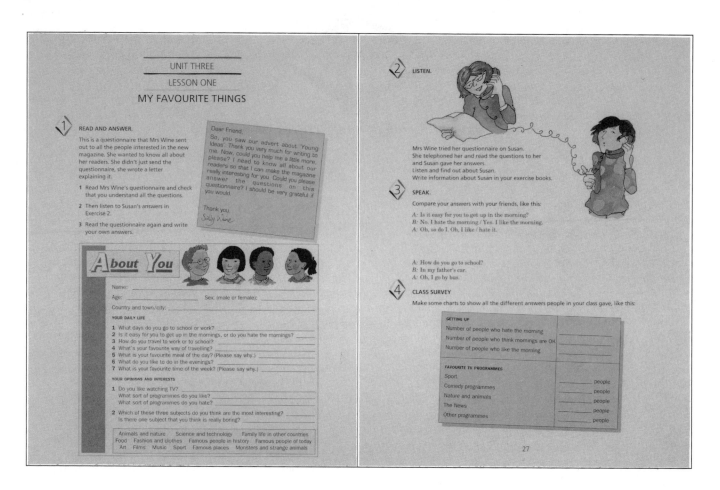

UNIT THREE

LESSON ONE

MY FAVOURITE THINGS

1 READ AND ANSWER.

This is a questionnaire that Mrs Wine sent out to all the people interested in the new magazine. She wanted to know all about her readers. She didn't just send the questionnaire, she wrote a letter explaining it.

1 Read Mrs Wine's questionnaire and check that you understand all the questions.

2 Then listen to Susan's answers in Exercise 2.

3 Read the questionnaire again and write your own answers.

Dear Friend,
So, you saw our advert about 'Young Ideas'. Thank you very much for writing to me. Now, could you help me a little more, please? I need to know all about our readers so that I can make the magazine really interesting for you. Could you please answer the questions on this questionnaire? I should be very grateful if you would.

Thank you,
Sally Wine

About You

Name: _____

Age: _____ Sex: (male or female): _____

Country and town/city: _____

YOUR DAILY LIFE

1 What days do you go to school or work? _____
2 Is it easy for you to get up in the mornings, or do you hate the mornings? _____
3 How do you travel to work or to school? _____
4 What's your favourite way of travelling? _____
5 What is your favourite meal of the day? (Please say why.) _____
6 What do you like to do in the evenings? _____
7 What is your favourite time of the week? (Please say why.) _____

YOUR OPINIONS AND INTERESTS

1 Do you like watching TV?
   What sort of programmes do you like? _____
   What sort of programmes do you hate? _____

2 Which of these three subjects do you think are the most interesting? _____
   Is there one subject that you think is really boring? _____

Animals and nature   Science and technology   Family life in other countries
Food   Fashion and clothes   Famous people in history   Famous people of today
Art   Films   Music   Sport   Famous places   Monsters and strange animals

2 LISTEN.

Mrs Wine tried her questionnaire on Susan.
She telephoned her and read the questions to her and Susan gave her answers.
Listen and find out about Susan.
Write information about Susan in your exercise books.

3 SPEAK.

Compare your answers with your friends, like this:

A: Is it easy for you to get up in the morning?
B: No, I hate the morning / Yes, I like the morning.
A: Oh, so do I. Oh, I like / hate it.

A: How do you go to school?
B: In my father's car.
A: Oh, I go by bus.

4 CLASS SURVEY

Make some charts to show all the different answers people in your class gave, like this:

SETTING UP	
Number of people who hate the morning	_____
Number of people who think mornings are OK	_____
Number of people who like the morning	_____

FAVOURITE TV PROGRAMMES	
Sport	_____ people
Comedy programmes	_____ people
Nature and animals	_____ people
The News	_____ people
Other programmes	_____ people

27

KEY VOCABULARY	comedy, comment, daily, female, get up, male, meal, nature, negative (adjective), news, positive (adjective), programme (TV), questionnaire, sex, technology
KEY GRAMMAR POINTS	Simple Present for daily routine and habits
SKILLS	Integrating information from a class survey into chart form, (optional) expression of these facts and figures on a bar chart

LESSON 1   MY FAVOURITE THINGS

1 ◖◗ READ AND ANSWER.

Read the introduction and Mrs Wine's letter to establish the situation. Mrs Wine wants to know all about the future readers of **Young Ideas** to help her to choose articles that will be interesting for them. Do question (**1**). Check that all the questions are understood. Some students may want to start answering for themselves (even though the book suggests that they wait until question (**3**). Let them try for a few minutes. They can write in their exercise books, but they will probably not have enough language yet to complete the questionnaire fully.

Do question (**2**). The instructions for this are at the top of page 27. Play the cassette for them to collect information about Susan in their exercise books. (Note: Susan has a slight Midlands accent on the cassette. This should not pose any comprehension problems since her speech is clear, but you might want to talk about the different vowel sounds if your students notice them.)

Return to the students' own answers in question (**3**).

2 ◖◗ LISTEN.

See ideas above about integrating Susan's answers with the students' own answers. At this point you can turn to the Workbook and do Exercise 1 and Exercise 2 which allow comparison of their answers with Susan's.

3 SPEAK.

Students use the questionnaire to guide them in mini-interviews with friends.

4 CLASS SURVEY

Collect answers to some of the questions in the questionnaire by saying *Hands up!*, counting out loud and putting numbers up on the board. Use the questions that appear in the grey box.
Students can, if you wish, make bar charts to show morning moods, means of travel to school and TV programme preferences in the class, etc.

WORKBOOK

See above. The Workbook activities are best integrated with the work in the Student's Book, Exercise 2.

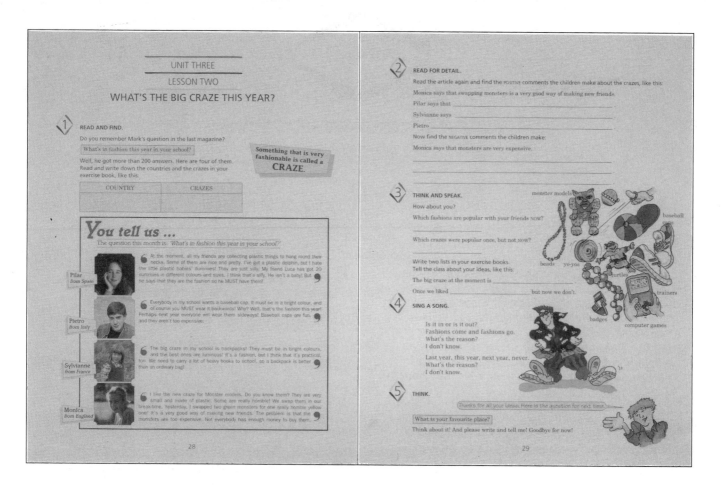

KEY VOCABULARY	backpack, beads, craze, dummy, luminous, swap (verb), trainers, turtle, yo-yo
KEY GRAMMAR POINTS	*Must* to express fashion imperatives, *They must be in bright colours;* Indirect Speech in the Present, *Monica says that ...;* Past and Present tenses contrasted, *Once we liked yo-yos, but now we don't.*
SKILLS	Extracting essential information from a fairly long article; Distinguishing detailed Positive and Negative comments; Advantages and Disadvantages; Contrasting past enthusiasms with present ones

LESSON 2   WHAT'S THE BIG CRAZE THIS YEAR?

1 READ AND FIND.

Remind students of Mark's '**You tell us**' question. Look at the green box which explains the meaning of the word CRAZE. Look at the grey INFORMATION BOX. Make sure that students understand that this shows the information that they must get from the article in a first, quick, reading. Ask them to copy the headings from the grey box into their exercise books. Give the students a time-limit of two minutes to read the '**You tell us**' article and put the information under the headings. They will probably exceed this, but push them, just the same, to make the point that they should sometimes read quickly just to get information. Reassure them that they will have time to read more slowly in Exercise 2. Circulate in the class and check progress. Stop the students after three minutes maximum and collect answers orally from the whole class.

2 READ FOR DETAIL.

Establish that the students understand what **positive** and **negative** comments are, by looking at the answers that Monica gives, which are printed in the book. Give them time to read again more slowly and collect more answers of each type from the other children in the article. (They can write these in their exercise books.) Circulate and help individuals. Then collect answers orally, insisting on the *Monica says that …* structures.

3 THINK AND SPEAK.

Look at the pictures with the students and make sure that they understand the meanings of the captions. Collect any other ideas that they may have and supply the English words if they do not know them (e.g. skate boards). Give them time to think and discuss with friends, then collect answers orally, following the language models in the book. They can write sentences based on this oral work if you wish.

4 ⚆ SING A SONG.

Play the cassette with the song for the students to follow the words in the book. Then play it again for them to join in.

5 THINK.

Draw attention to Mark's question, *What is your favourite place?* This gives the theme for Unit 4, and the next issue of the **Young Ideas** magazine. Students can think about this, but you do not need to do any work on it until Unit 4 starts.

WORKBOOK

All the Workbook activities are suitable for follow-up homework. Exercise 1 challenges students to complete the words of the song. Exercise 2 is cultural information about 'old' crazes. Exercise 3 invites comments on present crazes, and Exercise 4 gives guided writing practice for fuller written expression about a present craze.

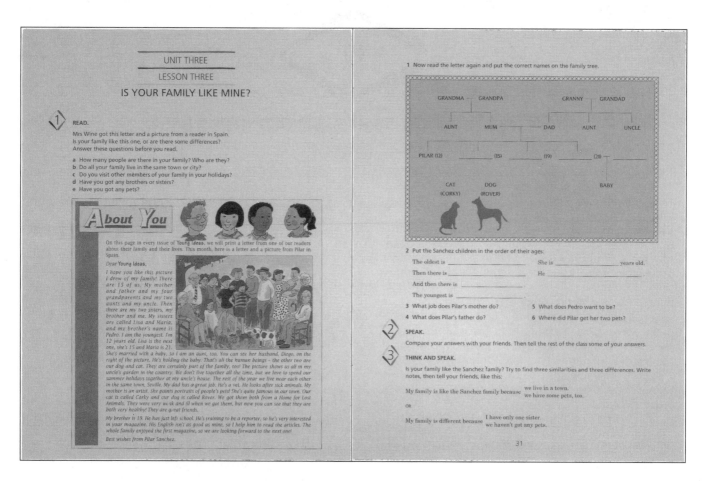

KEY VOCABULARY	aunt, baby, brother, daughter, family, granddad, grandma, grandparents, granny, great, healthy, husband, job, married, member, near, parents, pet, portrait, relations, reporter, similarity, sister, together, train (*verb*), uncle, vet
KEY GRAMMAR POINTS	Present Simple (**revised**) for general description of family; Present Continuous (**revised**) for actions seen at the moment: *She's holding the baby* (in the photograph). *He's training to be a reporter. We are looking forward to the next one!* Superlative of Adjectives (**revised**): *youngest/oldest*
SKILLS	Comparison of own life (family) with that of someone else; Finding similarities and differences

42

LESSON 3   IS YOUR FAMILY LIKE MINE?

1 READ.

Set the scene by reading the introductory sentences. Then, BEFORE the students read the article, ask them personal questions about their own families. Give them time to read the questions and think before you ask.

Then let them read the article at their own pace, but set a time limit of five minutes maximum. Then encourage them to move on to Exercise 1, the family tree and Exercise 2, the detailed questions about the Sanchez family.

2 SPEAK.

Let students compare their answers in pairs. Then collect answers orally. Draw the family tree on the board to collect the correct names.

3 THINK AND SPEAK.

Ask students to think about their own families and find three similarities and three differences. Give them time to read again and take notes, and prepare their answers. Let them practise the answers in pairs, then collect answers round the class.

WORKBOOK

The Workbook activities can be used in class as part of the lesson, but the letter in Exercise 3 can be finished for homework.

Exercise 1 is Language Awareness work. Many languages (e.g. Italian) have a word which sounds like 'parents' which in fact means something more general (all relations) than the English word 'parents' (which means only mother and father). Check this, in class discussion.

In Exercise 2 ask students to draw a family tree. (**NB** because in the modern world there are many non 'standard' families, i.e. many one parent families and separated parents, do not insist too much on students revealing every last detail if they are reluctant. Let them concentrate on brothers and sisters and pets if this suits some students better.)

In Exercise 3 Pilar's letter/article is repeated in the Workbook to form a handy reference for students to take ideas and language from when they attempt their own 'pen friend' letter. Start this in class, if possible, pointing out ways in which individuals can adapt the language Pilar uses to their own needs.

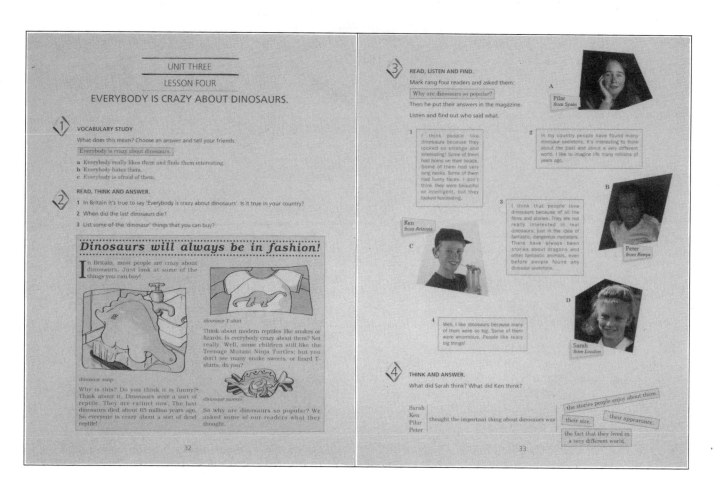

KEY VOCABULARY	appearance, crazy, horn, ring (*verb*), size, skeleton, strange, sweets
KEY GRAMMAR POINTS	Phrases expressing attitudes: *crazy about, interested in*; Passive recognition of indirect speech in the Past: *Sarah thought the important thing about dinosaurs was their size*; Link between adjectives, verbs and nouns: *They were enormous/their size; They looked strange/their appearance*
SKILLS	Recognising pictures from descriptions; Guessing who the speakers are using clues from the information they give

LESSON 4   EVERYBODY IS CRAZY ABOUT DINOSAURS.

1 VOCABULARY STUDY

Students have already met 'craze', so they should be able to generalise and choose the right answer. (Their general knowledge – that in many countries dinosaurs are very popular – will also help them get the answer.)

2 READ, THINK AND ANSWER.

Deal with question (1) first. Find out if people in your country are interested in dinosaurs. If not, it's a piece of cultural information about Britain that many British people are!
Then look at questions (2) and (3), and make sure that students understand them **before** they read. Tell them to look at the article very quickly to find the answers. Make it a light-hearted competition, *Who can finish first?*
Check the answers orally and discuss (in the native language, if necessary) if people can buy 'dino-products' in your country.
Then let the students go back and read more slowly, asking you for any help they need. As an oral task ask them to list the three other types of reptiles mentioned in the passage (snakes, lizards, turtles).

3 ⊡ READ, LISTEN AND FIND.

This task follows on directly from the last sentence of Exercise 2, *We asked some of our readers what they thought.*
We hear the words of the four readers that Mark telephoned. Let the students read the words in boxes 1-4 in the book before they hear the cassette, and guess who they think said them. The words on the cassette are similar but we must imagine that Mark 'edited them down' for the magazine.

4 THINK AND ANSWER.

Students summarise what each of the four children in Exercise 3 said. This activity gives guided practice in indirect speech (*is* in the direct words is changed to *was* after the past *thought*). Practice is also given in 'summarising' nouns like 'size' and 'appearance', e.g. *they* **looked** *so strange and interesting* (appearance) and *they were so big* (size).

WORKBOOK

The Workbook activities are all suitable for follow-up and consolidation work after the Student's Book lesson. Exercise 1 consolidates the idea of 'summarising nouns' started in the Student's Book, Exercise 4. To *size* and *appearance* are added *age* and *characters*. Different sentences from the same box can go under two headings, e.g. *People like to think about life millions of years ago* (age), *Many dinosaurs were enormous* (size). Good students can add ideas of their own under each heading.
Exercise 2 picks up two uses of the word *so*, both found in this lesson and in other parts of the book. It is best done in class with you to guide and check.
Exercise 3 is a puzzle for those students who enjoyed the idea of the tangram introduced earlier. They need to have the pieces to solve the puzzle. The solution is given below.

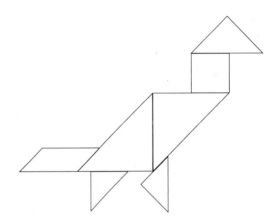

Exercise 4 is an optional extension of writing work. Students can get more ideas and language support from the Student's Book, Exercise 3 and the Workbook, Exercise 1. It would perhaps be a good subject for the class magazine.

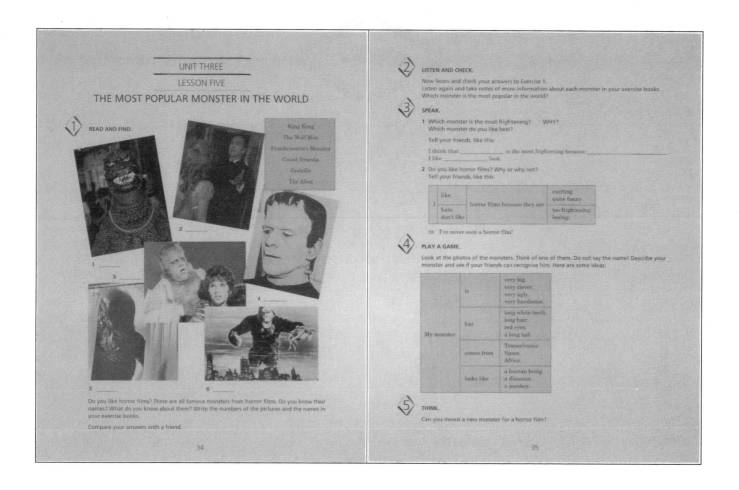

THE MOST POPULAR MONSTER IN THE WORLD

1 READ AND FIND.

King Kong
The Wolf Man
Frankenstein's Monster
Count Dracula
Godzilla
The Alien

Do you like horror films? These are all famous monsters from horror films. Do you know their names? What do you know about them? Write the numbers of the pictures and the names in your exercise books.

Compare your answers with a friend.

34

2 LISTEN AND CHECK.

Now listen and check your answers to Exercise 1.
Listen again and take notes of more information about each monster in your exercise books.
Which monster is the most popular in the world?

3 SPEAK.

1 Which monster is the most frightening?   WHY?
Which monster do you like best?

Tell your friends, like this:

I think that _____ is the most frightening because _____
I like _____ best.

2 Do you like horror films? Why or why not?
Tell your friends, like this:

	like		exciting.
I	hate	horror films because they are	quite funny
	don't like		too frightening.
			boring.

OR   I've never seen a horror film!

4 PLAY A GAME.

Look at the photos of the monsters. Think of one of them. Do not say the name! Describe your monster and see if your friends can recognise him. Here are some ideas:

	is	very big. very clever. very ugly. very handsome.
My monster	has	long white teeth. long hair. red eyes. a long tail.
	comes from	Transylvania. Space. Africa.
	looks like	a human being. a dinosaur. a monkey.

5 THINK.

Can you invent a new monster for a horror film?

35

KEY VOCABULARY	alien, frightening, gorilla, handsome, horror film, ugly, wolf

KEY GRAMMAR POINTS	Language of description (**revised**):
	noun + *be* + *very* and adjective
	        + *has* + adjective + noun
	        + *looks like* + *a* + noun
	I like/hate/don't like (**revised**)

SKILLS	Recognising pictures of characters from an oral description; Describing pictures

LESSON 5   THE MOST POPULAR MONSTER IN THE WORLD

1 READ AND FIND.

Students are encouraged to use and share their background knowledge in this activity. Let them make their guesses by themselves, writing the number of the picture and the name in their exercise books. Emphasise that this is not a test, but a preparation for the listening in Exercise 2. Then let them compare with friends. Encourage them to speak, and look at the pictures, rather than just looking at each other's exercise books. They could say, e.g. *I don't know no.4, do you?* or *I think no.6 is King Kong.* If they need help, say the sentences yourself and put them on the board. Collect ideas from the whole class, but do not confirm the right answers at this stage. Pretend not to be sure about some. (The idea is to reinforce the strategy of making guesses before they listen, because having some expectations, and knowing what information you need to listen very carefully for, helps them to become more efficient listeners.)

2 🔊 LISTEN AND CHECK.

Say, *Now listen to the cassette. It will give you all the answers.* Students should look at their guesses for Exercise 1 and confirm or change the names they guessed for each picture.
The descriptions of each monster on the cassette should make it quite clear what name goes with each picture.
Answers: 1 Godzilla **2** Dracula **3** Wolf Man
4 Frankenstein's monster **5** Alien **6** King Kong
If you wish, use the tapescript to help you ask questions about each monster, e.g. *What did King Kong look like?* (a huge gorilla).

3 SPEAK.

Let the students think about the two questions and prepare sentences to say to a friend and then the rest of the class. Weaker students may want to write their sentences first. The language models give support. Ask them to practise in pairs, then ask individuals to say what they think.
Then do a quick Class Survey. Put the six monster names on the board and ask each child round the class to say: *I like .... best.* Put a tick on the board under the appropriate name for each vote. Students then count the votes and write (then say), *The most popular monster in this class is ....* The Workbook, Exercise 1, goes into more detail about the most popular monster in the world – Dracula – but your class may prefer another monster!

4 PLAY A GAME.

Demonstrate and practise the game with the whole class first. Pretend to think of a monster yourself, and describe it/him, using language from the blue language box. The students guess which one it is. Then ask some individuals to challenge the class. Now they should be ready to play the game in pairs.

5 THINK.

Students often enjoy inventing their own characters. Individuals work alone – inventing a name and perhaps drawing a sketch, and preparing a description. They then tell the rest of the class, using the language box in Exercise 4 to help them.

WORKBOOK

The Workbook activity, Exercise 1, can be used in class for further reading practice (immediately, or you could save it for a later stage in the course, as revision). Alternatively, a good class could do the reading at home for homework. The language in the passage is quite easy by this stage.
Exercise 2 is good for a 'time-filler' in class if you need one, now or later, or it can be done for homework. (The names of some of the characters, e.g. Sherlock Holmes and Ben Hur could provide a starting-point for a general knowledge lesson on popular characters in the media, books or British folklore.)
Exercise 3 is optional extra writing work. Ideas for narrating the story can come from Workbook, Exercise 1. It could also provide an idea for class magazine articles.

CULTURAL NOTES

Many people dismiss horror stories and films as rubbish but many film-experts accept some films, e.g. 'Nosferatu'' and Francis Ford Coppola's recent Bram Stoker's 'Dracula' as valid works of art. Most people find 'King Kong' and the 'Godzilla' films funny rather than frightening. See if anyone knows about the 1993 Dinosaur horror film 'Jurassic Park' by Stephen Spielberg.
Many science fiction books, e.g. those by Isaac Asimov, A.C. Clarke and J.G. Ballard are becoming more and more accepted as valid works of literature.

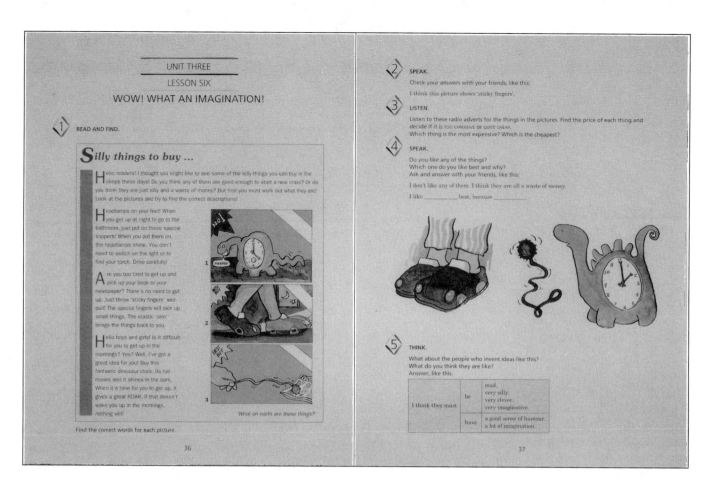

KEY VOCABULARY	description, headlamps, headlights, imaginative, mad, might (*verb*), pence, pick up, roar, sense of humour, slippers, stick (*verb*), sticky, stretch, torch, wake up, waste, what on earth...?
KEY GRAMMAR POINTS	Imperative (**revised**) used in recommendations and adverbs: *Just throw 'sticky fingers' and pull/Buy this fantastic dinosaur clock; Must* used to express certainty: *I think they must be very clever.*
SKILLS	Recognising pictures from a description; Learning about British money

LESSON 6   WOW! WHAT AN IMAGINATION!

1 READ AND FIND.

Look at the three pictures with the class and discuss what they show: (**1**) and (**2**) are easy to guess but *What on earth is number 3?* (Teach the idiomatic expression *What on earth ......?* It will be very useful in later lessons on strange events and mysterious objects.) Explain that these things are typical of the 'novelties' that British children (and adults) like. Read the first paragraph of the article, then ask the students to read the rest by themselves, to find the correct paragraph to go with each picture.

2 SPEAK.

Students check with a partner that they agree about which description goes with which picture. With a confident class, extend the speech work. Ask, *Which one makes a noise? Which ones shine in the dark? Which one picks things up?* (Recycle the word '*luminous*' to describe the dinosaur clock.)

3 👓 LISTEN.

Make sure that the students realise that the first time they listen to the cassette, their objective is to find out the three prices. (They can listen again later, for other details.) Remind them about British money (all they need for this activity are the words *pounds, pence/p.*) Invite some guesses about the possible prices for each item before they listen, like this: *How much is the clock? What do you think? £10, £20, £5.50p?* Collect different guesses and put them on the board. When the students hear the cassette, they can see whose guesses were the closest. (Students may have little idea of the equivalences of the English prices to their own money at this stage, so check the current rate of exchange and give them a 'rough and ready' equivalence for £10.)
That will allow them to express an *opinion* about the price of each item as well as to discover the price itself. The stages of working are like this:
   1 Collect the three prices.
   2 Find out the cheapest and most expensive items.
   3 Give an opinion if any of the things are too expensive or quite cheap.
Students can then listen again for more details. (The language on the cassette contains many of the same items as in Exercise 1, but has extra features such as, *Please don't throw it at your dog or cat ... .*)

4 SPEAK.

Students can give their opinions about the item they like best, OR reject them all because they are a waste of money.

5 THINK.

Make the point that it is actually some people's JOB to invent novelties like this! Ask the students what type of person they think this is. They give answers, supported by the language table. (**NB** *must* is used here to express a very strong *probability*.) You can turn this activity into a brief Class Survey of students' opinions. Put the headings MAD CLEVER IMAGINATIVE SILLY on the board and see how many people 'vote' for each opinion.

WORKBOOK

Exercises 1 and 2 consolidated the listening work done in Student's Book, Exercise 3 and can, if wished, be done in class immediately after the listening work. Alternatively, they can be done at the end of the lesson. Exercises 3, 4 and 5 expand on the theme of how different people show their talent. In Exercise 3, students group the famous people next to sentences describing a type of talent, e.g. Kodaly and Chopin go with *good at music*.
In Exercise 4 they decide which talents they themselves have (every student should be encouraged to find something that he or she is good at). Exercise 5 suggests some research to find out more about the talented people mentioned in Exercises 3 and 4.

CULTURAL NOTE

Your students may be shocked or amused at the ways in which some British people like to spend their money. Point out that not *every*one does this, but that these 'toys' are very popular. Many of them are bought by mail-order and there are many catalogues of mail-order novelties. Even institutions like The Natural History Museum and the World Wide Fund for Nature have a mail-order business that helps them to make money to support their work.

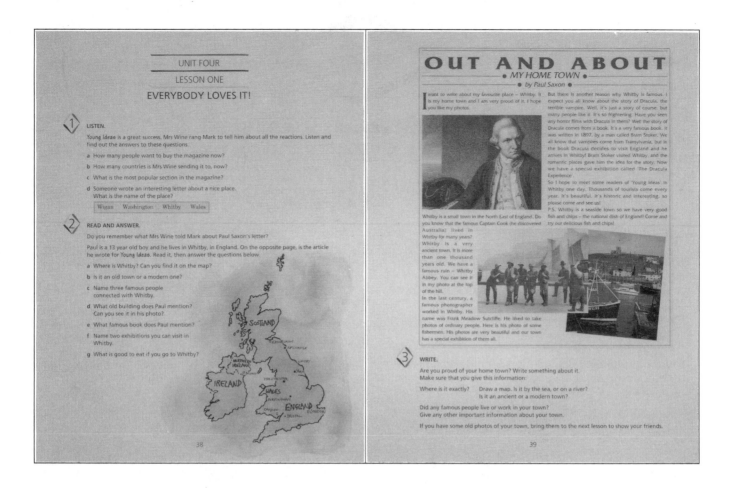

KEY VOCABULARY	abbey, captain, century, connected, discover, fisherman, hill, historic, national dish, opposite, place, reactions, ruin, success
KEY GRAMMAR POINTS	Present tense (used in the physical description of Whitby, in Exercise 2 and in the summary of the story of Dracula) integrated with Past tense (used in the historical narrative sections of the passage). Students should note the appropriate choices of each tense made in the article.
SKILLS	Using comprehension questions to help guide and support listening and reading. Students look for these information points first. Freer writing using the passage in Exercise 2 as a guide

LESSON 1 EVERYBODY LOVES IT!

1 ⊙⊙ LISTEN.

Read the four questions with the students **before** they listen and make sure that they understand what information they must find. Elicit some good strategies, e.g. if they see a question with *How many...?* in it they should listen for a **number.** For **c)** ask them to recall some of the sections that they know are in the magazine. Elicit a list orally. Perhaps one of these sections will be the one named on the cassette as the 'most popular'. Question **d)** is easy to guess if they look at the following exercises. It is there to raise awareness of the new name 'Whitby'. The recording is quite long and Mrs Wine and Mark have a good friendly chat, so the students will probably not understand every word. Impress upon them that this does not matter, so long as they can find the answers to the four important questions. Play the cassette as often as needed, then elicit answers orally. When answers have been given, play the cassette again, stopping at the points where the answers are to be found and check if everyone still thinks their answers are correct.

2 READ AND ANSWER.

The instructions suggest that the students read the article and then answer the questions, but it is of course good practice to go quickly through the questions with them orally **before** they read. This will guide their reading since they will have an idea of what sort of information to look for. Once these questions have been answered, you can ask supplementary questions of your own, to make them go back and look quickly at the by now 'familiar' article to find the information, e.g. *Who can tell me first – Why is Captain Cook famous? When was 'Dracula' written?*

3 WRITE.

Allow the students to make some notes before they write, and encourage them to look at the passage in Exercise 2 to find good ideas for useful expressions. The students' efforts will probably not be perfect at the first attempt, but try to act as an 'editor' rather than as a 'judge' and make helpful suggestions about what needs to be improved. **Then** let them try again, and if you wish, you can at this stage 'mark' the work.

WORKBOOK

The Workbook picks ups two themes of cultural information:

- Different food in different countries. The fish and chip shop menu in Exercise 1 is intended to arouse students' curiosity (see CULTURAL NOTES below).

  Exercise 2 encourages students to try to write something about food in their own country. The questions provide heavy guidance for the type of information needed and the order it should come in. The passage in Exercise 1 contains many useful expressions for this.

- Exercise 3 contains a more detailed account of Captain Cook's life. (See if some students notice that it is quite funny that his name was 'Cook' and that much of this lesson is concerned with food!) Exercise 4 contains some traditional word-play jokes about country names, to link with the 'travel' theme.

CULTURAL NOTES

Most of the information in the Student's Book and Workbook is self explanatory. If you wish to develop any of the themes more, most encyclopaedias will offer adequate information on all the topics.

The address of The Yorkshire Tourist Board is:

Yorkshire and Humberside Tourist Board,
Burniston Road,
Scarborough,
North Yorkshire,
YO12 6PE

The fish and chip shop menu contains some possible strange items. Cod, plaice and haddock are three types of common North Sea fish. 'Curry sauce' is a fairly modern item. Most British people love Indian food, so the idea of putting curry on your chips was a natural mixing of cultures! Pickled onions and eggs are preserved in vinegar and are highly spicy.

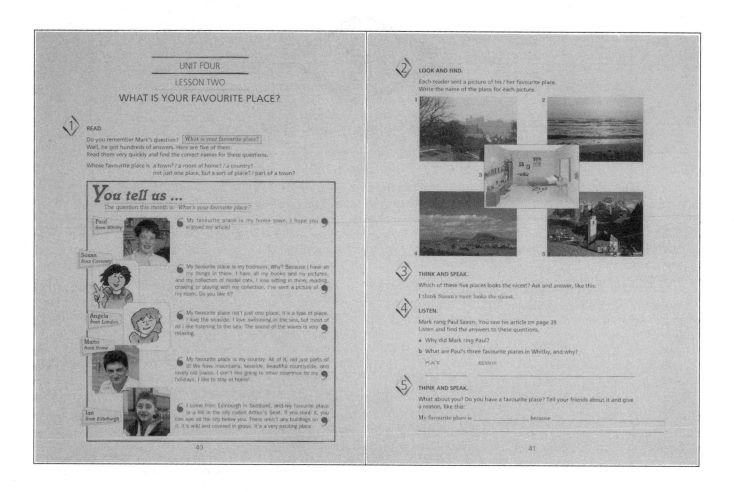

KEY VOCABULARY	collection, countryside, relaxing, room, talent, waves
KEY GRAMMAR POINTS	*My favourite place is ...* ; revision of superlatives – *the nicest*; revision of language for giving reasons: *Why? Because ...*
SKILLS	Fast reading to find limited information; Listening for specific information

LESSON 2   WHAT IS YOUR FAVOURITE PLACE?

1 READ.

Remind students of the '**You tell us**' format. Point out that the first time they read, they must try to find out the **name** of the boy or girl who likes:

a town (**answer**, Paul, Whitby)
a room (**answer**, Susan, her bedroom)
a country (**answer** Mario, Italy)
a type of place (**answer** Angela, the seaside)

Encourage the students to read quickly by asking the first question orally, then saying *Now look and find out. Who can be first?* Once the correct answer has been given, the activity becomes progressively easier, since the pupils can work by elimination. This is fine, since the purpose of the first activity is to encourage quick skimming to find out very simple information.

2 LOOK AND FIND.

At this stage, the student must read the '**You tell us**' section much more carefully, to find the pictures that correspond to the students' answers.

Answers   1 Whitby, 2 seaside, 3 Susan's bedroom, 4 Edinburgh, 5 Italy

3 THINK AND SPEAK.

Here the students are encouraged to bring in some personal taste in their choice of the 'nicest' place. They do not have to say **why** at this stage, though faster students may wish to and should be allowed to. (Everyone must say **why** in Exercise 5 once Exercise 4 has prepared them for it.)

4 ⌧ LISTEN.

The conversation between Paul and Mark is long and 'chatty' and the students may not understand every word! Let them listen once and take notes. Then let them compare answers with a friend, but don't ask for answers yourself at this stage. Then play the cassette again and let them check their answers. Elicit answers and play the cassette once

more, pausing it at the appropriate places to make sure that everyone hears the information correctly this time.

5 THINK AND SPEAK.

Students can now prepare a sentence or two about their favourite place. Language from Exercise 1 and from the cassette in Exercise 4 will be useful for this. Let everyone have a turn to speak. If you wish, turn it into a Class Survey, by listing the places mentioned on the board and putting a tick for each mention opposite a particular place. Perhaps there will be no 'most popular' place, but it will be interesting to find out!

WORKBOOK

Exercise 1 encourages students to collect the ideas from Exercise 5 in the Student's Book, and to write them in '**You tell us**' form. This can provide material for one of the first class magazine items, and students are encouraged to select about 10. This means looking at everybody else's work. Interesting ideas are more important than perfect English, since the English can later be 'edited' to make a perfect product for the magazine. Exercise 2 follows up Mark's promise to become Paul's penfriend, heard in Exercise 4 in the Student's Book. The letter is used first as a reading comprehension, then in Exercise 3 as a useful source of expressions for a 'penfriend' letter, which should now be more sophisticated than that attempted in Unit 1, Lesson 2.

CULTURAL NOTES

Notice how Ian from Edinburgh in Exercise 1 in the Student's Book, is very specific that he comes from Scotland. The people of the three different countries (apart from England) that make up the United Kingdom are very proud of their origins, and the Welsh, the Scottish and the Northern Irish become very offended if anyone makes the common mistake of calling them all English!

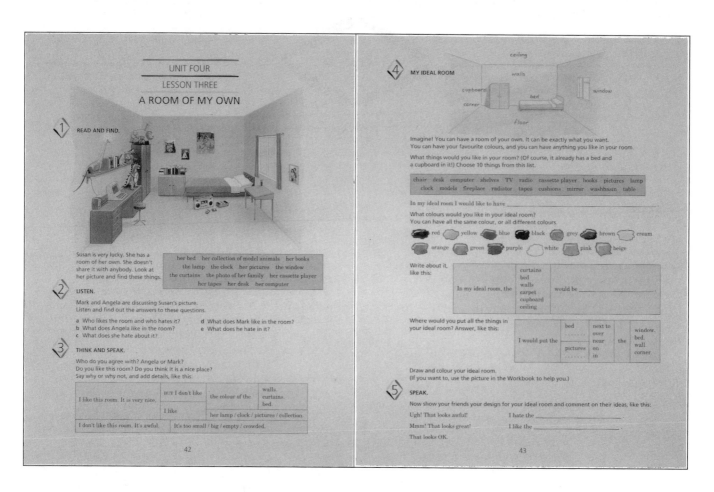

KEY VOCABULARY	beige, cream (and all the other previously met colour words), bright, carpet, cassette player, corner, crowded, curtains, fireplace, ideal, lamp, own, radiator, shelves, tapes, wall, washbasin
KEY GRAMMAR POINTS	*I like/don't like ... ; It's too ...*
	Would in hypothetical sentences: *In my ideal room the walls would be white. I would put the bed next to the window.*
SKILLS	Expressing and comparing personal tastes, trying different colour-combinations

LESSON 3   A ROOM OF MY OWN

1 READ AND FIND.

Not all children are lucky enough to have their own room, and there is no attempt in this lesson to assume that they do, but they can dream. Look at the picture of Susan's room and ask students to find and point to the things listed in the vocabulary box – most words are recycled from earlier in this book and from *Tiptop 1* to *Tiptop 3*. Check that all the words are understood. Then ask the class's opinion of the room. Is it nice or not? Do not go into detail at this stage since this type of language will be extensively practised in Exercise 3. Your question is just to prepare them for Exercise 2 in which Angela and Mark disagree about it.

2 🔲 LISTEN.

Read the questions and check that the students understand them before they listen. Play the cassette and let the students take notes. Then let them compare notes before you play the cassette again for the next try. Collect answers orally.

Answers
a Mark likes the room. Angela hates it.
b She likes the collection of animal models.
c She hates the green walls, the purple curtains and the purple bed.
d He likes the dinosaur clock, the collection of model animals.
e He hates the curtains.

3 THINK AND SPEAK.

Use the information gathered in Exercise 2 to help the students compare their ideas with Angela's and Mark's. They can then prepare sentences giving their own opinions, using the language table as a support. Take an informal 'hands up' vote to see who likes the room and who does not.

4 MY IDEAL ROOM

Encourage students to use fantasy and to really exaggerate, both about the colours and about the things they would like in their 'dream' room. Most parents would object to red walls, but if a student would like them in the 'dream' room, he or she should say so! Workbook Exercise 3 gives space for drawing and writing about the ideal room, so after the students have given oral answers, turn to the Workbook and do Exercises 1 to 3.

5 SPEAK.

Students look at each other's 'designs' in the Workbook and comment, using the language models suggested in the Student's Book.

WORKBOOK

Exercises 1 to 3 have been covered in the Student's Book lesson notes above. Workbook Exercises 4 and 5 are to deepen awareness of different design possibilities for students who are interested in visual arts, and can be done as a homework option.

CULTURAL NOTES

Point out that not many British children of 11 or 12 have a room of their own, and many prefer to share with a brother or a sister. Do not let the rather affluent lifestyle shown in Susan's room seem the norm. It was pointed out in Student's Book, Exercise 1, that Susan is lucky.

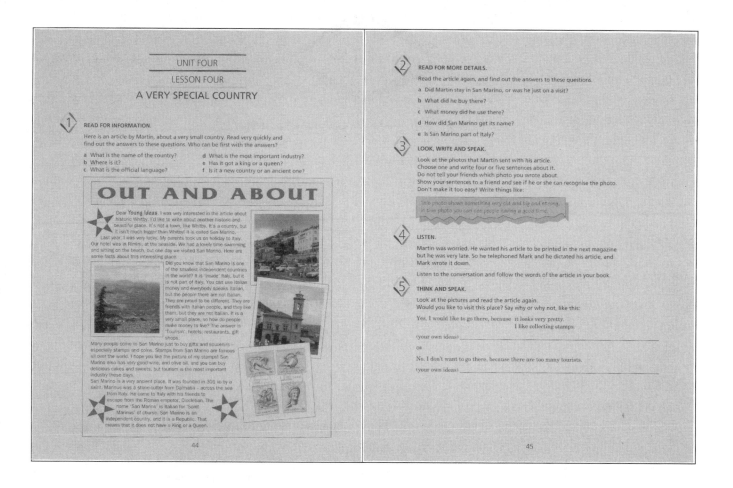

KEY VOCABULARY	beach, emperor, found (*verb*), independent, industry, olive oil, Republic, saint, stay, tourism, wine
KEY GRAMMAR POINTS	*I would like ... because ... ;*
SKILLS	Identifying a place from a description

UNIT 4

LESSON 4   A VERY SPECIAL COUNTRY

1 READ FOR INFORMATION.

Read questions (a)-(f) before the students look at the
article, and make sure that they understand them.
Ask students to look at the article to find the answers
as quickly as they can, to encourage rapid scanning
for information. Say that you will give them only
two minutes. Collect answers orally.

2 READ FOR MORE DETAILS.

Let the students read again more slowly to find the
answers to questions (a)-(e). Collect answers orally.
(Spend some time looking at the photos and
enjoying them.)

3 LOOK, WRITE AND SPEAK.

Students choose one of the pictures from the article
and write an accurate (but mysterious) description of
it, using the ideas in the Student's Book. They show
this to a friend who tries to identify the correct
picture.

4 ☞ LISTEN.

This activity allows students to listen and follow the
words in the book. The objective of this is to allow
them to make a subconscious link between the
sounds of whole words and the way they look in the
written form. It is also a preparation for the more
difficult dictation activities which will be found later
in the course (beginning with Unit 6, Lesson 1).

5 THINK AND SPEAK.

This activity encourages students to give their own
opinions. They must justify their opinions, and for
this they need to read the article in Exercise 1 again
to help them. They prepare their answers using the
language models in the book. They can write them
first if they wish.

WORKBOOK

All the activities here can be done for homework.

Exercise 1 is a simple wordsearch activity to
reinforce the adjectives used in the article in the
Student's Book, Exercise 1.

Exercise 2 is a gap-filling activity to reinforce the
language used in the article in the Student's Book,
Exercise 1.

Exercise 3 is a freer writing activity, building on the
oral work done in the Student's Book, Exercise 5.

Free writing is introduced gently throughout this
level of the course, alternating with guided writing
for more demanding topics.

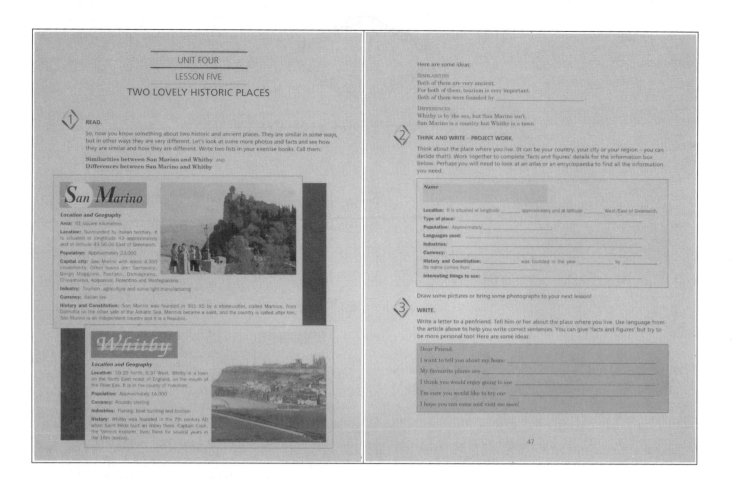

KEY VOCABULARY	agriculture, ancient, approximately, area, atlas, boat-building, constitution, county, currency, encyclopaedia, explorer, fishing, kilometre, latitude, location, longitude, manufacturing, mouth (of a river), personal, population, region, several, situated, sterling, surrounded, territory
KEY GRAMMAR POINTS	No new grammar points, since the lesson is heavy on geography-related vocabulary
SKILLS	Understanding and composing formally-expressed information about the geography, economy, history and administration of places; Transforming this type of information to a more personal mode suitable for penfriend letters; Reading to find similarities and differences between places

This lesson offers obvious possibilities for cross-curricular work where this is appropriate, but it can also be treated in a 'lighter' way, with less emphasis on technical matters such as latitude and longitude.
It will be useful to have an atlas or a big map of Italy and of Britain in class for this lesson. Geography textbooks or encyclopaedias in the native language might also provide useful comparisons for how formal information about places is presented. See CULTURAL NOTES for information on such terms as *county*.

1 READ.

The two places are already familiar from Unit 4, Lesson 1 and Unit 4, Lesson 4. The information here is

expressed in a more formal way, in the style found in encyclopaedias and other works of reference. Pay particular attention to the headings, such as **currency** and **population**.
Before the students do the note-taking activity for Exercise 1, give the following 'read and find' tasks orally. Collect the answers one at a time, and then ask the next 'search' question to encourage the students to **scan** the passages very quickly to find the information. Make it into a lighthearted competition: *Who can find the answer first? Hands up!* Examples of suitable 'search' questions:
How many people live in San Marino/Whitby?

LESSON 5   TWO LOVELY HISTORIC PLACES

Which is older San Marino or Whitby?
Who founded Whitby/San Marino?
What is the name of the river in Whitby?
Then let the students read the two passages more
slowly. Tell them that they can ask you for help with
any difficulties. Let them decide what to ask about.
Many of the 'new' words should not cause
difficulties in the clear context, since geographical
information in their own language probably contains
the same elements in the same sort of order.
It may be helpful for you, then, to read both passages
aloud to give them the model for saying some of the
expressions containing numbers. The latitude and
longitude figures should be read like this:
59.29 *Fifty nine point two nine.*
0.37 *Zero point three seven.*

For classes who are not yet dealing with latitude and
longitude in their geography lessons, do not
emphasise this aspect of the information. It has been
included to form a 'link' for teachers in countries
where this aspect of geography is already being
taught.
The students should now be ready to do the
similarities and **differences**, note-taking work. Ideas
and support for this are given at the top of page 47 of
the Student's Book. Encourage them to find as many
of each as they can by themselves, and then to
compare ideas in pairs or small groups, and add to
their own lists. Then write the headings, SIMILARITIES
and DIFFERENCES on the board. Elicit answers orally
from the whole class, and see how long a list for each
you can build up as a cooperative effort. Encourage
students to say whole sentences like those at the top
of page 47.

2 THINK AND WRITE – PROJECT WORK.

The chart to fill in is only an indication of types of
information that could be included. Students can
redesign it, leaving out or putting in some things.
Form pairs or small groups for working together. If
all the students come from the same big town or city,
they may produce similar information, but some
students who come from a village outside the city, or
who have 'roots' somewhere else may choose that
place. Atlases and reference books will be useful
here, but do not insist that the more technical
information is included if this is outside students'
current studies in their geography lessons.
You will probably have only one or two reference
books available, and certainly not enough for each
pair or group to have one. This does not matter. In

fact, you can turn it into an advantage. Encourage
students to fill in all the information they can, and
then to put up their hands for permission to come to
the front to consult the books. Help them as they do
this. Alternatively, you can act as 'Information
Centre'. They put up their hands and ask e.g. *Can
you tell me the population of Madrid, please?* Make a
great show of consulting the book, and then give the
answer.
Encourage students to draw illustrations (maps,
pictures) or to find photos at home for follow-up in a
future lesson. This activity could then be developed
into an illustrated wall display or part of the class
magazine.

3 WRITE.

The point of this activity is to show that we present
information in a rather different way when we are
writing something personal. A penfriend would
probably not be very interested in too many 'facts
and figures'. Encourage students to write to a
penfriend about the same place as in Exercise 2 but
ask them to be more personal and less detailed.

WORKBOOK

The Workbook, Exercise 1, picks up the idea of more
personal information about a place and integrates
Family and Friends information from earlier lessons.
Students extract information from the letter and fill it
in on the grid. Exercise 2 is a 'magic word' puzzle
with clues taken from the geography language of the
Student's Book. The answer is *Budapest.* In Exercise 3,
students are challenged to make a similar puzzle
about a place name, again recycling language from
the Student's Book. This type of puzzle would be
very good for the class magazine.

CULTURAL NOTES

A *county* corresponds roughly to a *region* in many
places. Each county is an administrative district with
its own principal town or city. People feel fiercely
loyal to their counties. It is probably not worth
spending a lot of time on the complications of the
modern British system of *counties.* There have been
many modern administrative changes of county
boundaries, and many smaller counties have been
'absorbed'.

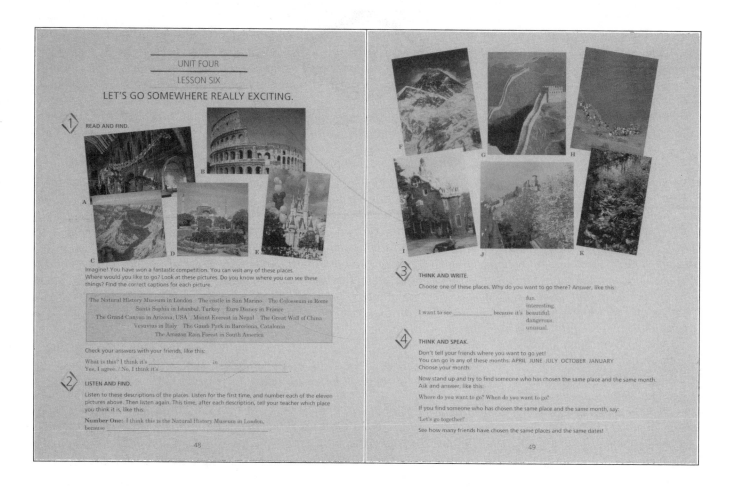

KEY VOCABULARY	architect, Christian, country, Moslem, mosque, natural, unusual, volcano, and month names revised
KEY GRAMMAR POINTS	*I want to ...; When/where do you want to go?* (**revised**)
SKILLS	Asking questions and listening carefully to the answers to see if the other person is your 'partner' (has chosen the same things) or not

1 READ AND FIND.

Read the introduction to the students. They must imagine that they have won a prize of a visit to any of the places in the pictures, but first they must name the places. The green caption box gives the names of the places for the students to match. Some of the pictures are obvious, but others need a careful look. Ask students to write the letters **A** to **K** in their exercise books, like this:

A
B
C
etc.

They then copy what they think are the correct names next to the letters. Then they compare their lists with a partner, discussing them in the way suggested in the model language at the end of Exercise 1. After some discussion in pairs, collect answers from the whole class, asking the rest of the class after each contribution, *Do you agree?*

Answers · **A** The Natural History Museum
B The Colosseum
C The Grand Canyon
D Santa Sophia
E EuroDisney
F Mount Everest
G The Great Wall of China
H Vesuvius (looking down into the crater)
I Gaudi Park
J San Marino, the castle
K The Amazon Rain Forest

LESSON 6   LET'S GO SOMEWHERE REALLY EXCITING.

2 🔲 LISTEN AND FIND.

Now that the lists are complete and correct, ask the students to listen to the radio quiz, and on their lists to write the numbers of the places mentioned. There is an example in the book and on the cassette: no. 1 is the Natural History Museum. When they have heard the cassette once, rewind and play it again, pausing it after each description for the students to give their answers orally. When all the answers have been agreed upon, you may play the cassette once more using the gap-filling activity, Exercise 1 in the Workbook for consolidation.

3 THINK AND WRITE.

Each student chooses one place (this must be kept a secret) and writes the reason for wanting to go there. Circulate and see what students are choosing, but do not let anyone know what others have chosen. This activity is preparation for the game in Exercise 4.

4 THINK AND SPEAK.

Remind the students of the imaginary competition that they have all won. They can go to visit the place they have chosen, but they must decide in which month to go. (They can only choose one of five months – the ones in the book or any other five or the game will not work so well.) Their choice of month is a secret, too, until the game begins. They must write down the month as well as the place to prevent 'cheating' and changing of minds during the game.

Students stand up and move around the class asking, *Where do you want to go?* If their friend has chosen a different place, they move on to the next person. If they find someone who wants to go to the same place, they next ask, *When do you want to go?* If they find a friend with the same place and the same month, they say, *Let's go together!* and go and stand together at the front of the class. Other students can join them, too, if they have chosen the same place and month, but they must ask the questions first.

This may seem a noisy activity, but it need not be. If you do not want all the students walking about at the same time, start with everybody sitting down and appoint four or five people to walk around quietly asking people near them the questions. If they find a 'partner', they say *Let's go together!* and stand next to them. If they find no-one, they go back to their places. In either case, a new person may stand up and move around. The aim of the game is **not** to finish first, but to see how many groups or pairs of people with the same ideas can be formed. A good follow-up to the game is to put this grid on the board and check round the class, asking *Where did you want to go? When did you want to go?* (since the event is now over), and putting a tick on the grid for every person who chooses a particular time and place. Then you can discuss whether there was a **most popular** place or month.

PLACE	APRIL JUNE JULY OCTOBER JANUARY
Natural History Museum	
Colosseum	
Grand Canyon	

WORKBOOK

As mentioned before, Exercise 1 could be used in class **after** the listening comprehension has been completed, as a way of letting students see the words of the quite complex radio broadcast. Exercise 2 develops the language in the Student's Book, with students having to give reasons for wanting or not wanting to see each of the places. It could be done in class or for homework. Exercise 3 is a wordsearch puzzle which challenges students to find, not only the place names, but some suitable adjectives to describe some of them, also hidden in the puzzle.

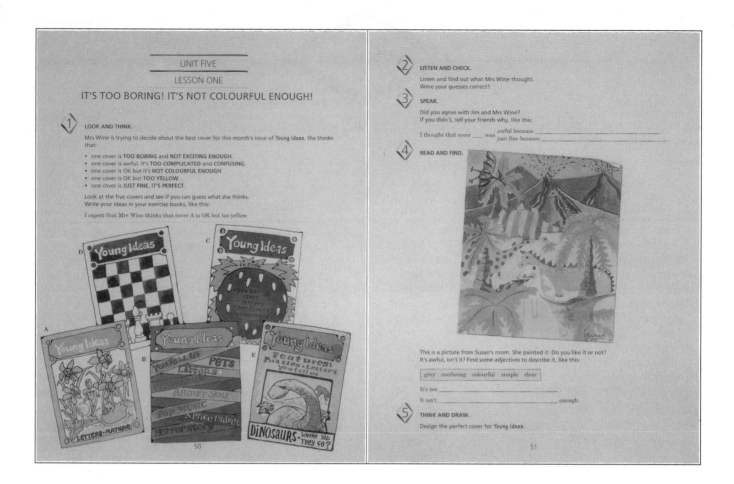

UNIT FIVE

LESSON ONE

IT'S TOO BORING! IT'S NOT COLOURFUL ENOUGH!

1 LOOK AND THINK.

Mrs Wine is trying to decide about the best cover for this month's issue of *Young Ideas*. She thinks that:

- one cover is **TOO BORING** and **NOT EXCITING ENOUGH**.
- one cover is awful. It's **TOO COMPLICATED** and **CONFUSING**.
- one cover is OK but it's **NOT COLOURFUL ENOUGH**.
- one cover is OK but **TOO YELLOW**.
- one cover is **JUST FINE. IT'S PERFECT**.

Look at the five covers and see if you can guess what she thinks. Write your ideas in your exercise books, like this:

I expect that Mrs Wine thinks that cover A is OK but too yellow.

2 LISTEN AND CHECK.

Listen and find out what Mrs Wine thought. Were your guesses correct?

3 SPEAK.

Did you agree with Jim and Mrs Wine? If you didn't, tell your friends why, like this:

I thought that cover ____ was awful because _____
                                 just fine because _____.

4 READ AND FIND.

This is a picture from Susan's room. She painted it. Do you like it or not? It's awful, isn't it? Find some adjectives to describe it, like this:

| grey confusing colourful simple clear |

It's too _____

It isn't _____ enough.

5 THINK AND DRAW.

Design the perfect cover for *Young Ideas*.

KEY VOCABULARY	complicated, elegant, simple
KEY GRAMMAR POINTS	*too* + adjective; *not* + adjective; *enough*
SKILLS	Exercising and expressing choices based on personal taste

LESSON 1   IT'S TOO BORING! IT'S NOT COLOURFUL ENOUGH!

1 LOOK AND THINK.

Look at the five possible covers, A,B,C,D,E, with the students before they read. They are deliberately extreme in their designs to draw strong reactions from the students. (They may, of course, not agree with Mrs Wine's preference!) Ask which one they prefer and take a vote. Then go back to Mrs Wine's situation. She must choose the 'best cover'. Let them read her five opinions. (*Complicated* is a new word, but it is in the same sentence as *confusing*, so this should help students to guess its meaning.) Ask them to guess which of Mrs Wine's opinions, matches which cover, and say, e.g. *I expect that Mrs Wine thinks that.......* . (This language model is in the book.) This raising of expectations will prepare them for the listening in Exercise 2.

2 ☉☉ LISTEN AND CHECK.

Students listen to Mrs Wine and Jim talking and confirm or change their guesses in Exercise 1. When they are happy with their answers, play the cassette again asking the students to 'collect' (noting down or trying to remember) some of the comments Mrs Wine made. You can use the Workbook, Exercises 1 and 3, and the tapescript later to select some of the phrases you would like the students to learn. (*Elegant* is a useful new word from the cassette.)

3 SPEAK.

Students may not agree with Mrs Wine and Jim. Ask them to choose one cover each and to prepare some comments on it. They can practise their comments in pairs. Then ask individuals to tell the whole class their ideas. The rest of the class should be encouraged to say, *Yes, I agree, That's right*, or *I don't agree*.

4 READ AND FIND.

The big picture is an enlargement of Susan's painting from her room in Unit 4, Lesson 2. The Student's Book says that it's awful, but do the students agree? Find out how many students do *not* like it, and ask them to prepare negative comments, using the language model in the book. The students who *do* like it can prepare a defence, saying, e.g. *I don't agree. I think it's attractive/interesting*, etc.
Try to encourage discussions about personal taste throughout the course wherever an opportunity presents itself.

5 THINK AND DRAW.

This is an optional opportunity for students to express their personal taste by designing a cover that is both clear and attractive. They can criticise each other's efforts using the language modelled in this lesson. This activity is best done in conjunction with Workbook, Exercise 3.

WORKBOOK

Exercise 1 consolidates the language used by Mrs Wine about the covers seen in the Student's Book. Exercise 2 is a completion activity using the tapescript of Mrs Wine's conversation with Jim, and reinforcing the 'personal taste' language it practises. Exercise 3 is a support for Student's Book, Exercise 5. Here the students are invited not only to comment orally, but to write a report about someone else's design, as if they were editors. Each student should write comments in their friend's Workbook. The design work can be done at home, but the Workbooks should be exchanged in class and the comments written (and discussed) then. This need not be done in the lesson immediately after Exercise 5, but could be kept as a 'filler' activity for a later lesson, when it would supply valuable revision work.

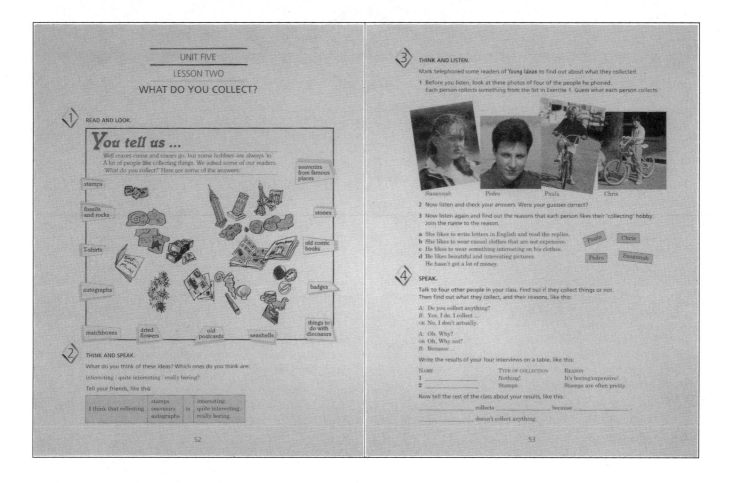

UNIT FIVE

LESSON TWO

WHAT DO YOU COLLECT?

1 READ AND LOOK.

You tell us ...

Well crazes come and crazes go, but some hobbies are always 'in'. A lot of people like collecting things. We asked some of our readers 'What do you collect?' Here are some of the answers:

stamps

fossils and rocks

T-shirts

autographs

matchboxes

dried flowers

old postcards

seashells

souvenirs from famous places

stones

old comic books

badges

things to do with dinosaurs

2 THINK AND SPEAK.

What do you think of these ideas? Which ones do you think are:

interesting / quite interesting / really boring?

Tell your friends, like this:

| I think that collecting | stamps souvenirs autographs | is | interesting. quite interesting. really boring. |

52

3 THINK AND LISTEN.

Mark telephoned some readers of *Young Ideas* to find out about what they collected.

1 Before you listen, look at these photos of four of the people he phoned. Each person collects something from the list in Exercise 1. Guess what each person collects.

Susannah   Pedro   Paula   Chris

2 Now listen and check your answers. Were your guesses correct?

3 Now listen again and find out the reasons that each person likes their 'collecting' hobby. Join the name to the reason.

a She likes to write letters in English and read the replies.
b She likes to wear casual clothes that are not expensive.
c He likes to wear something interesting on his clothes.
d He likes beautiful and interesting pictures. He hasn't got a lot of money.

Paula   Chris

Pedro   Susannah

4 SPEAK.

Talk to four other people in your class. Find out if they collect things or not. Then find out what they collect, and their reasons, like this:

A: Do you collect anything?
B: Yes, I do. I collect ...
OR No, I don't actually.

A: Oh. Why?
OR Oh. Why not?
B: Because ...

Write the results of your four interviews on a table, like this:

NAME	TYPE OF COLLECTION	REASON
1 _____	Nothing!	It's boring/expensive!
2 _____	Stamps	Stamps are often pretty.

Now tell the rest of the class about your results, like this:

_____ collects _____ because _____

_____ doesn't collect anything.

53

KEY VOCABULARY	actually, autograph, casual, fossil, matchbox, seashell
KEY GRAMMAR POINTS	*I think that ...* (indirect speech)
SKILLS	Interviewing each other, listening carefully to information and tabulating it; Summarising information collected

LESSON 2   WHAT DO YOU COLLECT?

1 READ AND LOOK.

The objects collected and the captions in the big picture are in the correct places, near to each other. Students look at it together, pointing from caption to picture to check and to remind themselves of the vocabulary, most of which has been met before. Invite students to add any ideas of their own about things that they collect. If they don't know a word, encourage them to ask you.
(Repeat the Rhyme from Unit 1, Lesson 4, *What can you do if you don't know a word ...?* on this and other suitable occasions.)
Please, how do you say ... in English? If you don't know a word (and words to do with collecting can be very obscure!), do not be embarrassed. Say, *Aha! That's an unusual word! I'll look it up!* Show how quickly you can look it up and find it. Students should see you as a role-model in this – someone who knows a lot of English, but is equally good at 'finding out' efficiently, when really unusual words are needed. Put all the 'extra' words for things that students in the class collect on the board. You could make a joke like, *Now let's **collect** some words!*

2 THINK AND SPEAK.

Students now give their opinions about all the collecting ideas (the ones in the box in Exercise 1 and the ones that they contributed themselves). They can do this in pairs and/or to the whole class. See if any collecting hobby comes out as very popular or very unpopular.

3 ◯◯ THINK AND LISTEN.

Before listening, students look at the four photos and answer question (**1**) trying to guess what each person collects. There is the opportunity with a good class to do a little 'character analysis' or 'amateur psychology' and ask *Why do you think this?* Possible answers could be, *Well, he/she looks serious/boring/ clever so I think he/she collects ....* The main point, however, is to make predictions to prepare the students' minds for possible words to listen for in the telephone conversations. It doesn't matter if the guesses are correct or not. The important thing is to build up expectations.

Play the cassette to check the guesses by doing question (**2**). The first time the students need only listen for the items collected. They do not need to get all the details. (**Note:** Some of the children have slight 'foreign' accents. These are not intended as stereotypes, just to make the point that acceptable and clear speech does not always sound exactly like received pronunciation.)
Question (**3**) invites the students to listen again for the **details** – why each person likes their hobby. They are heavily supported by having the four reasons printed in the book next to the four names. This makes it a 'matching' exercise (and the pronouns should help, too)! In the later 'Listen for detail' activities in this book there will be gradually less and less support of this kind.

4 SPEAK.

The language on the cassette in Exercise 3 should have given adequate preparation for the students to conduct 'mini-interviews' with four other people in the class, and to take notes and to prepare a table of results. Note that there is scope for 'non-collectors' to be honest!
Students then use their notes and their tables as support for a 'report back' session on what they found out.

WORKBOOK

The puzzle in Exercise 1 can be done for homework to consolidate the 'collecting' vocabulary. The '**You tell us**' suggestions in Exercises 2 and 3 allow for the oral work in the Student's Book, Exercise 4 to be developed into a possible magazine section. This is not obligatory, of course. If the option is taken up, encourage students to show each other their '**You tell us**' replies and to make suggestions for improvement, before you come in as the Editor and help with final corrections of mistakes and improvements of content or expression.

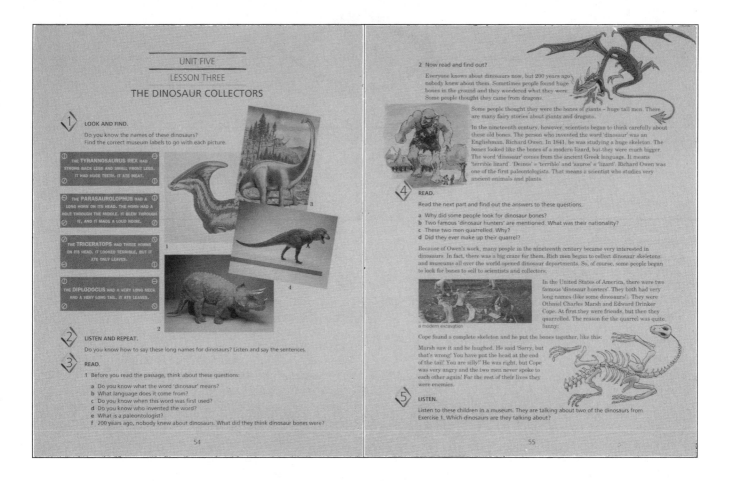

KEY VOCABULARY	blow (*verb*), bone, diplodocus, enemy, expect, fairy story, giant, hole, loud, palaeontologist, parasaurolophus, triceratops, tyrannosaurus rex, wonder (*verb*)
KEY GRAMMAR POINTS	Past tense in narrative; Language of description: *It had a ...*
SKILLS	Analysing words for their origins and the meanings of their components, e.g. *dino - saur* – terrible lizard, from Greek; Reading a fairly complex passage to find detailed information

LESSON 3   THE DINOSAUR COLLECTORS

1 LOOK AND FIND.

This is a familiar 'matching' activity. The descriptive language gives clues to the identities of the four creatures. The Parasaurolophus is the only 'new' dinosaur on the list, but it will be a 'star' later in the book!

2 ⊙⊙ LISTEN AND REPEAT.

The sentences to repeat are to help students to 'get their tongues round' these extremely odd and long words. Treat this activity in a light-hearted way. Actually even palaeontologists do not seem to agree whether to say 'DipLODocus' or 'DiploDOCus'!!

3 READ.

The article is divided into two parts, each with its 'pre-reading' questions, to encourage students to read quickly the first time to 'search' for information. They can read more slowly the next time.
Go through the pre-reading questions for Exercise 3 and make sure all students understand them. Then have a *Who can find the answers first? Hands up!* competition to encourage rapid 'scan' reading of this part of the article. You can either set one question at a time for students to search for (this will mean six rapid 'encounters' with the text) or set all the questions at once for students to take notes for each answer and then put their hands up. Try to prevent the 'quicker' students from shouting out answers when they find them. Stick to the *Hands up!* rule, and go to the student and collect the answer quietly, asking him or her to point to the sentence where it was found. This will give the others time to catch up. Finally, go through the answers with the whole class, and ask them to point to the relevant sentences as you collect the answers orally.

4 READ.

Repeat the procedure above with the second part of the article.
Allow time for the students to go back and read both articles at their own pace, and to enjoy the pictures without you hurrying them this time. Encourage individual students to call on you to help with any difficulties. Point out that these are two different ways of reading and that each way is important for different purposes.
Finally, check understanding of key new words like *enemies* (last word of the article) by asking for translations, if you wish, but many teachers do not like to do this. Try getting paraphrases like, *They weren't friends* or *They hated each other*, or do an 'Opposites quiz' The opposite of *friend* is *enemy*.

5 ⊙⊙ LISTEN.

Ask the students to look again at the words and pictures in Exercise 1. Play the cassette. They can write down the names of the two dinosaurs or just point to the pictures and the words.

WORKBOOK

Exercise 1 looks at the meaning and derivation of suffixes and prefixes, and challenges students to find the precise definition of the three words.
Exercise 2 gives some cultural information about the famous writer, Sir Arthur Conan Doyle. There is a thematic link between his detective character Sherlock Holmes and the 'Dino Detective' theme which follows in Unit 9, Lesson 4.
Exercise 3 revises names for parts of the body and challenges the students to re-assemble the jumbled bones of the dinosaur skeleton in a drawing. The possible names for the dinosaurs are invented, but they are possible since they are made up of the same sort of Greek root-words as 'real' dinosaur names.

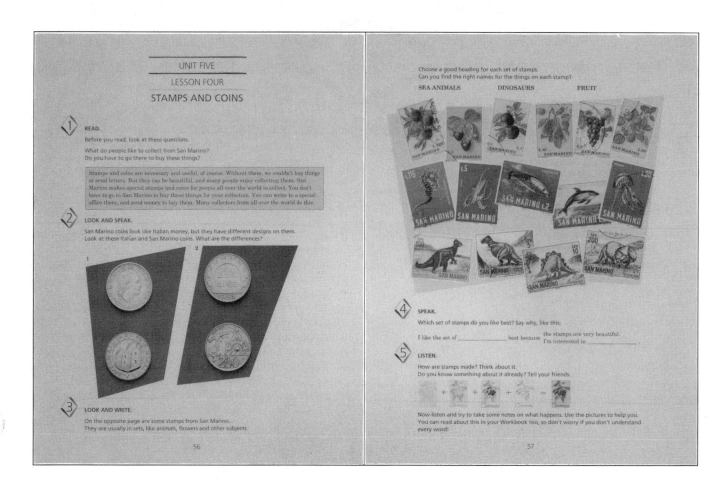

UNIT FIVE

LESSON FOUR

STAMPS AND COINS

1 READ.

Before you read, look at these questions.

What do people like to collect from San Marino?
Do you have to go there to buy these things?

Stamps and coins are necessary and useful, of course. Without them, we couldn't buy things or send letters. But they can be beautiful, and many people enjoy collecting them. San Marino makes special stamps and coins for people all over the world to collect. You don't have to go to San Marino to buy these things for your collection. You can write to a special office there, and send money to buy them. Many collectors from all over the world do this.

2 LOOK AND SPEAK.

San Marino coins look like Italian money, but they have different designs on them.
Look at these Italian and San Marino coins. What are the differences?

3 LOOK AND WRITE.

On the opposite page are some stamps from San Marino.
They are usually in sets, like animals, flowers and other subjects.

56

Choose a good heading for each set of stamps.
Can you find the right names for the things on each stamp?

SEA ANIMALS   DINOSAURS   FRUIT

4 SPEAK.

Which set of stamps do you like best? Say why, like this:

I like the set of _____ best because the stamps are very beautiful.
I'm interested in _____

5 LISTEN.

How are stamps made? Think about it.
Do you know something about it already? Tell your friends.

Now listen and try to take some notes on what happens. Use the pictures to help you.
You can read about this in your Workbook too, so don't worry if you don't understand every word!

57

KEY VOCABULARY	coin, cyan (a colour used in printing), have to = 'must', magenta (a colour used in printing), original set (*noun*)
KEY GRAMMAR POINTS	Passives (in the description of how stamps are made)
SKILLS	Finding good category headings for sets of similar things; Putting information about a process into the correct sequence

LESSON 4   STAMPS AND COINS

1 READ.

Students read the two questions before they look at the passage. The answer to the first is obvious, but they will have to search the passage for the answer to the second. See if anyone in the class collects either stamps or coins. You may have found this out already from Unit 5, Lesson 2. Check that the students understand that in San Marino making stamps and coins is an industry. The best artists and designers are chosen, and many different sets of stamps are produced each year.

2 LOOK AND SPEAK.

The top two pictures show the 'head' and the 'tail' of an Italian coin, and the bottom two show the corresponding San Marino coin.
Encourage comments like, *They are the same size, but the designs are different.*

3 LOOK AND WRITE.

Let the students have a good look at all the stamps. See which ones they think are the most attractive/colourful/interesting. Ask them to give the correct title for each set, e.g. *The ones at the top/in the middle/at the bottom have ... on them.*
If you wish, you can extend vocabulary about fruit and sea creatures (the dinosaurs should be well-known by now! and their names can be read on the stamps in English). From left to right, the 'fruit' stamps are: *peaches, strawberries, apples, pears, grapes and apricots.* The sea animals are: *sea-horse, octopus, fish, dolphin* and *jelly fish.*

4 SPEAK.

Students prepare a sentence to say about their favourite set of stamps and the reason. If you wish you can collect the 'votes' for each set on the board. (Put a tick by the name of the set for each 'vote'.) Then find the most popular set.

5 ⊙⊙ LISTEN.

The previous stages in this lesson have been gentle preparation to raise the students' interest so that they can tackle this quite demanding listening passage, which is about the process of making stamps (and of colour-printing in general). This may be a subject already studied in art or technical studies lessons. If so, try to exploit the cross-curricular link. If not treat it as general knowledge. What will probably interest students most is how the four 'basic' colours shown in the book mix on the page to make all the colours of any printed picture. Point to the first four small pictures and tell the students their 'official' names. From left to right they are: yellow, cyan, magenta, black. See if they can guess how the colours mix before you listen to the cassette. Ask: *How do you make green? (yellow and cyan) red? (yellow and magenta) purple/violet? (cyan and magenta).* Point out (in the native language if necessary) that the different shades of each colour come from mixing a little of other colours in, too. (Dark green has some black in it, too, for example.) Let the students listen and try to take notes. They may not understand very much at first, but do not let them panic! This is a good challenge. Then turn to the Workbook, Exercise 1, which gives the words of the cassette for them to put in the correct order. Let them study the words, then play the cassette again.

WORKBOOK

As mentioned above, Workbook Exercise 1 can be used in the lesson to support the difficult listening passage. Once the students are confident that they know what happens, let them draw a picture to illustrate each stage in the process. If you can bring some reference books which show this process, so much the better.
The 'design a stamp' activity in Exercise 3 will really help to check if the students have understood all about the colour-printing process! They should enjoy using coloured pencils to experiment and work out how to make the final stamp. This activity has obvious cross-curricular links with art and technology.

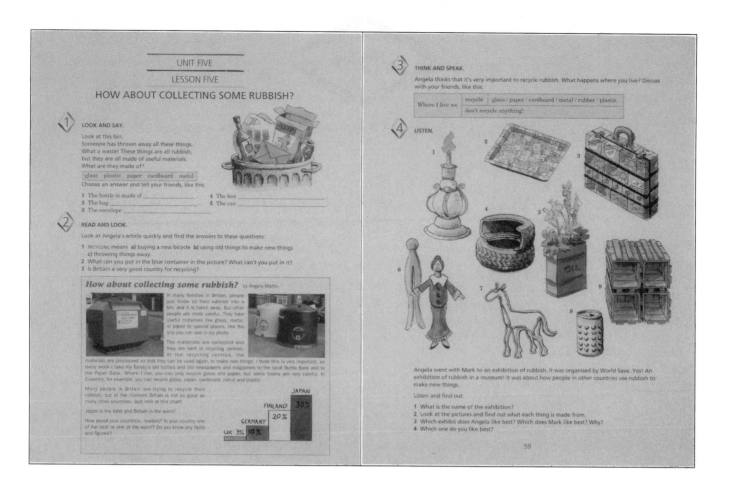

KEY VOCABULARY	cardboard, carry, container, doll, fussy, glass, grater, hunter, light bulb, material, metal, papier maché, process (*verb*), recycling, rubber, throw away, toy, tray, tyre, wire, wooden
KEY GRAMMAR POINTS	*The ... is made of ...* ; *How about ...?* (as a suggestion); Passives for talking about processes, *The materials are collected, and they are sent to recycling centres*; Comparisons, *Britain is not as good as many other countries.*
SKILLS	Interpreting charts and facts and figures; Listening to a conversation with many irrelevant pieces of information in it and selecting only the important information

LESSON 5   HOW ABOUT COLLECTING SOME RUBBISH?

1 LOOK AND SAY.

Check and revise the 'materials vocabulary' in the small yellow box by asking students to point to things in the class made of *glass/rubber/paper/ cardboard/ metal*. Say, *Show me something made of ... .* Then ask them to 'look in the bin' and point to the *box/bag/envelope/ bottle/can*. (You can also use the more British English word *tin* though even British English tends to use the word *can* for containers of drinks.)

Then ask the students to prepare sentences about what the things in the bin are made of, using the language model given in the book. They can write the sentences first, or proceed directly to speaking.

2 READ AND LOOK.

Read the three questions before the students look at the article. Then have a 'Who can finish first?' competition to encourage quick scanning of the passage to find the answers.

Let the students read the passage again, more slowly and ask for any help they need. Ask why Coventry is better than London about recycling. Then look at the chart and at the last paragraph. Ask them if they think that their country is good/bad/better than Britain/worse than Britain.

3 THINK AND SPEAK.

This activity follows naturally from the discussion at the end of Exercise 2, but provides a language model to help less confident children to say something.

4 ☐☐ LISTEN.

The tasks for this passage are relatively simple. Read the four questions before the children hear the cassette. They can probably answer question (**4**)

before they listen. The language on the cassette is not difficult, but Mark and Angela do talk about all sorts of other things (and Angela is definitely **not** enjoying the exhibition very much!). This means that students must listen to select only the information they need to answer questions (**1**) to (**3**) and can ignore the 'rest' the first or second time around.

Exercise 1 in the Workbook provides more support for the matching of objects in the exhibition to the materials they are made from, and can be brought in at this point if wished.

If the students want to listen again and get more of the whole conversation, use the tapescript at the end of this book for them to listen-and-read, but only **after** the comprehension tasks have been done.

WORKBOOK

Exercise 1 can be used during the listening part of the Student's Book lesson, or it can be used for consolidation for homework.

Exercise 2 is suitable for class or homework. If time is limited, you could set a 'target' number of words to be found (25 would be reasonable) or you could set up a 'word-recycling' competition and see who can create the most new words, with or without the help of a dictionary.

Exercise 3 consolidates the use of the Present Passive to describe processes. The pictures are in the correct order, but the sentences are not. Students could simply find the correct sentence to go with each picture, or they could copy out the whole passage in the correct order. The answers are: **1A, 2D, 3B, 4E, 5C, 6F, 7G.**

Exercise 4 is optional, but would give a good opportunity to artistic children to make their own contribution to the class magazine.

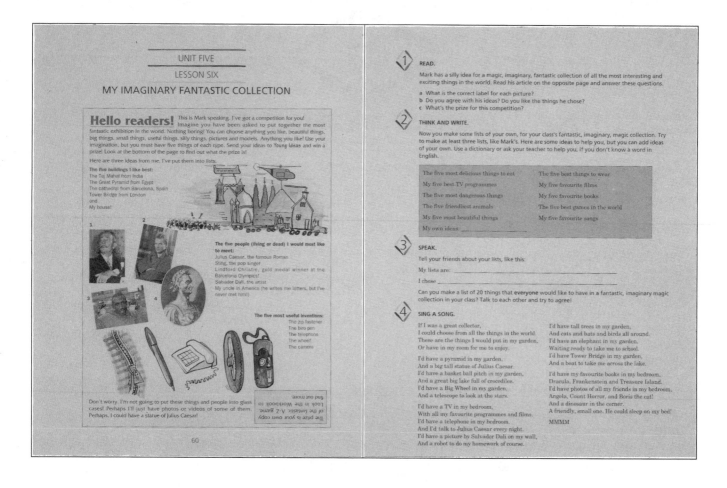

KEY VOCABULARY	biro, cathedral, competition, lake, medal, office, pitch, prize, pyramid, statue, wheel, zip fastener, + country names revised
KEY GRAMMAR POINTS	Second Conditional *If* + Past tense + *would*: *If I met a crocodile, I would be very frightened.*
SKILLS	Putting vocabulary items into groups; Using a dictionary to find new words needed for a list

LESSON 6   MY IMAGINARY FANTASTIC COLLECTION

1 READ.

The instructions for the activity are at the top of page 61, while the article fills page 60. Read the introduction to the questions on page 61, and stress that the article is about fantasy ideas. Mark is imagining his 'ideal collection'. Question (**a**) invites the students to look at the text and the pictures (the pictures are in the correct order) and to find the objects or people named in each section. In the 'buildings' section, the Taj Mahal, Barcelona Cathedral, the Great Pyramid, Tower Bridge and Mark's house are all seen being carried off by lorry or by helicopter to join Mark's collection – a deliberately silly idea to stress the fantasy. In the famous people section, picture **1** shows Salvador Dali, **2** shows Sting, **3** shows Lindford Christie and **4** shows an old engraving of Julius Caesar as imagined by a Renaissance artist. (Mark's uncle is not shown.) For Inventions, students should point to the zip fastener, the biro, the telephone, the wheel, and the camera, which are shown left to right in the right order. (They could add these words, plus small drawings, to their Word Books.)

For (**b**), ask students to read the passage slowly and think about Mark's ideas, then think about what things they would choose in each category. Elicit answers using the forms, *I would choose* .... or *I would like to have* .... . Discuss answers. (They do not have to find five things in each category if this is too difficult, one or two would be enough.)

For (**c**) the prize is the A-Z game, shown in the Workbook, Exercise 3.

2 THINK AND WRITE.

This extends the ideas of fantastic collections. Let students choose three categories from the grey box (or invent categories of their own).

This is a good way of revising and bringing together vocabulary already covered as well as stimulating students to use a dictionary for any special words they may want to use.

3 SPEAK.

Students prepare to report on their lists, then tell the rest of the class about their choices, using the language model in the book.

Listen carefully as they speak. At the end, see if the class can remember if any items were mentioned by several speakers.

Do a mini-survey to see if the class can agree on 20 things that they would *all* like to have in a silly imaginary collection (if 20 proves too many, reduce the list to 10).

4 ⊙⊙ SING A SONG.

Play the song for the students to follow the words in their books. Then play it again for them to join in and sing.

WORKBOOK

Exercise 1 shows the pictures of some of Mark's ideas, and follows this by some grammatical explanation of the Second Conditional. Do this activity in class since the students will need your guidance and extra help with the grammar. It was thought worthwhile to include this rather formal statement of a grammar rule, since English (unlike many languages) does not have a separate form for the hypothetical use of a verb after IF, when talking about impossible or improbable situations, but uses the Simple Past tense. (Older grammar books talk about the English 'subjunctive' in this context, by analogy with languages which have a Subjunctive Mood, but this is inaccurate.) Let the students study the grammar table and encourage them to see that all the situations are untrue or most unlikely to occur. Exercise 2 provides gentle guided practice in forming correct sentences of this type. This activity can be done in class, or for homework once the rule has been understood.

In Exercise 3 the A-Z game provides more practice in gathering together and revising vocabulary. Another version of it appears in the Student's Book, Unit 9, Lesson 6.

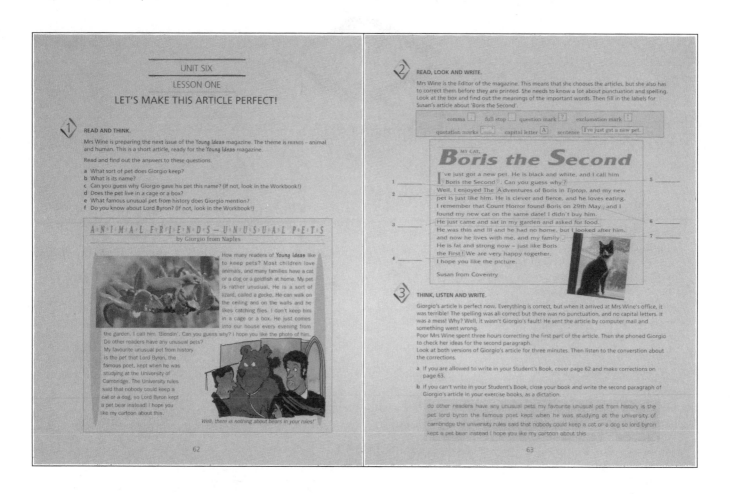

KEY VOCABULARY	cage, capital letter, comma, computer mail, don't mention it! exclamation mark, fault, full stop, gecko, instead, literature, Lord (title), paragraph, poet, punctuation, quotation mark, spelling (*noun*), university, version
KEY GRAMMAR POINTS	No new grammar points since the lesson concentrates on punctuation
SKILLS	Scanning a reading text quickly to find information; Learning English punctuation conventions; Editing (correcting) a faulty text; Taking a text down from dictation, including use of punctuation

LESSON 1 LET'S MAKE THIS ARTICLE PERFECT!

1 READ AND THINK.

Before the students read the article, look quickly with them at the title and the pictures and ask what they think it is about (Pets). Ask who wrote the article. Then read through the questions (**a**) to (**f**), and tell the students to read the article very quickly and find as many answers as they can. They probably will not be able to answer questions (**c**) and (**f**) fully at this stage, but tell them not to worry too much about these unless they know the answers from general knowledge. They can find out more from the Workbook later. Collect answers orally and ask them to quote the sentences where they found the answers. Let them look at the Lord Byron cartoon and read the caption. Check that they understand the joke, by asking, *Who is the man on the left?* (a university teacher), *Why is he angry?, Who is the young man on the right?* (Lord Byron). Let them read the whole article again at their own speed, asking you for any help they need.

2 READ, LOOK AND WRITE.

Read the introduction with the students and point out the punctuation marks and their names in the yellow box. Let them study the box for a few minutes. Then ask them to cover the box. Write the words, comma, full stop, question mark, exclamation mark, quotation marks, capital letter on the board and invite students to come to the board and draw the appropriate symbols or letters next to the words. Then let them read the article about 'Boris' for meaning, first. Ask some oral questions to check understanding, like *Who wrote the article?, Why is the cat's name Boris?, Did Susan buy Boris?, When did she find him?, Where was he?*
Then draw the students' attention to the punctuation marks and the lines from each going to a number. They write the numbers in their exercise books and write the name of the punctuation marks next to them. They can refer to the yellow box to help them.

3 ◯◯ THINK, LISTEN AND WRITE.

Read the introduction to make sure that the students understand the situation. The green box below shows the article in its damaged state as it appeared on the computer screen. You can use this in several ways as suggested in the Student's Book.
1 This is suitable for an 'average' class. Let them study the 'perfect' version on page 62, then cover it and try to correct the green version (either on

page 63, if they can write in Student's Books, or by rewriting it correctly in their exercise books). They can then listen to the cassette to check their versions before looking back at page 62 for a final correction.
2 This is more challenging, and suitable for a very 'quick' class. They study the perfect version on page 62 as before, then close their books and listen to the cassette and write down the passage as a dictation. They compare their versions with a partner, make any alterations they want, then check their versions with page 62.

WORKBOOK

All these activities can be tried at home, but will need discussion in the next class. Alternatively, they may be done in class as a follow-up to the Student's Book work.
Exercise 1 answers questions (**c**) and (**f**) more fully, by giving biographies of Lord Byron and the 'real' Blondin. Students need to refer to Exercise 1 in the Student's Book as they work.
Exercise 2 is a crossword puzzle which practises and reinforces grammar, spelling and punctuation terms, by making students search in the 'Boris' article in Exercise 2 in the Student's Book to find the answers. A completed puzzle appears below for checking purposes.

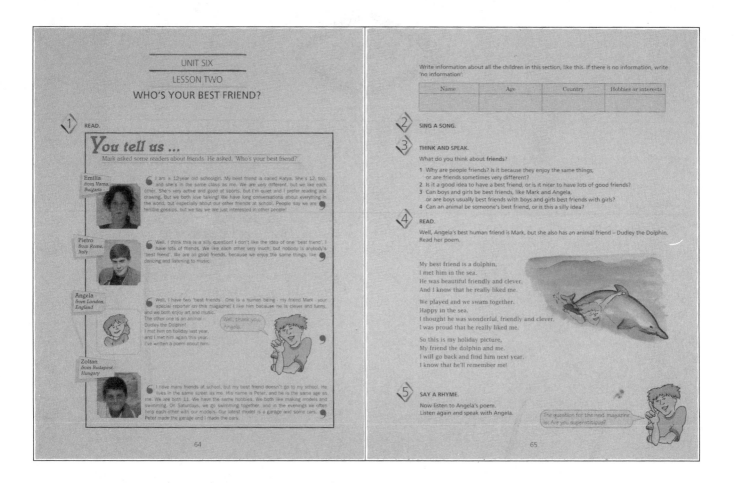

KEY VOCABULARY	garage, gossip (*noun*), model, poem
KEY GRAMMAR POINTS	*We like **each other***
SKILLS	Extracting information from a fairly long piece of text and putting it in a table; Reflecting on friendship, especially if having a 'best friend' is a good idea or not; Pronunciation – speaking with rhythm in unison with a cassette

UNIT 6

LESSON 2   WHO'S YOUR BEST FRIEND?

1 READ.

Let the students read the '**You tell us**' article at their own pace, without any pre-questioning. The language it contains is not very demanding. It is intended for enjoyment and to make them think about a subject probably close to their hearts. Let them ask for your help as they need it. Allow a maximum of ten minutes.

Then ask the students to tell you all the names of children mentioned in the article (not just of the writers themselves but of their friends too). Dudley, the dolphin, is a friend too, but he is not a human being so he doesn't go on the list.

Look at the information table at the top of page 65, and ask the students to go back to the passage and collect as much information as they can for each name on the list. They can build up their own tables in their exercise books. Let them compare notes with people near them after a few minutes.

Then elicit answers orally, e.g. *What do we know about Peter? Where does he come from? How old is he? What are his hobbies? Has he got a best friend?* and so on for all the names.

2 ▭ SING A SONG.

Play the song, which is a repeat of the song first met in Level 2. The Workbook contains the words of the song, so you might like to turn to the Workbook at this point if students do not understand all the words easily. Then replay the cassette for the students to join in with singing the song.

3 THINK AND SPEAK.

By now the students should be thinking carefully about the topic of FRIENDSHIP. Let them read all the questions and think about their own responses. Ask each question to get answers from individuals. If you wish, you can take a vote and put the numbers of answers of each type on the board for some of the questions to do a Class Survey. Questions (**2**) and (**3**)

should elicit the most disagreement in the class. Question (**2**) is there to comfort those students who may not actually be anybody's best friend.

As a follow-up, ask which children from the article in Exercise 1 have opinions that individuals, or the class as a whole, agree or disagree with (e.g. Pietro does not believe in 'best friends' and Angela – a girl – is happy to be 'best friends' with Mark – a boy). Unit 6, Lesson 6, goes into much more depth about the question of friendship and *What is a good friend?*

4 READ.

The 'dolphin' poem follows on from question (**4**) in Exercise 3. Let the students read it by themselves. The language is very simple and it should present no difficulties.

5 ▭ SAY A RHYME.

Play the cassette once, then rewind for the students to 'join in' with the speaker.

Draw attention to Mark's *Are you superstitious?* question, which gives the theme of Unit 7. Explain the word *superstitious* if necessary, but do not do a lot of work on it. Just say that this will be the subject of the new issue of the **Young Ideas** magazine, so perhaps they would like to think about superstitions and beliefs in the meantime.

WORKBOOK

Exercise 1 gives the words of the song and would be useful as support in the lesson or for homework follow-up. Exercise 2 refreshes adjectives that people use about their friends, many of which appeared in Exercise 1 in the Student's Book. Exercise 3 provides writing support for a description of a friend. Students can also look back at what the children wrote in Exercise 1 in the Student's Book to get ideas and language support. Exercise 4 provides optional class magazine ideas for a '**You tell us**' section.

KEY VOCABULARY	abandoned, adventure, chihuahua, dachschund, disappear, disaster, earthquake, fierce, fight (*noun*), guard (dog), guide (dog), hospital, labrador, local, locked, Mexican, middle-sized, mixed, mongrel, proper, properly, rescue, sniffer (dog), stroke, window
KEY GRAMMAR POINTS	No new grammar because of heavy vocabulary load in this lesson; Present Simple for description of appearance and roles of different types of dog; Past tense in narrative of the 'Rory' story
SKILLS	Matching descriptions (of physical appearance and of activity) to pictures; Following a complicated narrative and working out its sequence

LESSON 3 MAN'S BEST FRIENDS

1 READ AND FIND.

The title of the lesson 'Man's Best Friends' is taken from the well-known English saying 'A dog is Man's best friend'. **Note:** no sexism is intended here! 'Man' with a capital 'M' still often means 'people in general'. Although modern British political correctness demands that we say 'Chairperson' and not 'Chair-man' or 'woman' no-one has yet suggested that we change all our proverbs. With a very sophisticated class you might discuss, in the native language, this odd use of 'Man' but most children of this age will probably not be very interested.

Ask, *Who has a dog at home? What is his (or her) name? How old is he (or she)?*

Cultural note: British people usually use *he* or *she* to refer to their pets, though they often say *it* for babies! Let the students look at the four photos and decide on the best title for each one. Ask, *Are sheep dogs used in your country? What breed of dog is the most popular?* The article below gives two more unusual and modern functions for dogs. Sniffer dogs are, of course, also used at airports to detect drugs and explosives. You can bring in this information if you think it is appropriate. Find out if students know if 'Visiting dogs' are used in your country. If not, do they think it is a good idea? See if they can demonstrate the meaning of the word *stroke*. Then demonstrate *pat*.

Students then match the descriptions of different breeds of dog to the pictures at the top of page 67. They can point, or write, the number of the description next to the letter of the picture in their exercise books. If the name of the breed is similar in your language, the task will be easy, but for some types of dog the students will have to read the description very carefully.

Follow up with some oral questions like: *Which type of dog is the smallest in the world? Which type of dog looks like a wolf?*

2 ☐ LISTEN AND FIND OUT.

The story on the cassette is deliberately long and complicated. It 'stars' two types of dog (alsatian and dachschund), already introduced in the first part of the lesson. There is a lot of word play in the story (the rhyming names Rory, Maury, Bernard Glory, and the new name for the abandoned dog 'Floory'). You do not need to insist on this. The Workbook provides support for the stages in the story, and it might be useful to turn to this after the first listening.

1 Read all the questions with the students **before** they listen. See if the questions give them any expectations about the story. Play the cassette.

2 Turn to the Workbook, Exercise 1 and let the students read the stages in the story, and try to put them in the right order. Then play the cassette again. The students do not have to understand every word, but if you want them to read the story **after** their attempts at listening, reproduce the words of the tapescript.

WORKBOOK

The pictures in Exercise 1 can be used for support during the listening lesson. The ordering activity can then also be done for homework. Exercise 2 is a 'grammar awareness' activity which can be looked at in class and then attempted for homework.

CULTURAL NOTES

The listening introduces the Battersea Dogs' Home which is the major topic of Unit 6, Lesson 4 and Unit 6, Lesson 5. Find out if there are any similar animal charities in your country. Perhaps one of the children in your class adopted a lost dog or cat from one of these places.

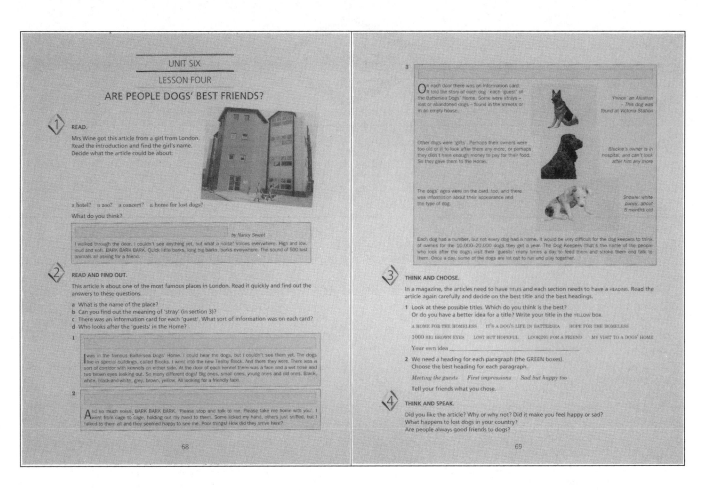

KEY VOCABULARY	abandoned, feed, gift, guest, hard=difficult, heading, homeless, hopeful, impression, lick, lost (*adjective*), pay for, puppy, sniff, station, stray, stroke, voice, woof
KEY GRAMMAR POINTS	Past tense in narrative; The placing of the apostrophe in singular and plural nouns (Dogs' Home, Blackie's owner)
SKILLS	Summarising, shown by choice of the best title and the best headings for an article; Emotional response to a deliberately emotive article

LESSON 4   ARE PEOPLE DOGS' BEST FRIENDS?

1 READ.

Read the title of the lesson. It is a deliberate variation on the title of the last lesson. (Dogs are Man's best friends, but are people always good friends to dogs?) It will probably give your students a clue to the answer to the question about the topic of the article. The photo of the new building at Battersea Dogs' Home may distract them. It looks quite like a block of flats, but it is, in fact, a scientifically designed home for hundreds of dogs.

Read the question about the subject of the article. Ask the students to guess privately and then to read the paragraph in the blue box and tell you what they think. (The yellow box is to be used later in Exercise 3 when they choose a good title for the article.)

2 READ AND FIND OUT.

Read the four questions **before** the students look at the rest of the article. Do a 'Who can find the answers in four minutes?' competition. **Note:** This time, it is not a 'Who can finish first?' but a realistic time-limit which gives all students an idea of the time within which you think they should be able to find the answers. After four minutes, collect the answers orally.

Then let the students read again more slowly and ask you for any help.

Follow up with some oral questions like: *Give me some reasons why dogs arrive in the Battersea Dogs' Home* or *How old is Snowie?*

If you wish, this lesson gives many opportunities to draw attention to the placing of the apostrophe in singular and plural nouns and names (after the plural **s** ending, but an apostrophe and **s** for singular nouns and proper names). Remember, this is a refinement of English that many native speaker children have not mastered well by this age, so do not expect too much.

3 THINK AND CHOOSE.

This activity is quite demanding. There are no 'right' answers, but the activity should stimulate the students to find the most 'powerful' and expressive title and section headings in their opinions. If they think of ideas of their own, accept them enthusiastically. Even if they do not seem perfect to you, it will be a sign that the students are trying to make English their 'own' to express their own meanings. Let them discuss their ideas before they tell you their choices.

Note: *It's a dog's life* is a well-known English saying meaning, *It's a terrible life.*

4 THINK AND SPEAK.

This section asks for an emotional response, and asks about the situation in the students' own country. It does not need to take up a lot of time unless you have a class of real animal lovers.

WORKBOOK

Exercise 1 gives more practice in matching descriptions to pictures. The puzzles in Exercises 2 and 3 are an introduction to a fascinating 'three-way' dominoes which can be used to help students memorise boring 'pairs' of words such as opposites (as here) or Present and Past tenses. There are developments of this idea in other Workbook lessons. Students who like the idea can make up their own puzzles and challenge their friends.

CULTURAL NOTES

Battersea Dogs' Home is most helpful to teachers. If you are in Britain, you can go there and buy a cheap video which your students may enjoy as well as pick up useful leaflets and buy a book about the history of the home. The address to write to is:

The Dogs' Home Battersea,
Battersea Park Road,
London SW8 4AA

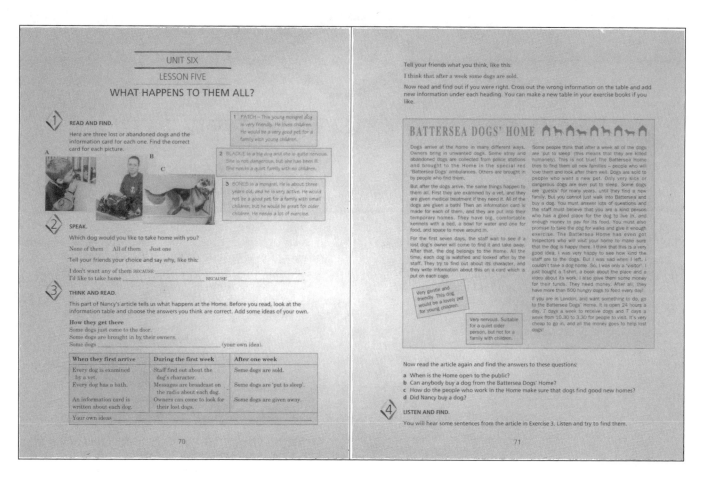

KEY VOCABULARY	ambulance, bowl, broadcast (*verb*), character = personality, examine, funds, gentle, give away, inspector, medical treatment, nervous, owner, public (*noun*), put to sleep, receive, staff, suitable
KEY GRAMMAR POINTS	*None of them; all of them; some of them;* Time expressions, *When they first arrive, during the first week, after one week;* Present Passive
SKILLS	Matching a description to a picture; Prediction of possible actions; Reading a long article and extracting detailed information to confirm or correct predictions; Reading for further detail

LESSON 5   WHAT HAPPENS TO THEM ALL?

1 READ AND FIND.

Students look at the three photos and find the most appropriate description to fit each one. The descriptions all include ideas about the dogs' suitability for different types of new future homes, a point which will be important later in the lesson, but which is not focal at this stage.

2 SPEAK.

Students use the language model to help them express their own feelings. There is scope for dog-haters to be honest here!

3 THINK AND READ.

The article is long and demanding, so the pre-reading preparation questions are a very important support for students. Spend enough time on them. The table has some correct and some incorrect information. Let the students study it and think about it. Collect any ideas that the students themselves may have. Talk about the possibilities. Check their understanding of *put to sleep*. (Is there a similar euphemism for *to kill humanely* in your language?)
Let the students tell each other (in pairs or to the whole class) what they think happens. (See the suggestion at the top of page 71.)
Let the students read the article to correct or confirm the ideas they formed. Give a time limit of five minutes **maximum** for this, but tell them that they will be allowed more time later to read more slowly. Collect answers orally about what was right or wrong on the yellow table at the bottom of page 70, and find out which of their own original ideas was right or wrong.
Read through the questions that appear on page 71 after the article. See if the students can already answer some of them without reading again. (They probably will be able to, in some cases.) Send the students back to the article to find the answers they cannot give (time limit of two minutes). Collect answers.

4 ▭ LISTEN AND FIND.

The cassette contains focal passive sentences and phrases. Play it, pausing after each sentence or phrase, and ask the students to scan the passage and point to them. Watch them as they work and help any students with difficulties.

WORKBOOK

The first part of Exercise 1 is best done in class, with your help and extra information. Exercise 1 starts with a simple matching activity, to make clear to the students that active or passive sentences can be used to refer to the same event. The explanation then shows how the *passive* sentences give more prominence to the dogs by putting them first. (Students need to realise that there is a 'reason' for choosing certain structures in any language.)
The table analyses the components of Present Passive sentences.
The transformation of sentences from active to passive can be started in class and finished for homework.
Exercise 2 re-uses the 'three-way dominoes' idea from Unit 6, Lesson 4 and encourages the students to actually make the puzzle, and experiment with different ways of putting it together.
Exercise 3 uses the six cards of the puzzle. By working out the 'opposites' of the words on the cards surrounding the space where the 'missing' card should be, students can remember part of the description of one of the six dogs from Unit 6, Lesson 4 (Blackie, Granddad, T. Rex, Snowy, Jumpy and Tiny).

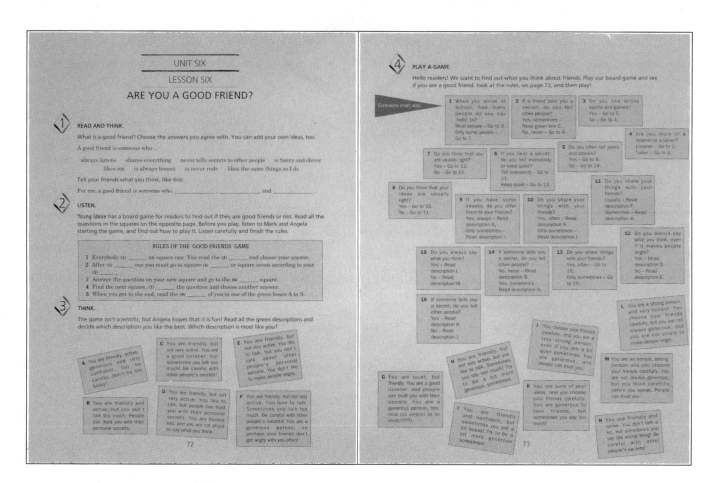

KEY VOCABULARY	board game, bossy, confident, generous, honest, listener, rude, scientific, secret (*noun*), talker, trust (*verb*)
KEY GRAMMAR POINTS	A _____ is someone who _____ ; Present Simple for habitual behaviour
SKILLS	Reading for detail and following instructions; Using own judgement to assess if a description of some one is accurate or not

LESSON 6   ARE YOU A GOOD FRIEND?

1 READ AND THINK.

This activity raises awareness of the issue, *What is a good friend? How should a friend behave?* and also practises the defining relative clause in e.g. *A good friend is someone who shares everything.* Let the students choose ideas from the list and write sentences in their exercise books, using the language model for support. They can add their own ideas too, of course.

Then ask individuals to read out their opinions to the rest of the class. See how much agreement or disagreement there is. Is any particular characteristic or behaviour generally agreed to be very important?

2 🔘 LISTEN.

The dialogue on the cassette gives the rules for playing the game in Exercise 4. Students listen to complete the missing information in the blue 'RULES' box. (They can write in their exercise books.) Let them compare notes and make sure that everyone has the same rules. If necessary, write the rules up on the board, or give out a photocopy of the complete rules at the end of this activity.

3 THINK.

Before students play the game in Exercise 4, let them read the 14 possible descriptions in the green boxes. Let them choose the one that they think (or hope!) describes them best. When they have all chosen, they can compare ideas.

4 PLAY A GAME.

Remind students of the rules on page 72. Students can play individually or in pairs, commenting on each other's progress. They answer the questions and follow the instructions about which square to

'visit' next, until they arrive at a green description square. Many students may land in a square different from the one they predicted in Exercise 3. They are at liberty to object – after all, Angela says the game is 'not scientific' – but their friends may think the final description is more accurate! When everyone has landed on a green square, ask around the class, *What's your square?* and *Do you think it's a good description of you?* If they think it isn't, ask the opinion of the rest of the class. Treat this in a light-hearted way. Nobody should feel hurt at the end. All the descriptions have something positive in them.

WORKBOOK

Exercise 1 reinforces the adjectives used in the descriptions of people's characters in the Student's Book. In Exercise 2, if all these adjectives are put in the right places in the puzzle, the (new) 'magic' word PERSONALITY will appear in the heavily-outlined vertical box. This word will be re-used as an alternative to *character* in Unit 7, Lesson 1 and onwards. Exercise 3 presents a fun way of thinking about the fact that people often interpret actions and characteristics in different ways. Barny thinks that he is *honest.* His friends say that he is sometimes *rude.* Students draw lines between Barny's views and his friends' views.

In Exercise 4, at the beginning of his summary, Barny uses the well-known ironic English saying, *With friends like mine, who needs enemies?* Point this out to students as an example of 'British humour'. Students read Barny's summary of the views in Exercise 3 and then use it to guide them in a short piece of writing about what they think about themselves and about what their friends say.

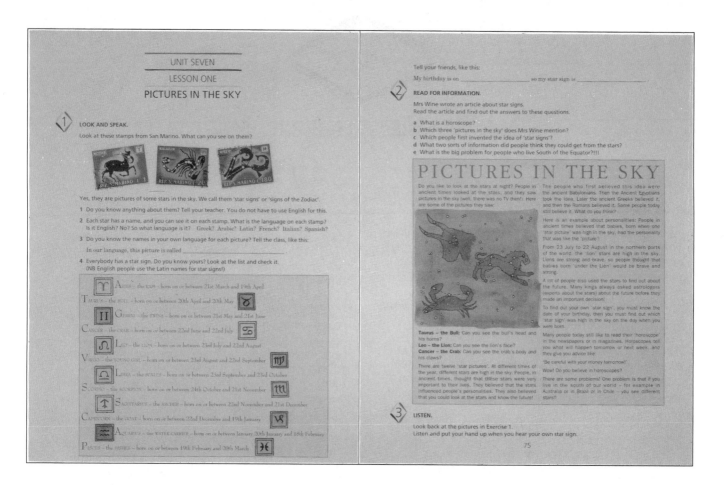

KEY VOCABULARY	bull, influenced, personality, scorpion, star sign, names
KEY GRAMMAR POINTS	Past tense and Present tense mixed in a description of a present situation (people's views of horoscopes) and of the history of horoscopes and astrology; Date expressions (**revised**); Use of the apostrophe in possessives
SKILLS	Reading a complex passage and extracting important information

LESSON 1 PICTURES IN THE SKY

1 LOOK AND SPEAK.

Look at the three stamps, and use the four questions to guide an oral discussion to help the students to 'tune in' to the topic of astrology. Question (1) may best be done in the native language, if students have a lot of complicated things to say. This is acceptable, since the aim is to orientate them to a complex topic, but encourage students to say what they can in English. For question (2) the language on the stamps is Italian. Students may recognise this, or they can guess this, since they already know that Italian is the language used in the Republic of San Marino.

For question (3), see if the students know the names of these three star signs (and then of all the others) in their native language (or perhaps your country uses Latin names, as does the UK).

For question (4), let them look at the blue star table and find their own star signs. (Remind them of the meaning of **NB** if necessary. It is the Latin *Nota Bene = please notice*.)

Then they use the language model at the top of page 75 for each student to say the exact date of his or her birthday and to say the star sign.

You could do a Class Survey from this information. Put the names of the signs on the board, and every time a student mentions a sign, put a tick by it. Total the ticks and see if there is a very common or rare sign in the class.

Students could also make a bar-chart to show the frequency of each sign, if this fits with maths work in other lessons in school.

2 READ FOR INFORMATION.

Look at questions (a) to (e) before students read, and then do the usual, *Who can find the answers first?* race, to encourage rapid scanning of the article. Collect answers, and discuss them. Then, let the students read more slowly, asking you for help if necessary. Give some oral questions after this reading, e.g. *How many 'star-signs'? What is the name of an expert about 'star-signs?' Who first believed in 'star-signs?'*

Then some questions about opinions and experiences:
Do you read your horoscope in the newspapers?
Do you believe in horoscopes?

3 🔲 LISTEN.

Students listen to the cassette, and put up their hands when they hear 'their' star signs. You can also use the tapescript to look at the details of what the speaker says about each sign.

WORKBOOK

In Exercise 1, the diagram of all the constellations is there for general knowledge (even if students do not believe in horoscopes, it is good to be able to identify the stars in the sky).

A second objective of this activity is to show how much imagination is needed to project the pictures on to the formation of the stars. Students write about their own star signs and then say if they can imagine the supposed pictures.

Exercise 2 is best done in class with your guidance and extra help. It picks up the correct use of the apostrophe for possessive expressions. The apostrophe has been used since Level 1, without comment, but we assume that you have been trying to correct any mistakes in written work throughout the course. Correct use of the apostrophe is a mark of a well-educated English writer, and we feel it is worthwhile to draw together the 'facts' at this stage. However, do not be too harsh when you encounter mistakes. Native speakers of English take many years to develop the ability to use it in the correct place.

Exercise 3 provides a challenge to put the apostrophe in the correct places in the underlined words, and will give a useful check on whether the explanation in Exercise 2 has been fully understood.
1 dinosaurs', **2** Susan's cat's, **3** children's, grown ups', **4** animals' lives, **5** Bram Stoker's book, **6** The Battersea Dogs' Home.

In Exercise 4 students guess which is Angela's and which is Mark's horoscope by the worried or happy expressions on their faces.

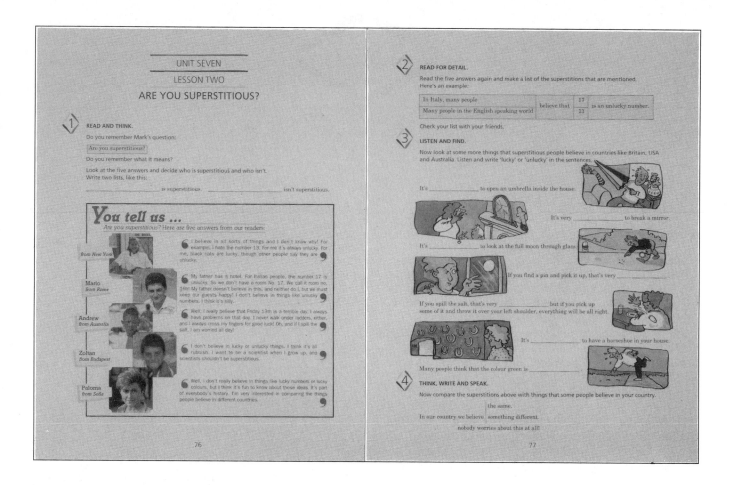

KEY VOCABULARY	horseshoe, ladder, lucky, mirror, pin, shoulder, spill (*verb*), superstitious, unlucky
KEY GRAMMAR POINTS	*if + will ...*, (First Conditional) (**revised**); *shouldn't* (for passive recognition) for moral obligation
SKILLS	Comparison of beliefs and superstitions in own culture with those in English-speaking countries; Correct completion of sentences using contextual as well as grammatical clues

LESSON 2   ARE YOU SUPERSTITIOUS?

1 READ AND THINK.

Refer back to Unit 6, Lesson 2 in which Mark first announced the '**You tell us**' question. Check that students have some idea of the meaning of the word 'superstitious'. The five opinions in the '**You tell us**' feature will show the use of the word in context. Ask the students to read the '**You tell us**' feature quickly to find out which of the five readers are or are not *superstitious*. They write sentences containing the appropriate names in their exercise books, using the language model in the book.

2 READ FOR DETAIL.

Let the students go back to the '**You tell us**' feature in Exercise 1 and first take notes on the superstitions mentioned there. Then they compose true sentences about the superstitions, using the language model in the book. Let them compare sentences with a partner or two other students, both to help each other with any possible mistakes, and to see which ideas their friends chose. Elicit some of the sentences orally and discuss briefly whether these superstitions are held in the students' own country or not. (Do not spend too much time on this, since Exercise 4 provides more structured practice of this kind.)

3 ▢▢ LISTEN AND FIND.

Look at the pictures with the students before they listen and ask them to guess which actions or events are probably lucky or unlucky. Then play the cassette for them to check their ideas. Let them compare answers with a friend before they listen again. Play the cassette to let them resolve any doubts or disagreements. Elicit answers orally. Play the cassette again, if you think this is necessary for your class.

4 THINK, WRITE AND SPEAK.

Point out that the students can consider both the superstitions in Exercise 1 and in Exercise 3. They should then each prepare at least five sentences following the language model in the book. If possible, include ideas about beliefs which are the same, different, and about which nobody worries or thinks at all. Let the students compare their answers. Move round the class to look at and help with

people's work. Then, elicit some ideas orally. You can collect comments too, in a mini-discussion, about which superstitions students think are really strange or silly.

WORKBOOK

The Workbook activities can all be done in class or for homework, but Exercise 4 needs discussion and completion in class.
Exercise 1 reinforces vocabulary already met in the Students' Book, Exercises 1 and 3, and reminds students of vocabulary they will need for Workbook Exercises 2 and 3. Students fill the words in on the puzzle, to reveal the mystery word SUPERSTITIONS.
Exercise 2 revises the information about superstitions given in the Student' Book and gives practice in first conditional sentences with *if + will* future forms.
Exercise 3 gives similar practice to Exercise 2 but this time the superstitions and beliefs have not been met in the Student's Book. Students have to piece together the two halves of the sentences, using the continuity of the syntax and the sense of the second halves to help them. The answers are:

1 If you really ...... fingers, *and then perhaps it will happen.*
2 If the sky ...... evening, *the next day will be fine and sunny.*
3 If you see ...... its face, *it will rain very soon.*
4 Many ...... butterflies, *are very unlucky.*
5 If ...... glove that means, *that someone is coming to see you.*
6 Remember ...... shoe on, *before the left one.*
7 Never ...... on a table like this, *because that's very unlucky.*

In Exercise 4, students compose their own answer to the question, draw a picture of themselves for the box, write their names, and copy their answer into the Workbook. This can be done at home or in class. In class, the students then look at each other's work and choose two answers by friends, to copy opposite the lower two boxes, along with names and pictures. Encourage students to help each other by looking for possible mistakes before they copy their answers.

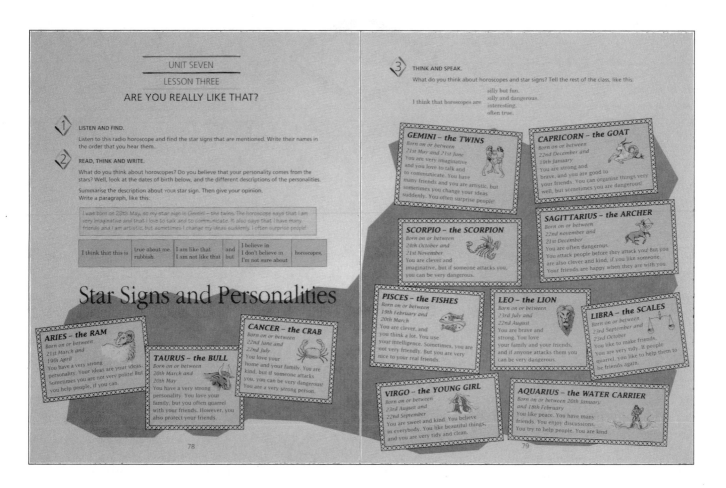

KEY VOCABULARY	archer, artistic, attack, brave, horoscope, polite, protect, ram, scales, sign, sweet, water carrier; Latin names of zodiac signs
KEY GRAMMAR POINTS	Present Simple in descriptions of tendencies and habits (**revised**); Indirect Speech: *I think that ......* (**revised**) *I am like that/not like that*
SKILLS	Listening for specific information; Summarising information (given in second person singular in horoscopes) and transforming it into first person singular; Evaluating information and giving personal opinions

90

LESSON 3   ARE YOU REALLY LIKE THAT?

1 🔘 LISTEN AND FIND.

Look at the horoscope boxes on pages 78 and 79 and say the names of the signs in Latin and in English for the students to repeat after you. Then ask the students to listen to the cassette and collect the star signs that are mentioned in the correct order. Collect answers orally.

2 READ, THINK AND WRITE.

Put the names of the twelve signs of the zodiac on the board. Ask individuals around the class what their dates of birth and their star signs are, and fill in the names on the board. They can check with the horoscope boxes. Then ask students to read their own horoscope, and to decide if the description of their personality is good or not. Then they write a paragraph summarising what the horoscope says (using the pale blue box as a model), substituting information in it to match their own star sign. They then add a sentence at the end, giving their own opinion of whether it is a good or a bad description, using the grey box as a support.

Let them read the work of a partner, commenting on the correctness of the English and on the information in it.

Then ask opinions round the class. Each student says his or her star sign, and then reads the summary of what it says and gives his or her opinion. Other students can comment to agree or disagree, saying e.g. *You're right/wrong! You are/aren't like that!* If the class is very large, just choose one representative of each star sign.

3 THINK AND SPEAK.

Students, now that they have read their own and heard about other people's star signs, can give their opinions round the class of horoscopes. You could develop this into a vote about who believes in horoscopes, who thinks they are silly but OK, and who thinks that they are wrong/and or dangerous.

WORKBOOK

The Workbook provides some activities which can be used in class as part of the lesson, to extend and deepen the horoscope work.

Exercise 1 is a good 'time-filler' in class for now or a later lesson. It can also be done for homework.

Exercise 2 provides guidance for class activity as a development of Exercise 1 in the Student's Book. It could be done as follow-up in class after the main Student's Book lesson, or used at the beginning of Student's Book, Exercise 1. Students find out how many people are born under each sign, using one of the two methods suggested (a simple *Hands Up!* or by interviewing each other) and fill in the appropriate number of squares on the chart to show numbers.

Exercise 3 can be done in class or for homework and is a written summary of the information found in the Workbook, Exercise 2.

Exercise 4 extends the summary of horoscope work done in the Student's Book, Exercise 2 to the use of the third person singular. They find out (or remember) the star sign of someone else in the class, summarise the horoscope from the Student's Book and give their opinion of whether it is a good or bad description.

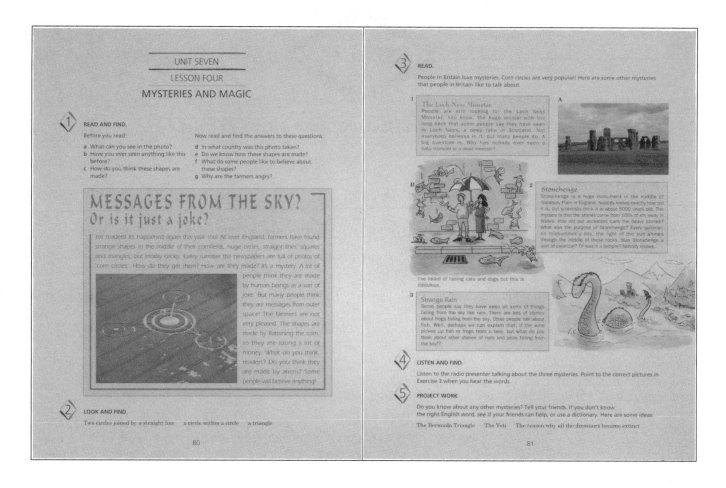

KEY VOCABULARY	calendar, corn, farmer, flatten (*verb*), heavy, message, midsummer, monument, mystery, nut, outer space, presenter, rain, shape, strike (*verb*), temple, wind, within, Yeti
KEY GRAMMAR POINTS	Present Passive in question forms: *How are they made?* Present Passive + *by* for agent: *They are made by human beings/aliens;* Present Passive + *by* for process: *They are made by flattening the corn;* Phrases describing shapes and positions; language of certainty and possibility – *probably, certainly, possibly*
SKILLS	Assessing possible explanations and comparing ideas with friends

1 READ AND FIND.

Ask students to look at the photo while you read questions **a**, **b** and **c** to elicit oral responses. (See Cultural Notes for a full account of 'crop or corn-circles'.) (**a**) Try to establish that we are looking down on a field of green corn from the air. (**b**) More and more corn circles are appearing in countries outside the UK, so your students may have heard about them or seen photos in newspapers or magazines. (**c**) Nobody

knows, but your students can guess. If they have no idea about corn-circles at this stage, that is fine – even an advantage! Ask them now to look at the title of the article and make a guess about the story. Then read questions (**d**) to (**g**). Make sure they understand them, and start the usual, *Who can find the answers first?* race, to encourage quick scanning of the passage. Collect answers, and then let the students go back and read the passage more slowly, asking you (or each other) for help as needed.

LESSON 4   MYSTERIES AND MAGIC

2 LOOK AND FIND.

Ask students to look at the photo again and point to the shapes. (See Workbook Exercise 1 for further work on this.) Students should then draw the shapes in their exercise books and write the correct captions under them, e.g. a circle within a circle ◎. **NB.** *within* is introduced here for passive understanding as a formal alternative to *inside*, often used in geometrical descriptions.

3 READ.

The pictures and the passages are in the wrong order. Look at the pictures first with the students. They will probably remember the Loch Ness Monster from Level 3. Then let them read the three titles to the passages and try to match pictures to passages. They can write the numbers and the letters in their exercise books, like this:
1 C, **2** A, **3** B.

Then let the students read the passages slowly by themselves.
Ask, *What are the questions about each mystery?* and send them back to the passages to find them, e.g. Loch Ness Monster, *Why has nobody ever seen a baby monster or a dead monster?*

4 ▭ LISTEN AND FIND.

The reading in Exercise 2 should have prepared students to understand most of the words of the radio programme. Ask students to point to the correct pictures as they listen.
Then ask some general oral questions based on the information in Exercise 2 and 3, e.g.
  How old approximately is Stonehenge?
  Where is it?
  Where is Loch Ness?
  Name the four types of strange rain.
Draw attention to the caption for the 'rain' cartoon in (2) and explain the idiom *raining cats and dogs* (= *raining very heavily*). Ask if there is an idiom like this in their own language.

5 PROJECT WORK

Students heard something about the three other mysteries in Exercise 4. See if they already know something about them. If they are interested, let them find out more for a possible class magazine article. (They could ask their parents or use an encyclopaedia, or look at any magazines or books that you have been able to find which mention any of them.)

WORKBOOK

Exercise 1 gives more practice in recognising the shape and position language, started in the Student's Book, Exercise 1.
Exercise 2 goes into some detailed investigation of the 'corn-circles' mystery. Students can use the language box to attempt their own explanations. You could do this activity in class, or check homework in class and then do a mini-survey to find the most popular explanation. (**NB** *Animals with a sense of humour* is not a totally silly idea. Some people have blamed some of the damage on moles or rabbits!)
Exercise 3 invites students to practise some of the vocabulary from the Student's Book by labelling the pictures, and to link the BIG QUESTIONS about each mystery to each picture. You should have prepared for this in the oral work for the Student's Book. This activity in Exercise 4 can be done for homework, or in conjunction with Exercise 5 in the Student's Book.
Exercise 5 is a hint about turning the Project work in Student's Book Exercise 5 into a **'You tell us'** feature with students' own explanations. They can use the language box in the Workbook, Exercise 2 to help them.

CULTURAL NOTES

'Corn-circles' started to be seen in the UK in the late 1980s. Many people became very interested and excited. Some people thought that the shapes were messages from outer space. Farmers became very angry when newspaper and TV reporters camped out in their fields every night, waiting for the next message. Scientists have tried to find explanations. Some jokers were caught making the shapes but many shapes have not yet been explained. There are even magazines and newsletters (e.g. 'The cereal-ogist') on the subject. In recent years, people in many other European countries have claimed to have seen them. Is this an example of a 'craze' spreading across the world?

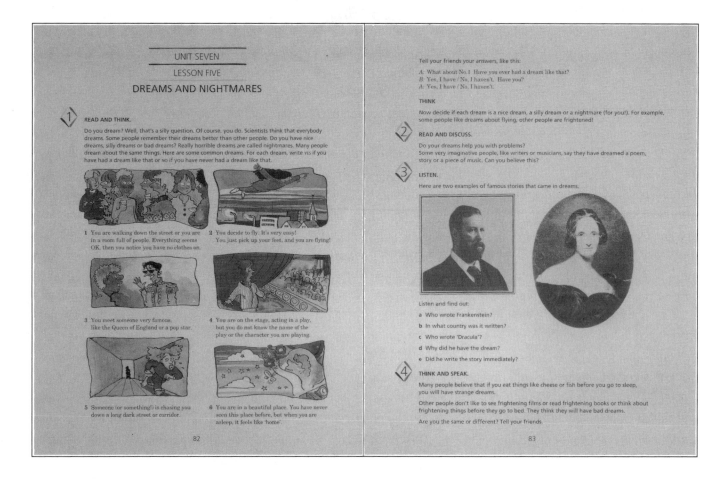

KEY VOCABULARY	asleep, character (in story or play), corridor, dream (*noun and verb*), folklore, indigestion, nightmare, notice (*verb*), play (*noun*), stage
KEY GRAMMAR POINTS	Present Continuous and Present Simple combined in descriptions of dreams in Exercise 1; Present Perfect (**revised**) for talking about life experiences: *Have you ever ... ?*
SKILLS	Personal interpretations of different situations e.g. is a dream about flying a nice dream or a frightening dream? Listening and finding causes for events (Stoker's and Mary Shelley's inspiration for their stories)

LESSON 5   DREAMS AND NIGHTMARES

1 READ AND THINK.

Help the students to understand the introductory paragraph by asking them to look at the six pictures (without reading yet) and guessing the situation. It should be obvious that they are all dreams. Ask these orally: *Do you dream?* If someone says *No*, say *Yes, you do.* Everybody dreams but perhaps they don't remember – that's all. Then build up with them a 'word family' on the board, like this:

DREAMS
nice dreams   silly dreams   bad dreams
horrible dreams (nightmares)

Read the paragraph and draw attention to the task. Students must write the numbers **1** to **6** in their exercise books and read the information under the six pictures. For each number, they must write YES or NO if they have ever had a similar dream. This information is then used for making and answering questions with their friends in pairs or groups, or around the class in a 'chain drill'. (Each student asks the person next to him while the others listen.) Use the language model at the top of page 83. In the THINK activity, they go back over the six types of dream and decide if for them they are nice, silly, or frightening. (It doesn't matter here if they have all actually had these dreams, this activity is to get their personal reactions to the situations in the dreams.)

2 READ AND DISCUSS.

This interesting question can be tackled in the native language if necessary. The important thing is to prepare their minds for the two strange stories of 'dream inspiration' which follow in Exercise 3. Many scientists and mathematicians also claim that they 'solve problems' in dreams. See if your colleagues in science can help you with more information or use this idea in some of their lessons.

3 ☉☉ LISTEN.

Look at the two photos and see if students can guess who the people are. The four pre-listening questions should help them, at least with Bram Stoker. Check that the four questions are understood, and impress on students that they need only find the answers to these the first time. They should not panic if they do not understand every word at first.

Answers
a Mary Shelley **b** Switzerland **c** Bram Stoker
d Because he had indigestion (crab for supper)
e No (He studied and took notes for many years).

When they have found the answers, you can go back and ask more detailed questions such as the dates, and where exactly Stoker was when he had his dream. The Workbook, Exercise 3, contains the words of the listening passage for completion, so you might like to do this activity at this point in the lesson.

4 THINK AND SPEAK.

Discuss, in English if possible, if students believe that eating cheese or fish causes bad dreams. Or is there some other food to avoid? Different cultures have different beliefs. Also ask, *Do you read frightening books before you go to sleep?* Act as 'chairperson' of the discussion, making sure that everyone says something, however limited.

WORKBOOK

Exercise 1 is best done in class. It can be integrated with the Student's Book lesson, and done immediately after Student's Book Exercise 1, or it can be done at the end of the lesson or at the beginning of the next lesson as a 'reminder'. Exercises 2 and 3 support the listening and the Student's Book, and allow students to come to grips with the exact words of the passage.

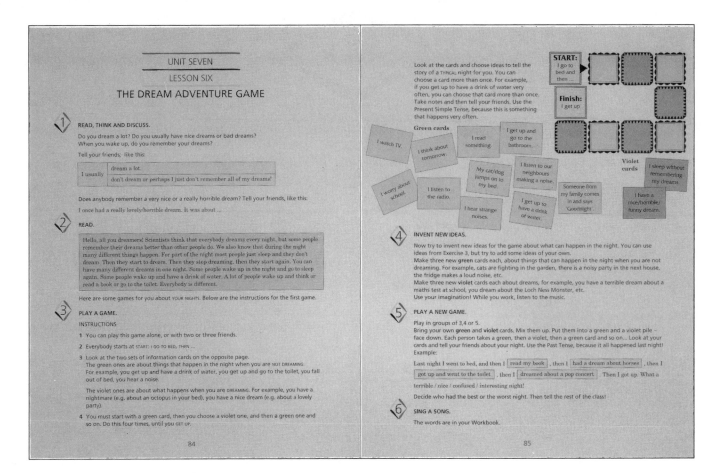

UNIT SEVEN
LESSON SIX

THE DREAM ADVENTURE GAME

1 READ, THINK AND DISCUSS.

Do you dream a lot? Do you usually have nice dreams or bad dreams?
When you wake up, do you remember your dreams?

Tell your friends; like this:

I usually	dream a lot.
	don't dream or perhaps I just don't remember all of my dreams!

Does anybody remember a very nice or a really horrible dream? Tell your friends, like this:

I once had a really lovely/horrible dream. It was about ....

2 READ.

Hello, all you dreamers! Scientists think that everybody dreams every night, but some people remember their dreams better than other people do. We also know that during the night many different things happen. For part of the night most people just sleep and they don't dream. Then they start to dream. Then they stop dreaming, then they start again. You can have many different dreams in one night. Some people wake up in the night and go to sleep again. Some people wake up and have a drink of water. A lot of people wake up and think or read a book or go to the toilet. Everybody is different.

Here are some games for you about YOUR NIGHTS. Below are the instructions for the first game.

3 PLAY A GAME.

INSTRUCTIONS

1 You can play this game alone, or with two or three friends.

2 Everybody starts at START: I GO TO BED, THEN ...

3 Look at the two sets of information cards on the opposite page.
The green ones are about things that happen in the night when you are NOT DREAMING. For example, you get up and have a drink of water, you get up and go to the toilet, you fall out of bed, you hear a noise.

The violet ones are about what happens when you are DREAMING. For example, you have a nightmare (e.g. about an octopus in your bed), you have a nice dream (e.g. about a lovely party).

4 You must start with a green card, then you choose a violet one, and then a green one and so on. Do this four times, until you GET UP.

84

Look at the cards and choose ideas to tell the story of a TYPICAL night for you. You can choose a card more than once. For example, if you get up to have a drink of water very often, you can choose that card more than once. Take notes and then tell your friends. Use the Present Simple Tense, because this is something that happens very often.

START: I go to bed and then ...

Finish: I get up

Green cards

- I watch TV.
- I think about tomorrow.
- I read something.
- I get up and go to the bathroom.
- I worry about school.
- My cat/dog jumps on to my bed.
- I listen to our neighbours making a noise.
- I listen to the radio.
- I hear strange noises.
- I get up to have a drink of water.
- Someone from my family comes in and says 'Goodnight'.

Violet cards

- I sleep without remembering my dreams.
- I have a nice/horrible/funny dream.

4 INVENT NEW IDEAS.

Now try to invent new ideas for the game about what can happen in the night. You can use ideas from Exercise 3, but try to add some ideas of your own.
Make three new **green** cards each, about things that can happen in the night when you are not dreaming. For example, cats are fighting in the garden, there is a noisy party in the next house, the fridge makes a loud noise, etc.
Make three new **violet** cards each about dreams, for example, you have a terrible dream about a maths test at school, you dream about the Loch Ness Monster, etc.
Use your imagination! While you work, listen to the music.

5 PLAY A NEW GAME.

Play in groups of 3,4 or 5.
Bring your own **green** and **violet** cards. Mix them up. Put them into a green and a violet pile – face down. Each person takes a green, then a violet, then a green card and so on... Look at your cards and tell your friends about your night. Use the Past Tense, because it all happened last night! Example:

Last night I went to bed, and then I read my book, then I had a dream about horses, then I got up and went to the toilet, then I dreamed about a pop concert. Then I got up. What a terrible / nice / confused / interesting night!

Decide who had the best or the worst night. Then tell the rest of the class!

6 SING A SONG.

The words are in your Workbook.

85

KEY VOCABULARY	neighbour, octopus, typical
KEY GRAMMAR POINTS	Present Simple for talking about general truths about oneself, e.g. *I dream a lot* or about routines and habits, e.g. *Some people wake up in the night and go to sleep again;* Use of the Past tense to narrate the events of last night; Words to signal sequence: *first, next, then*
SKILLS	Using imagination and cooperating to expand the 'option cards' in the Dream Game; Putting events in chronological order

LESSON 6   THE DREAM ADVENTURE GAME

1 READ, THINK AND DISCUSS.

You could start the lesson with the Class Survey from Workbook Unit 7, Lesson 5. If not, the brief question in Exercise 1 here is to remind students of the topic of Unit 7, Lesson 5. With a good class, you could ask for free contributions about particular dreams students have had, asking the *Does anybody remember ...?* question in this section. Correct gently, if necessary, and do not let students feel that this is a 'test', since they are taking a risk by talking about something so personal. Give value to the information they give, more than to the absolute correctness of their English. If they are slow to start, tell them about a funny or spectacular dream of your own, and see if they react.

2 READ.

This passage revises the Present Simple, but also gives some ideas for what happens during 'typical nights'. See how they react. Ask: *Who are you most like?* and give information about yourself e.g. *I often get up and have a drink of water.*

3 PLAY A GAME.

For this game and for Exercises 4 and 5 you need to bring some pieces of card or paper to make 'dream cards'. Ideally, they should be green and violet as in the book, but pieces of ordinary paper will do. You can put a coloured mark on the back of each piece. Look at the 'dream cards' on the next page, and read the instructions with the students.

Show how the game works using the examples in the book. To arrive, by chance, on a card in the book, you can close your eyes and point and see what card you find.

4 INVENT NEW IDEAS.

Put your students into groups of three to five people. Distribute your blank 'green' and 'violet' cards – at least three of each type for each student. Ask the groups to cooperate to copy out the cards shown in the book but also to make some new cards inventing their own ideas. It is better if they do this in their 'game' groups so that they do not make too many duplicates. Slower students in a group can be given the easier task of just copying the cards in the book while the others make up their own new ideas. You can play the song in Exercise 6 a few times while they work to provide 'background' music. Do not ask them to concentrate on the words of the song at this stage.

5 PLAY A NEW GAME.

When the cards are ready, ask the groups to mix them up and put them into two piles face down (green with green, violet with violet, of course). Then they take it in turns to 'collect' three of each without looking. They then arrange them green violet, green violet, green violet, to make a funny or sensible sequence. They use the language model to tell their friends about last night. Remind them to 'switch' to the Past tense because they are talking about 'last night'.

If this game is liked, collect the cards and keep them to use another time.

6 ⌒⌒ SING A SONG.

The words of the song are in Workbook activity Exercise 1. Play the song again, and ask them to put the lines in the correct order. Then they are ready to 'sing along' with the cassette when you play it again.

WORKBOOK

Exercise 1 has already been suggested as a good ending to the lesson. Exercises 2, 3 and 4 can be done for homework, since they consist of reading and writing consolidation of the language used in Student's Book.

UNIT EIGHT

LESSON ONE

WHAT CAN CHILDREN TEACH GROWN-UPS?

 READ AND ANSWER.

Do you have any computers
in your school?
Where?
Who uses them?
What for?

What do you think about computers?
Tick the answers that are true for you.

They are very useful.
I'm afraid of them.
I like playing computer games.
I don't know anything about computers.

Tell your friends.

 LOOK AND SPEAK.

Mark's school has some
computers. All the
children are learning to
use them. In Britain, it's
part of the Official
School Programme.
Twice a week, Mark
has a special lesson
about computers.

Can you find the
correct name for this
lesson on the school
timetable? What are
the days and the times
for this lesson?

	MONDAY	TUESDAY	WEDNESDAY	THURSDAY	FRIDAY
1	Music	Maths	Music	P.E.	Science
2	Art	Science	Geography	P.E.	Maths
3	Science	English	Science	French	Geography
4	Geography	Information Technology	Maths	P.S.E.	English
5	History	French	R.E.	English	French
6	History	R.E.	Drama	Information Technology	History
Homework	Science Geography	Information Technology English French	Maths R.E.	English French Geography	Maths Science

Look at the timetable again, and say how Mark's school is similar to or different from yours, like
this:

SIMILAR   In our school, we study _____ and so does Mark.
   Mark studies _____ and so do we.

DIFFERENT In our school, we study _____ but Mark doesn't.
   Mark studies _____ but we don't.

 READ.

Information Technology means 'learning how to use computers'. It is a new subject in British
schools. Some of the teachers are very excited about it, but some teachers are a bit afraid.
Often, the children know more about computers than some teachers! Look at the article on the
opposite page from Young Ideas about a special computer course for teachers.

Read the first section and find out the **problem**. Can you guess the **solution**?

86

BACK TO SCHOOL FOR 'MISS' and 'SIR'
by Mary James, the Field School, Exeter.

The problem
Our school had a problem last term. All the pupils know how to use computers. Many of us have a computer
at home and we enjoy working and playing with computers. We really love them! Our special teacher for this
subject is called 'Information Technology' at school is Miss Ellen Locke. She is a very good teacher and
she teaches us new things about computers. She explains everything very clearly. So, we pupils have no
problems. We know that computers can be useful in many subjects and we want to use them in all our school
work.

The big problem was – the other teachers – the Maths teachers, the Geography teachers, the French
teachers, the History teachers, even the English teachers! Many of them knew nothing about computers, and
some of them were afraid of computers! They all wanted to learn more, and we all wanted to use computers
in all our lessons, so we needed to find a solution. So, what did we do?

Now read about the **solution** and find the answers to
these questions.

a Who taught the teachers in the school to use
   computers?
b Who organised the course?
c How many 'students' were there for this course?
d Was it a success?

The solution
Yes, we had a special course for all our teachers. We had it on a Saturday morning, and we used the
school's Computer Room. We have thirty computers in there, so there was one computer for each teacher in
our school. But who taught the course? Aha! Not Miss Locke. She organised it, but she didn't teach it. The
answer is ... WE taught 30 pupils from the school came in on Saturday and each pupil taught one teacher. It
was great fun. Everybody enjoyed it, and we all learned a lot.

Read about the **result** and find the answers to these questions.

a What do you think the grown-ups learned?   c Who was the best 'pupil'?
b What do you think the children learned?   d What was the best result of the project?

The result
The grown-ups – the teachers – learned how to use computers, of course. For example, Mr Jones, our history
teacher, said afterwards 'This is fantastic! Now I have all sorts of ideas about using computers in some of my
history lessons. It's very easy, and very interesting!' He was a very good 'pupil', but he was not the best!
Our best 'pupil' was our art teacher, Mrs Wolf – she understood everything immediately! The worst 'pupil' was
Mr Page, our maths teacher. He needed lots of explanations! He laughed about it afterwards, and he said
'Well, now I know how difficult it is to learn something new! I promise to be more patient with my classes this
year! I will explain everything very clearly, and I will ask for questions.'
We all had fun, and I think that pupils and teachers are now better friends. That was the best result of our
project. At the end of the day, we had a big party, and now everybody is looking forward to an exciting new
term with our computers.

 DISCUSS

Do you think it's important to know how to use a computer? Say why or why not.

Do you think that it is a good idea for children to try to teach grown-ups sometimes? Does your
teacher agree? Find out if he or she would like to learn something new from you.

87

KEY VOCABULARY	computer, course, homework, patient (*adjective*), pupil, problem, solution, subject (at school), timetable; Days of the week (**revised**) School subjects (mostly **revised**): art, drama, English, French, geography, history, information technology, maths, music, PSE (= Personal and Social Education), RE (= Religious Education), science Titles: *Miss, Mrs, Mr* and their pronunciation; The use of 'Miss' and 'Sir' to refer to teachers.
KEY GRAMMAR POINTS	Present Simple (**revised**): + *so do/does ....* + *don't* Past tense in narrative (**revised**): *more.... than* *Often the children know more about computers than some teachers!* *Many/some/all of them ...*
SKILLS	Speculating about solutions to given problems; Reading a long and complex text for information; Comparing own (school) life to that of others; Free discussion

98

LESSON 1   WHAT CAN CHILDREN TEACH GROWN-UPS?

1 READ AND ANSWER.

Set the scene by reading the questions. Give students time to think, and then collect answers.

2 LOOK AND SPEAK.

Let the students study Mark's timetable. This is a good opportunity for cultural comparisons. See if they can find the correct name for computer studies. (It's part of information technology on Tuesdays and Thursdays. The times of the lessons are not given on the timetable. They should answer, saying e.g. *It's the fourth lesson on Tuesday.*) Explain what RE and PSE are. Then ask the students to look at the timetable again and find similarities and differences between it and their own school timetables.

3 READ.

This text is deliberately long and complex, but the students work through it step by step. First they read the first section and identify the **problem** (many teachers knew nothing about computers). See if they can guess the solution. Discuss their ideas before moving on to the next section.

The second section and the questions before it help them to identify the **solution** (the pupils taught the teachers). Make sure that they read the questions before they read, since they will help them to focus on the important information. Discuss their answers before you move on.

Then let them read about the **result**. (Teachers learned about computers. Pupils learned about teaching. Some teachers also learned more about teaching, about being patient in particular. Pupils and teachers became better friends.)

Draw attention to the conventional titles *Miss, Mrs, Mr* and *Miss* for an unmarried woman, *Mrs* for a married woman, *Mr* for all men. (*Mrs* and *Mr* are abbreviations, and they are almost never written in full.)

See CULTURAL NOTES.

Finally, give students time to read the whole article again, at their own pace (10 minutes maximum is the suggested time-limit) and ask for any help they need.

4 DISCUSS.

Discuss the 'computer' question. Give ample time for the *Can children teach grown ups?* question. Exercise 4 in the Workbook provides support and can be used at this point in the lesson. Be prepared with a few ideas for what you might like to learn from your class, e.g. a game, a song, how to start a new hobby or how to look after a new pet animal. (This will not destroy your dignity as a teacher, but will rather make your relations with students (even) better and more relaxed.)

WORKBOOK

Workbook Exercises 1, 2 and 3 build on the Student's Book Exercises 1, 2 and 3. They can be done at home or integrated with the class lessons as you think best. Exercise 4 has been mentioned as a good support in class for the DISCUSS activity in the Student's Book.

CULTURAL NOTES

'Miss' and 'Sir' are the conventional ways in which British students call for the attention of or refer to their female and male teachers (respectively). Even married women are called 'Miss' in this context. At other times children do use the full name, often preceded by *Please ...* as in: *Please, Mrs Brown, may I be excused?* (go to the toilet). The use here, in the title to the article is humorous, and your students may enjoy hearing about this aspect of British school life. Politically aware students may enjoy hearing about the other title 'Ms' often used in writing when addressing all women, married or not, in response to feminist dislike of differentiating married from unmarried women. Few people use it in speech, and nobody is quite sure how to say it! (muz) is the usual attempt. In some countries, mature women, whether married or not are given the title often associated with married women (e.g. Signora in Italy, Madame in France). It might be interesting with an advanced class to investigate and compare the situations in your students' country with that in Britain.

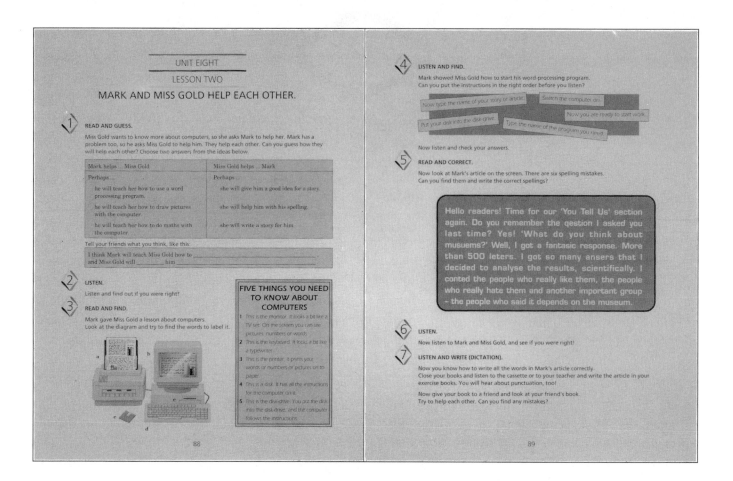

KEY VOCABULARY	disk, disk-drive, keyboard, monitor, printer, program (computer), screen, switch on, typewriter, word-processing
KEY GRAMMAR POINTS	*Each other* for reciprocal actions; Imperatives used in instructions; *Will* used for predictions; Consolidation of short forms of verbs and the correct use of the apostrophe; *more .... than ....*
SKILLS	Editing (correcting) mistakes in a text

LESSON 2   MARK AND MISS GOLD HELP EACH OTHER.

1 READ AND GUESS.

Read the introduction with students, and establish the situation. Ask students to predict what will happen. They can use the language models in the pink boxes to prepare their answers. Then ask pupils to speak and say what they think will happen.

2 ◉◉ LISTEN.

Students check their predictions by listening to the conversation between Mark and Miss Gold.

3 READ AND FIND.

This activity brings together the vocabulary connected with computer use. Ask the students to look at the pictures and match items (a)-(e) to the numbered descriptions in the grey box. Then they can draw and label a picture of a computer in their Word Books.

4 ◉◉ LISTEN AND FIND.

Let the students think about the correct order of the instructions before they listen. Then they listen and check their ideas. If you wish, you can then ask them to copy the instructions in the right order in their exercise books. Some students may want to copy them into their Word Books next to the computer drawing. (They can do this instead of using their exercise books.)

5 READ AND CORRECT.

See if the students can find the six spelling mistakes on the screen before they listen in Exercise 6. Let them work together. Say, *Help each other!* (to reinforce the *each other* expression).
The corrections are: *question, museums, fantastic, letters, answers, counted.*
They will probably miss a few, but do not give the right answers at this stage. Make them listen in Exercise 6 to check.

6 ◉◉ LISTEN.

Students listen and find the corrections on the computer screen.

7 LISTEN AND WRITE (DICTATION).

Students close their books and write the passage again in their exercise books as a dictation. This activity reinforces spelling and revises the punctuation words first introduced in Unit 6, Lesson 1. It also gives them the chance to practise editing and correcting a friend's writing. Let them exchange books in pairs and discuss any mistakes. Say, *Help each other!* once again.

WORKBOOK

Exercise 1 gives a context to the idea of 'helping each other'. It demands that one person knows more about something than another does. Students think about their own knowledge and that of a friend (or their teacher) using the language box to help them. Then they write two sentences, using the *more ... than ...* structure.

Exercise 2 extends the idea in the Student's Book, Exercise 4, of instructions, on how to check and edit their own work. This also links with the activity in Exercise 7 from the Student's Book. The correct order is:
Write notes.
Write your sentences.
Check the spelling and punctuation.
Ask a friend or your teacher.
Read it again.

Exercise 3 picks up and consolidates the use of apostrophes in short forms of verbs. (Practice of this was given in Level 3, but perhaps now is the time to look at this matter again.) This activity is best done in class under your supervision, but a good class could try the writing exercise for homework, after you have helped them with the grammar table in class.

The editing task in Exercise 4 will be a good check of whether they have understood the information in Exercise 3. It can be set for homework, with a thorough check in the next lesson, or done in class with the students helping each other and discussing their answers.

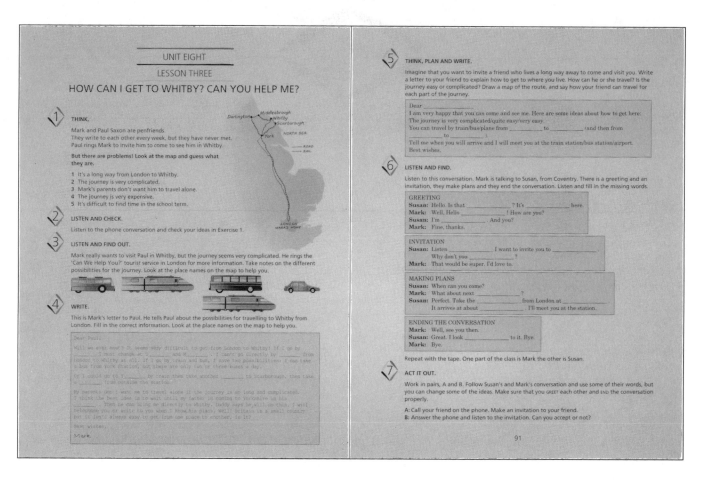

KEY VOCABULARY	change (*verb*) (trains, buses, etc.), direction, directly, during, greeting, moors, motorway, route
KEY GRAMMAR POINTS	*Could* for potential choices: *Mark could go by train or car; Can't* for impossibility: *He can't get to Whitby by coach; Must* for necessity: *He must change at Darlington;* Expressing distances: *It's a long way from London to Whitby.* *He lives a long way away.*
SKILLS	Solving problems; Processing complex information to find the best route; Learning more about places in Britain

LESSON 3   HOW CAN I GET TO WHITBY? CAN YOU HELP ME?

1 THINK.

Read the introduction to set the scene. Students look at the map to realise that Whitby and London are distant. Help them to 'read' the map symbols – the red line for roads and the black line for rail (train lines). Read the questions to get students to guess the problems. (All of them are problems!)

2 ▭ LISTEN AND CHECK.

Play the cassette for students to confirm their answers. Then ask, *What is Mark going to do next?* (He is going to ring the Tourist Information Service and find out more about the possibilities for travel.)

3 ▭ LISTEN AND FIND OUT.

Mark's conversation with the Tourist Service contains some complex information. Help students by looking first with them at the letter in Exercise 4 that Mark wrote to Paul as a result. The gaps will give them an idea of the information they must listen carefully for. Give them the hint that the missing words are either place names or names of means of transport. Play the cassette once or twice, and then let them compare their answers before you collect them orally. If your students need more help, turn now to Workbook, Exercise 1 which shows the computer screen information and let them write the sentences about how Mark could travel.

4 WRITE.

Students can copy the letter from Mark to Paul in their exercise books, using the information from Exercise 3.

5 THINK, PLAN AND WRITE.

Students now think about their own country and imagine that they are inviting a friend who lives a long way away to visit. The model letter will be very useful if your students are thinking of inviting penfriends to come to visit. Encourage them to draw a good, clear map, too.

6 ▭ LISTEN AND FIND.

Students listen to the conversation between Susan and Mark, and fill in the missing words. They can copy the conversation in their exercise books. Then they repeat with the cassette. The aim is to give them a good preparation for Exercise 7 and to provide them with language support if they need to telephone a penfriend to give an invitation.

7 ACT IT OUT.

Let the students adapt Susan's and Mark's conversation to fit a situation close to their own.

WORKBOOK

Exercise 1 can be used in class as support for Student's Book, Exercise 3, as mentioned above, or it can be used for homework to consolidate the information and the language in this lesson. The passage and puzzle in Exercise 2 aim to consolidate information about places in Britain. It is more suitable for homework, since it is quiet, absorbing work which will take some time to do well, especially the map-completion.

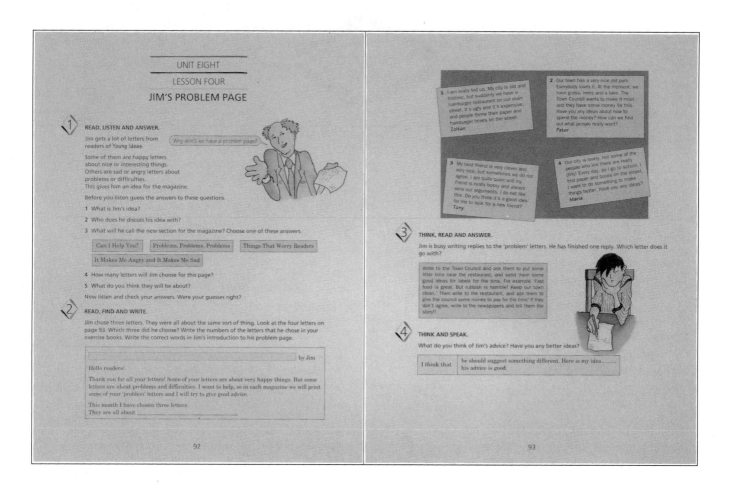

KEY VOCABULARY	advice, argument, difficulty, litter bin, problem
KEY GRAMMAR POINTS	*will* for predictions (**revised**); Imperatives (**revised**) for strong advice or instructions; *should* for gentle advice
SKILLS	Exercising personal taste in the choice of a name for the 'Problem Letters' page, recognising which three letters fit the same 'category' and distinguishing the 'odd one out'; Matching suitable advice to a particular problem

UNIT 8

LESSON 4   JIM'S PROBLEM PAGE

1 ⊙⊙ READ, LISTEN AND ANSWER.

Read the introduction and look at the cartoon of Jim to set the scene. Look at questions 1 to 5 before students listen and let them guess the answers. Most of the answers are easily guessed if students look at the title of the lesson and remember that he usually discusses things with Mrs Wine. The answer to question 3 is a matter of taste. You can discuss guesses at this stage. Quick students may note that 'Problems, Problems, Problems' is a bit negative and that 'Things That Worry Readers' is a bit boring. Play the cassette for students to confirm or change their guessed answers.

2 READ, FIND AND WRITE.

The yellow box contains Jim's letter to the readers. Students write the title he chose (Can I Help You?) using the information from the listening in Exercise 1 and they can then look quickly at the readers' letters in the box on page 93 to find the category of letter that he chose – problems about the places where readers live (Letter 3 is the 'odd one out').
Let the students read the four letters more slowly. Ask, *Which three letters go together?* (1,2 and 4) and *What are they about?* Then you can ask some more oral questions about the letters, e.g. *Who wrote about rubbish in the streets?* (Zoltan and Maria), *Who has a problem with his friend?* (Tony).

3 THINK, READ AND ANSWER.

Let students read Jim's reply to one of the letters and decide which one it answers (No.1, from Zoltan). The advice is very direct and given in the form of imperatives for instructions. (This will later be contrasted in the Workbook with more 'gentle' advice using *should*.)

4 THINK AND SPEAK.

Students give their opinions of Jim's advice in Exercise 3 using the language models in the book. If they don't like his advice, ask them to prepare a better idea. Check how many students agree with Jim and how many have better ideas. (The language model reintroduces *should* which was met briefly in Unit 7, Lesson 2.)

WORKBOOK

Exercise 1 can be done in class as a follow-up to Exercises 3 and 4 in the Student's Book. It could also be attempted for homework. Exercise 2 contrasts the use of the imperative with *should* in giving advice. (Examples of *should* are seen in Workbook, Exercise 1, in Jim's notes.) Exercise 2 needs introducing and explaining in class, then the students in Exercise 3 can try giving advice in the two ways in class or for homework. Exercise 4 allows students to use their imaginations in class or for homework, to write an answer to a new problem letter. The Workbook gives ideas under the headings of *nasty (cruel)* and *kind*. Discuss answers in class both for language and for suitability for the problem!

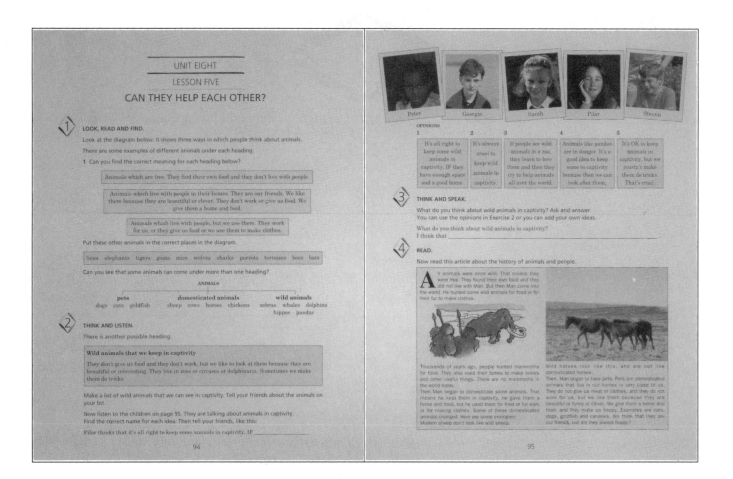

KEY VOCABULARY	mammoth, opinion
KEY GRAMMAR POINTS	Relative clauses used for restricted definitions (defining relative clauses): *Animals which/that are free; each other* used for reciprocal actions: *Can they help each other?*
SKILLS	Categorising ideas, using fine distinctions, e.g. wild animals and wild animals that are kept in captivity; Forming own ideas about a difficult moral issue (keeping wild animals in captivity) and expressing them clearly

LESSON 5   CAN THEY HELP EACH OTHER?

1 LOOK, READ AND FIND.

Look at the branching diagram at the end of this section. Check that the students remember the meanings of *pet*, *domesticated* and *wild* (the examples under each of these headings will help to clarify any doubts). Students match each of these headings with one of the definitions in the yellow boxes. Now ask them to draw a version of the branching diagram in their exercise books, adding the definitions under each heading, and putting in more examples of animals, taken from the green box. (**NB** It is, of course, possible to include an animal under more than one heading, if a justification can be found, e.g. some people keep goats as pets, some as domesticated animals for their milk and meat, and some types of goat live as wild animals. Goats are also popular in Children's zoos.)

2 ⊙⊙ THINK AND LISTEN.

A fourth and more subtle category is introduced here; animals which normally live in the wild, but which are also found in captivity. Discuss with students where they would put these 'zoo animals' on the diagram in Exercise 1. Do they want to add a fourth heading, like this ...

| Pets | Domesticated animals | Wild animals | Animals in captivity |

or do they think they should make a sub-category of WILD animals like this?

| Pets | Domesticated animals | Wild animals |
| | | free   in captivity |

Students then list individually the sorts of wild animals often seen in captivity. They compare their ideas with friends to build up a longer joint list.
Look with the students at the photos of the five children at the top of page 95. Their opinions about keeping wild animals in captivity are given in the boxes below, but we do not know who thinks what. Explain that the students must listen to the cassette and find the name that goes with each opinion. Ask them to write the numbers of the opinions **1** to **5** in their exercise books and then listen and write the names. Let them compare answers before you play the cassette again. Then collect answers orally round the class.

3 THINK AND SPEAK.

The opinions expressed by the children in Exercise 2 give support for the students as they prepare their own opinions. Give them time and take notes, then elicit answers orally round the class. Try to make it a real discussion. Make a chart on the board to collect the ideas, and see if there is a majority opinion in the class or not.

4 READ.

Let the students read the passage at their own pace (about four to five minutes is a reasonable time-limit). Then, with the books still open so that they can look back and find information, ask some oral questions about it, e.g. *Show me a picture of a mammoth, Are the horses in the picture wild or domesticated? Which domesticated animals are mentioned in the passage?*

WORKBOOK

All of the Workbook activities can be done at home or in class.
Exercise 1 offers two alternative endings for each sentence about wild, domesticated or pet animals. The endings are found by paying careful attention to the sense as well as to the grammar.
In Exercise 2, the short reading and completion passages offer interesting new (and true) information about how animals and people can help each other. The pictures support understanding and the correct answers are found by a combination of sense and grammar.
The puzzle in Exercise 3 revises most of the already-covered animal names, but also includes some new and more unusual names. Comprehension of these is assisted by captioned pictures of 'new' animals around the puzzle.
In Exercise 4 both magazine ideas are optional, but give ideas for extending work on animals to include use of reference books to find out more.

KEY VOCABULARY	dungeon, haunted, outing, poster, ride (*noun*), show, ticket
KEY GRAMMAR POINTS	*I would / I'd like to* (**revised**)
SKILLS	Making and expressing a choice, based on own personal preferences; Deciding on what information should go into a visual or radio advert

LESSON 6   THINGS TO SEE AND DO

1 🔲 **LOOK AND LISTEN.**

Look at the four posters carefully with your
students. Ask, *What can you see in the picture?* for each
poster. See if they can guess what type of things they
can do and see in each place. Elicit, e.g. *fish, sea
animals (Scarborough), scientific things (Eureka!),
horrible things / a dungeon (London dungeon is the
world's most famous medieval horror museum), haunted
house, shows, rides for Alton Towers.*
Then play the cassette. The task is simple: to number
the pictures according to the order in which the
radio presenter mentions them. Students may write
the numbers in the small red box next to each of the
four pictures, or they can first copy the name of each
place into their exercise books and then write the
numbers next to them. Check the answers by playing
the cassette again and asking pupils to put up their
hands and say the name of the place being described.
(The Workbook, Exercise 1, offers support for
students for follow-up work to this listening task.
These activities can be done now, or after the
Student's Book lesson is completed.)

2 LOOK AND THINK.

By this stage in the lesson, students should have
enough information about each place to allow them
to form a personal opinion about which of the four
places they would like to go to. Give them time to
prepare their sentences in writing, then put up the
names of the four places on the board, and ask
around the class what each student chose, to elicit
oral answers. For each 'vote', put a tick by the
appropriate place-name. Total the ticks to find the
most popular place.

3 LOOK AND FIND.

Look at the map of the British Isles with the students
and ask them to find the locations of each of the four
places. With a good class, ask questions about all the
places on the map to elicit oral answers revising the
points of the compass and location.

4 THINK.

This activity gives a starting point for follow-up
work. Students do not have to do **every** task.

You may decide on the poster-design, for example,
or for the choosing of suitable words for a radio
advert. (With a good class, you could record the
students' efforts, perhaps adding suitable music to
introduce their 'advert'.)

WORKBOOK

As mentioned before, Exercise 1 can be done during
the Student's Book lesson, to give more support to
the listening, or the whole Workbook lesson can be
carried out at the end of the Student's Book
activities. Activity 1 picks out some key phrases from
the cassette, and challenges students to recognise
which place they refer to. The cassette should be
played again, if this activity is done in class-time.
Activity 2 reinforces vocabulary, but also encourages
students to see that the same vocabulary item can
'belong' under more than one heading, e.g. you
might see a skeleton in the London Dungeon (horror
exhibition) and in the Eureka Museum (scientific
exhibit).
Exercise 2 expands the theme into vocabulary and
phrases connected with paying and waiting to go
into an exhibition or show. The questions require
problem-solving and close reading by the students,
e.g. they must calculate the price that the whole
family must pay to go in. This involves calculating
full-price tickets for the two adults, half-price for the
children, and remembering that, according to the
rules, the baby goes in free.
In Exercise 3, the word *outing* is introduced as a
useful general word to use for any pleasure visit, and
students are invited to choose their personal
favourite. As usual, it is suggested that students
have the chance to compare their answers and try to
find the most popular idea for an outing. This can be
done in class when the pupils bring in their
Workbooks, if you have set this activity for
homework.
Exercise 4 is optional, but the story of a really
successful or a really disastrous outing (told in a
humorous way) could be a good idea for the class
magazine.

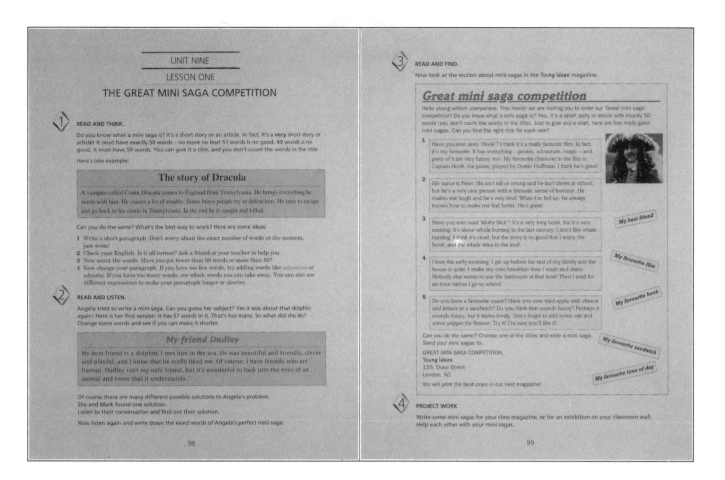

KEY VOCABULARY	defeat (*verb*), expression, flavour, mini saga, snack
KEY GRAMMAR POINTS	No new grammar points, since students are concentrating on demanding skills work
SKILLS	Practising editing to arrive at the exact number of words required. This will involve: removing or adding words without changing other expressions (the easiest operations), or reformulating expressions in different words (more challenging); Cooperative work, looking at other's as well as one's own attempts and making suggestions

1 READ AND THINK.

This section explains what a mini saga is, gives an example of one – and lists useful strategies for succeeding in inventing one. It needs to be understood well before the students can go on to the next activities. Mini sagas are popular in many countries, so try to find examples from your local newspapers or radio competitions if you know of any. Sometimes the target figure is 100 words, but the **very** mini length of 50 words – although more difficult in one way – being brief and to the point, is more suitable for young learners. The passage to write is shorter and should take less time and it is less difficult to estimate and count 50 words accurately!

2 🔲 READ AND LISTEN.

The 'My Friend Dudley' example is too long by seven words. Before students listen to the cassette, which gives just one possible solution to this problem, let them look at it and make their own suggestions about ways of making it shorter. Do not demand that each student arrives at exactly 50 words at this stage. Accept and list on the board all suggestions about how to shorten it. When the cassette has been heard, you can look back at the list to see if any of the students' suggestions were used by Mark and Angela. Ask, *What did Mark and Angela do? How did they change the passage? Were your ideas the same – or better?*

LESSON 1   THE GREAT MINI SAGA COMPETITION

If wished, the students can then close their books and listen to the cassette again, writing down the exact words of the new perfect mini saga in their exercise books. You will need to pause the cassette to allow them time to write. A quicker, less demanding way is to let them look at the passage as they listen, and take notes on the changes made (but without writing in the Student's Book). Then they write out the perfect mini saga as before.

3 READ AND FIND.

Students read the five mini sagas very quickly to try to find the correct title for each. Make it into a competition. They do not have to read every word to find these answers, they should skim through for key words. Ask, *Who can finish first? (Hands up, and check silently.)* This will prevent the rest of the class 'giving up' when the faster children have found the answers. Make sure that everyone has finished before you elicit and check the answers with the whole class. Then let them go back and read the five mini sagas more slowly to get the full meaning. Ask a few oral questions of your own to suit the class's interests, both about the information in the passages and about their own feelings and experiences, e.g. *Who has seen 'Hook'? Did you enjoy it? Do you like the early morning, or do you prefer the evening? Would you like to eat that sandwich?*
Ask each student to choose one of the five titles and try to produce his or her own mini saga on a similar subject. Students should be encouraged to look at each other's work and make suggestions and you should circulate and help, too. Make sure that they follow the suggestions about procedure in Exercise 1. This will take at least 20 minutes or more, and can be continued for homework if necessary, with a 'report' session at the beginning of the next lesson.

4 PROJECT WORK

Very able classes, who finish Exercise 3 quickly, can start on new topics for mini sagas for the class magazine. This stage is not essential. Slower classes can stay with the five topics from Exercise 3 where they have support from the examples on the page.

WORKBOOK

Workbook, Exercise 1 picks up the grammar point *too many/too few*, and Exercise 2 puts the grammar into use when the students count the words in two imperfect mini sagas and write sentences about each and about what they need to do to improve them. Then they take action to arrive at 50 words exactly. Exercise 3 offers more possible topics for more mini sagas.
Your students do not have to attempt all the mini saga ideas in the Student's and Workbook at this point in the course. If they seem bored with the idea, drop it, or come back to some of the Workbook activities later on in the course. Mini sagas are supposed to be fun, not a chore!

GRAMMAR AND CULTURAL NOTE

The Student's Book in Exercise 1 uses the more 'relaxed' and generally used phrase *no more, no less* about the number of words. Purists may object that it should be *no **fewer**.* This is strictly correct, but modern English usage allows the use of *less* in this context. There was, however, an amusing debate recently about notices in Supermarkets which were put over special 'fast' check-out desks for people with *Five items or less.* The media took up the discussion and as a result, several Supermarket chains changed the notices to read, *Five items or fewer!*
In the *too many/too few* phrase, the word *few* is obligatory.

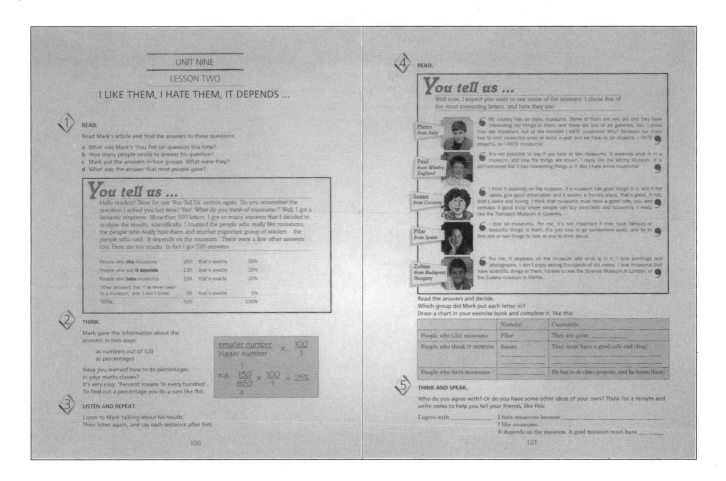

KEY VOCABULARY	analyse, depend, gallery, old-fashioned, percent, percentage, scientifically, total (numbers revised and consolidated, including very large numbers)
KEY GRAMMAR POINTS	100 out of 520 (to express proportions); *It depends on ....;* *If* + Present Simple (**revised**) to express real conditions (First Conditional); *How many ......?* (**revised**) Relative clauses: *people who ...* (**revised**)
SKILLS	Scanning a text quickly to find required information; Working out percentages and proportions from simple questionnaires, and facts and figures; Distinguishing a main opinion from comments which elaborate it or support it

LESSON 2   I LIKE THEM, I HATE THEM, IT DEPENDS...

1 READ.

Look at the first paragraph of Mark's article with students and check that they understand the situation. Mark asked the question, *What do you think of museums?* and now he is reporting on the answers. Then read the questions (**a**) to (**d**) with the students and ask them to scan the text quickly to find the answers. Encourage light-hearted competition and (*Hands up!*) as before, to motivate them to read quickly. Collect answers orally, then let them read again more slowly. Ask oral questions to practise numbers (not percentages yet) e.g. *How many people wrote to Mark?* (520), *How many people like museums?* (260) etc.

2 THINK.

Most students of this age will have 'done' percentages in their maths lessons. Look at the article in Exercise 1 again and see if the students can see how Mark arrived at his percentages. Look at the calculation in the grey box and check that they see how he got his result of 25% – people who said that it DEPENDS. (Maths specialists may want to develop this work more at this stage, but this is optional.)

3 ▭ LISTEN AND REPEAT.

Students repeat the words after Mark on the cassette, to consolidate the expression of percentages and proportions in English.

4 READ.

Let the students read the five answers chosen by Mark as the most interesting. Before they do the chart exercise, ask, *Which person do you agree with most?* and collect brief answers round the class, e.g. *I agree with Susan.* Then ask the students to copy the table into their exercise books and fill it in with information from '**You tell us**'. Make sure, before they do this, that they understand the difference between the MAIN opinion and COMMENTS which support it.

5 THINK AND SPEAK.

This activity was prepared for, if you did the oral work suggested for Exercise 4. Now, the students prepare an answer in written form, so that they can give a longer oral answer about museums, along with their comments. Then elicit answers around the class. If you wish, you could do a quick Class Survey to find out the majority opinions. Put up the headings LIKE DEPENDS and HATE on the board and put a tick under the appropriate heading as each student gives his or her answer. Then total the ticks and give the Class Result.

WORKBOOK

Exercises 1 and 2 can be done in class or for homework with discussion later in class. Exercises 3 and 4 are best done in class, with discussion and explanation on the spot.
Exercise 1 starts as a pure matching activity, to see if students can relate numbers and percentages. Then they fill in the diagram to show their comprehension.
Exercise 2 contains new cultural information, about pets in Britain, but it is basically another matching activity, to match the words and the numbers mentioned.
Exercise 3 uses information from Exercise 2 to encourage a cultural comparison about pets in Britain and in your students' native country. They may not have all the exact 'facts and figures' necessary for a scientific comparison, but they can guess, and a class discussion of the questions after guessing will be most useful. In Exercise 4, students may be surprised about the multi-ethnic/multi-language situation in modern Britain, which is why this activity is best done in class, with discussion (some of it possibly in the native language) comparing Britain with your students' own country. Scots Gallic and Welsh are languages native to Britain for thousands of years, but the other languages mentioned have been used in Britain since recent times.

CULTURAL NOTES

A teacher who wants to give a true cultural picture of modern Britain (and not just a stereotyped version, full of white men in bowler hats!) really needs to do a lot of research. Please do not give the impression that Britain is a place where only English is spoken, and that all British people speak English with a 'standard' accent. We are proud of our multi-cultural society. People from many other lands live in modern Britain, and most of us appreciate the cultural and linguistic richness that this brings. The 'xenophobic' cat which you will meet in Unit 9, Lesson 6, (a cat who hates 'foreign' people) is certainly not a role-model. Educated people in modern Britain enjoy cultural and linguistic diversity. This, of course, will make Britain a much happier destination for your own students, if they have the chance to visit us!

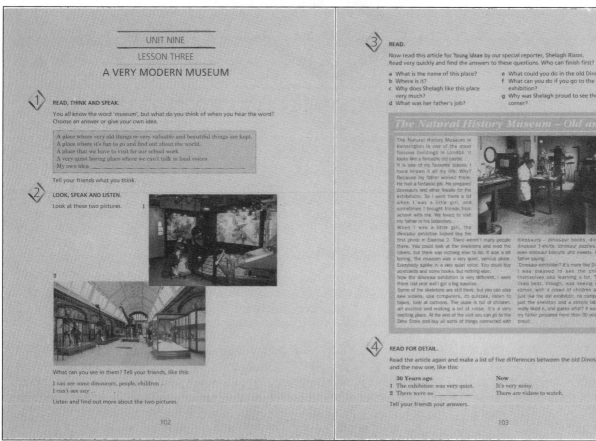

KEY VOCABULARY	crowd, laboratory, valuable
KEY GRAMMAR POINTS	Present and Past tenses integrated in a description of a place (Past for the narrative of events, Present for the description of the place) – revision of the same point from Unit 4, Lesson 1; Expressing similarities and differences over time: *30 years ago it was ... now it's ...*
SKILLS	Reading a fairly complex passage and extracting factual information **and** the author's personal feelings

LESSON 3   A VERY MODERN MUSEUM

1 READ, THINK AND SPEAK.

The introductory question allows students to give their own opinions about museums (see also Unit 9, Lesson 2, where Mark conducts a survey). It also raises their awareness about the differences between 'fun' and 'serious' museums, which is the point of the rest of the lesson.

2 ⌕ LOOK, SPEAK AND LISTEN.

Students look at the two pictures and say what they can or can't see in each. Ask, *What are the differences between the two pictures?* Then play the cassette, which reveals that the two pictures are of the same place (the Natural History Museum in London) but with 30 years' difference!

3 READ.

Read the questions **before** the students read the article. Will they notice that 'Shelagh Rixon' is in fact the author of their textbook? This is a true story, and as you can see I have strong feelings about the museum because of family reasons. Part of the purpose of this passage is to show that facts and opinions or feelings can appear in combination in some passages. Impose a time limit for finding the answers, to encourage rapid reading at this stage, or make it into a competition, *Who can find all the answers first?* Collect answers orally.

4 READ FOR DETAIL.

Students go back and read the passage more slowly, collecting the information they need to contrast the '30 years ago' and 'Now' features of the museum. They should write their answers: make sure they use the Past tense for '30 years ago' answers and the Present for 'Now' answers. Then let the students compare answers, telling the person next to them (and not just looking at the other person's book!).

WORKBOOK

Do all these activities after the Student's Book lessons as follow-up. Exercise 1 demands that students scan another fairly complex article (but with most of the language already well-known from previous lessons) to find the old wrong ideas and the new, better ideas about dinosaurs. Exercise 2 focuses on 36 adjectives from the passage. They put the adjectives into 18 pairs of opposites, and then may, if they wish, make a '9 square' puzzle to practise matching them. See Unit 6, Lesson 4 for an earlier use of this idea.

CULTURAL NOTES

Most museums in Britain used to be free, but now many, such as the Natural History Museum, charge for entry at most times (though there are limited 'free' periods at the ends of some days). Is this the same or different in your country? More sophisticated students might like to discuss whether they like or dislike the 'commercialism' of some museums, e.g. is it a good idea or a bad one to have a 'Dinostore' where they can buy dinosaur gifts?

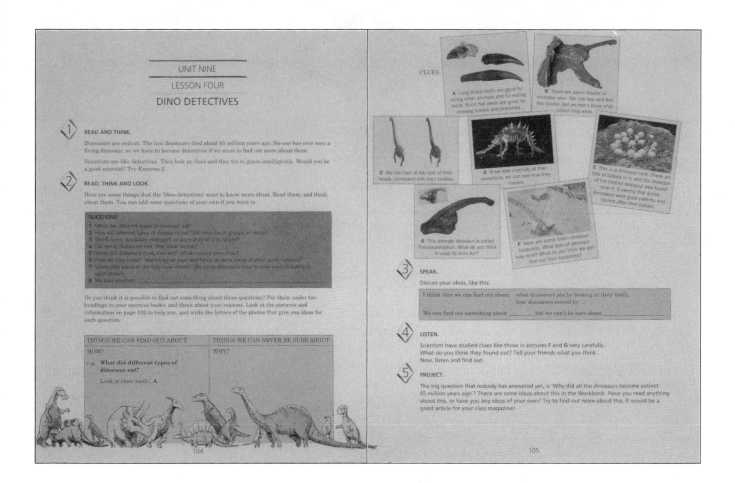

KEY VOCABULARY	blunt, branch, chew, clue, find out, flat (*adjective*), footprint, guess, intelligently, nest, scales, sharp, silent, skin, stupid
KEY GRAMMAR POINTS	Past tense for talking about dinosaur's habits and characteristics; 'Reduced' relative clauses (no 'that'): *Things (that) we can find out about;* Indirect questions: *We can find out about how dinosaurs moved ... ; by + ing: We can find out by looking at their teeth; Couldn't have a*nd *must have* for logical deduction about the past
SKILLS	Using inductive skills to use visual 'clues' about dinosaurs and make intelligent guesses

1 READ AND THINK.

The short paragraph sets the scene. Talk if you wish in the native language about how detectives (and scientists) use clues to find out facts or to guess intelligently. If there are any popular TV or film detectives known to your students, use them as an example.

2 READ, THINK AND LOOK.

This activity will take up most of the lesson. It is demanding both conceptually and linguistically, so work through it in careful stages, like this:

1 Go through the seven questions with the students and make sure that they understand them. Find out which questions the students think are the most interesting or the most difficult to find out about. Encourage them to think of one more question of their own. (They can help each other in pairs if they wish.)

2 Let the students tell you their extra questions. (If they do not have many ideas, there is one **big** question 'missing' – *Why did they all die 65 million years ago?* Real dino enthusiasts may also know about the big discussion, *Were they really all cold-blooded?* Other questions might be, *Could they swim?*, *How often did they eat?*, *Did they go to sleep at night?*

LESSON 4   DINO DETECTIVES

3 Now ask them to put the seven questions, plus their own question into two groups, in their exercise books, as shown in the table in the book. This is quite a demanding activity, and students can work in pairs to help each other if they wish. For the A group (things we can find out about) they should also add a suggestion about **how** as shown in the example. The **clues** section on page 105 will give them many ideas. If they do some of the discussion in the native language, this is not important, since they will be getting a better grasp of the concepts, but their 'results' should of course be written in English.

3 SPEAK.

Compare the answers of each individual or pair, by asking round the class, *What do you think about Question 1, What did different types of dinosaur eat?* etc. through all the questions. The students reply using the language box as a support. Individuals may vary in whether they think people can or cannot find out about some questions, and they may have more or less good ideas about **how** (e.g. for 1, we could also see if any small dinosaurs are found inside the stomach area of big dinosaur skeletons). Encourage them to say which **clue** pictures were useful.

4 ⊙⊙ LISTEN.

Look at **clues F** and **G** with the students and see if they can guess what scientists can find out from them. (They may remember the Parasaurolophus with its loud trumpeting noise from Unit 5, Lesson 3.) Collect ideas on the board. Then listen and ask students to take notes.

5 PROJECT.

This section just sets students thinking about this **big** question, if they have not already mentioned it in Exercise 1. It can be followed up through the Workbook. Use Workbook, Exercise 4, MAGAZINE IDEAS.

WORKBOOK

Exercise 1 builds on the thinking skills practised in the Student's Book, and develops the ideas of what can be discovered from the study of skeletons and footprints. The correct answer to the question is Number 3, of course. Exercise 2 practises the grammar needed to express what **must have** happened and what **couldn't have** happened, in the situation in Exercise 1. In case of doubt, the answers are given below.

Answers

We know that the big dinosaur **must have** been alive ...

The big footprints are close together so the big dinosaur **must have** been moving slowly.

It **couldn't have** been running.

The small footprints are far apart, so the small dinosaur **must have** been running.

It **must have** surprised the big dinosaur and attacked it.

The small dinosaur lost some teeth, so the two dinosaurs **must have** had a fight.

Some of the bones of the skeleton are missing, so the small dinosaur **must have** carried them away.

In Exercise 3, this grammar and information is carried over into a piece of continuous writing – a scientific report about the deductions from the picture in Exercise 1.

Exercise 4, MAGAZINE IDEAS, gives some possible guesses about what happened to all the dinosaurs. Students may take up the option to make a magazine article about it, but this is not essential if you feel that the subject has been exhausted!

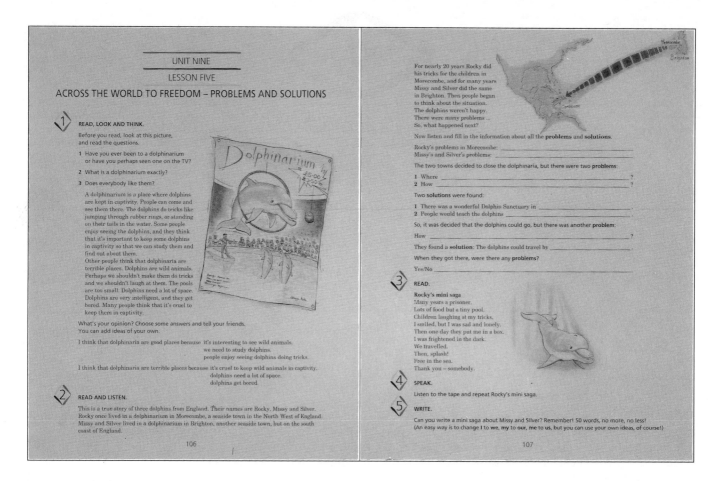

KEY VOCABULARY	coast, dolphinarium (plural: dolphinaria), lonely, prisoner, sanctuary, shore, splash (*noun*), still (*adverb*)
KEY GRAMMAR POINTS	*should/shouldn't* for moral issues; Passive understanding of indirect questions when the main verb is in the Past tense; Pronoun practice
SKILLS	Seeing the relationship between problems and their solutions; Listening to a complex narrative and taking notes

LESSON 5   ACROSS THE WORLD TO FREEDOM
– PROBLEMS AND SOLUTIONS

1 READ, LOOK AND THINK.

Look at the picture with the students, and get their reactions. Ask, *Does the picture make you happy or sad?* (Many modern children dislike the idea of keeping dolphins in captivity. If yours don't, they soon will after reading this article!)
Look at questions (1)-(3) before the students read. The questions relate to the children's own experience rather than to the passage. Collect ideas in English, where possible, but also allow discussion in the native language since the moral issues are complex. Let the students read the passage at their own pace. Then draw attention to the question below the passage. Ask them to think carefully and to prepare their answers, using the language models in the book to help them.
Collect answers orally round the class. Put on the board the two headings: FOR DOLPHINARIA and AGAINST DOLPHINARIA. For each answer, ask the class *Is he/she FOR or AGAINST dolphinaria/keeping dolphins in captivity?* and put a tick under the appropriate heading. Count the ticks under each heading at the end, and find out if the class 'vote' at the moment is FOR or AGAINST. (At the end of the lesson, see if there is any change in opinion.)

2 ⏺ READ AND LISTEN.

Read the introduction with the students and make sure that they understand it. Ask them to find Brighton and Morecambe on the map. Look at the **problem** and **solution** headings and check that they understand the words. Say that now they will listen and that their task is to find the problems and the solutions. Then play the cassette for them to take notes. (This is a very demanding listening exercise, but the Workbook will give full support later.) Play the cassette several times and let the students compare notes between listenings and help each other. Ask questions to help, like, *Where is the dolphin sanctuary?* (refer to the map) *How did the dolphins travel to the sanctuary?*
Let the students do as much as they can, then turn to the Workbook. Let them read the words (these are the exact words of the tapescript) and look for the 'missing' words in the big box. Play the cassette again and let them fill in all the words they can.

Build up on the board a **problem → solution** network diagram, like this:

Problem	Solution
1 Where could they go?	To a dolphin sanctuary in the Caribbean.
2 How could the dolphins feed themselves?	People would teach them to catch fish for themselves.

(Return to Student's Book, Exercise 3.)

3 READ.

The mini saga tells Rocky's story. Let the students read it for themselves. The language is simple, but the emotional interest is high.

4 ⏺ SPEAK.

Rewind and play the cassette again, for the students to join in for pronunciation and rhythm practice.

5 WRITE.

If the students simply change the pronouns as suggested in the Student's Book, they will be doing a useful substitution-drill-type practice, which does have a creative element. Good students may, however, want to try to create their own mini sagas. This should be encouraged.

WORKBOOK

As suggested above, the gap-filling exercise may help most students to follow the complex narrative on cassette, and it should be used in class as support for listening, **after** one or two note-taking attempts with the cassette. A good class can, however, do the listening without this support, and then do the gap-filling for homework. In this case, check the homework in the next lesson by playing the cassette again.

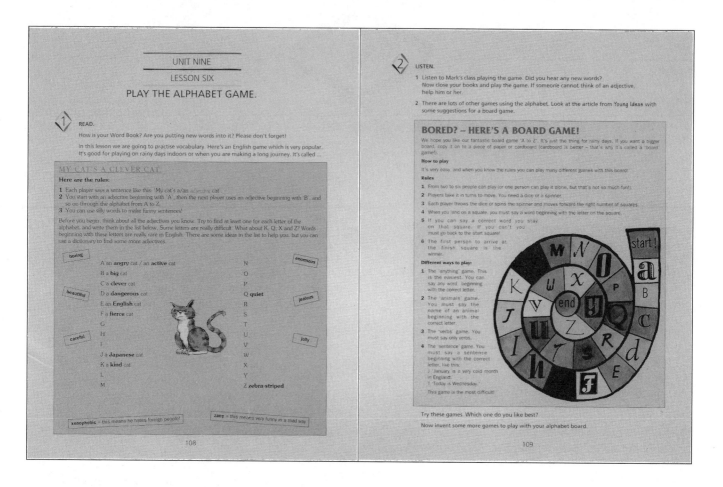

KEY VOCABULARY	dice, jealous, jolly, spinner, take it in turns, xenophobic, zany, zebra-striped, (and consolidation of all adjectives in the 'My cat's a clever cat' game)
KEY GRAMMAR POINTS	No new grammar since the focus is on vocabulary
SKILLS	Alphabetical order; Recalling words (adjectives in Exercise 1, other classes of words in Exercise 2) at speed; Creativity – creating deliberately humorous or 'silly' sentences within the framework of the games

LESSON 6   PLAY THE ALPHABET GAME.

1 READ.

The first sentence is a 'reminder' about the students' own Word Books. If you have not checked on their progress recently, do so now!

The game which follows is a 'real' game, part of English speaking culture, though it may be found in other countries. The 'official' name for it in many places is 'The Minister's (or Parson's) cat', but I have changed the name to one that will be more generally understood. Of course, you can play it in other versions with e.g. 'My Mum's car' or 'My little sister's a ....girl', but I have kept the 'classic' cat version for the Student's Book. The aim is to make sensible or silly sentences, which contain adjectives that progress through the alphabet. You might like to give students some time working with a dictionary or looking at their Word Books to prepare for the 'difficult' letters of the alphabet like J K Q X and Z. (Sentences with these in are sure to be humorous or silly!) Read the rules with the students and demonstrate by reading the examples given in the book. See if students can suggest other adjectives to continue through the alphabet. Make sure they see the suggestions for X and Z in the small grey boxes: the two words *zany* and *xenophobic* are definitely **not** high on the priority list for an English course for children, but they may amuse students and give them an insight to the strange words that can be found in a dictionary.

2 🔊 LISTEN.

Play the cassette for students to hear a class of children playing the game. If you want to exploit this recording more, play the cassette again and ask the students to write a list of all the adjectives the children used. Individuals probably will not be able to remember or to write down all the words, but let them do their best and then compare notes with one or two friends to see if they can combine their notes to complete a full list of 26 adjectives. Collect the list on the board, eliciting answers orally round the class. Then play the game yourselves. You can play it in two ways:

1 Round the class with all students standing and each student trying to find an adjective to fit his or her 'letter' as the alphabet progresses. Students who fail to find an adjective within five seconds are 'out' and must sit down. This is the way the game is played in the 'classic' form, but unless your class is small or very patient, students who are eliminated may get bored and disruptive.

2 As a cooperative effort. You still go round the class, but if someone cannot answer after five seconds, other people can suggest a word and nobody is 'out'. The fun is in the silliness of the sentences. This version is probably better for class management in most situations.

Then look at the board game, which is an elaboration of the basic game idea. (Students have already met this game in Unit 5, Lesson 6, in the Workbook, but this is a more challenging version.) Students need a dice or a spinner to help them decide on which squares they should 'land'.

Let them try the game in class, alone, in pairs or in small groups. They can use a dictionary for five minutes before they start a game to help them to 'collect' and take notes on words that may help them. Then they start the game with dictionaries closed! The progression of games suggested in the book goes from easy to more difficult, but let the students choose the game(s) they want to play. A good extra rule is that they must explain or translate any 'new' word that the other players do not understand. The final sentence in the Student's Book suggests that the students invent some more categories for further games. Examples are personal names or place names.

Note: Ideas for difficult letters in the 'animals' game J – jaguar K - kangaroo Q – quagga (a sort of wild horse) X - xebu (a sort of antelope) and of course Z - (zebra).

WORKBOOK

The Workbook contains work on alphabetical order, but also on the personal associations students make with particular words. The activities can be done in class or started for homework, but it is best to discuss results for Exercises 2, 3 and 4 in class. Exercise 1 checks the 'facts' about English and compares it with the native language. The English alphabet has 26 letters, and the commonest letter is 'e'. In Exercise 2, students choose ten words and put them under the most appropriate of the three headings. It is good to compare and discuss results in class. In Exercise 3 they give the reasons for their choices. Again, the answers will provide material for a good class discussion. Exercise 4 can be done alone, at home or in class, but a class discussion of the silly ideas would be good fun. The joke in Exercise 5 first appeared in *Tiptop*, Level 3, but it had been 'recycled' here to place emphasis on dictionary use and alphabetical order.

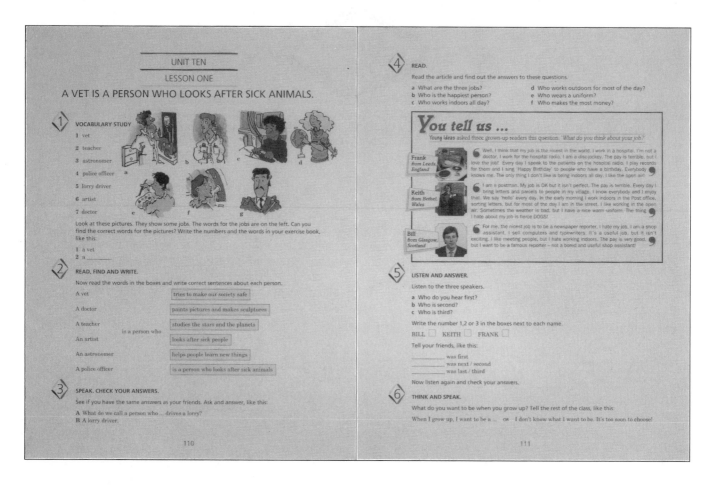

KEY VOCABULARY	job words: acrobat, architect, artist, astronaut, astronomer, astrologer, builder, disc-jockey, dentist, doctor, fashion designer, lorry driver, model, palaeontologist, pilot, police officer, postman, sailor, shop assistant, teacher, vet
KEY GRAMMAR POINTS	Defining relative clauses: *A vet is a person who looks after sick animals; I want to be a …* (**revised**)
SKILLS	Matching job-names to definitions; Scanning a text for important information; Listening to identify speakers; Expressing personal ambitions

LESSON 1 A VET IS A PERSON WHO LOOKS AFTER SICK ANIMALS.

1 VOCABULARY STUDY

Look at the job words on the left and ask students to write the words in their exercise books, and next to them the letters of the pictures that go with them. Elicit the answers orally, like this:
Picture a? Students: *Picture a is a vet/shows a vet.*

2 READ, FIND AND WRITE.

Let the students match the first and second halves of the sentences and then copy them into their exercise books.

3 SPEAK. CHECK YOUR ANSWERS.

Let students check their answers to Exercise 2 by discussing them in pairs or groups of three, using the language model in the Student's Book. Then elicit the answers to Exercise 2 orally round the class. If wished, you can extend the practice of the question and answer in Exercise 3 to make a quiz or guessing game. Students challenge the rest of the class with questions like, *What do we call a person who looks after people's teeth?* (a dentist). They can ask questions about any job-names they happen to know.

4 READ.

Read questions (**a**) to (**f**) with the students, then start a scanning race, asking students this time to scan and find the answers to the questions one at a time, e.g. start with (**a**) elicit the answer, then move on to (**b**), etc. sending the students back to the text each time. Then let them read the whole text at their own speed, asking you or each other for any help they need.

5 ⌒ LISTEN AND ANSWER.

Tell the students that they will hear the three people from Exercise 4 talking about their jobs. The task is simply to put a number next to each name to show the order of the speakers. The aim of this simple activity is to give them more experience in hearing

native speakers saying something quite complex in a natural way, but with the support of already being quite familiar with their words. Let them check their answers together, using the ___ *was first/second/third* language model in the Student's Book.

6 THINK AND SPEAK.

Students may have no idea of what they want to be when they grow up, so accept the second alternative in the language model where necessary. Ask around the class. The purpose of this activity, apart from recycling the *I want to be ...* structure is to introduce the idea of ambitions, which is a theme of the rest of this unit.

WORKBOOK

All these activities can be done in class or for homework, but the answers need discussing in class. Exercise 1 is an extension of the matching Exercise 1 in the Student's Book but it includes some new job-names, so the students need to try the strategy of elimination to help them guess. Exercise 2 provides more written practice in defining relative clauses, but this time the students need to think of their own definitions of what the jobs involve. Exercise 3 is an awareness-raising activity based around the Greek root ASTRO. The students work out who does what, then write sentences to show the correct answers. Exercise 4 demands a little general knowledge, but Bram Stoker and Lord Byron are already familiar from the rest of the book, and Sean Connery is *very* famous. Helen Sharman is a new figure, but she can be guessed as the only woman here! She is introduced here to familiarise her to the students before they meet her in Unit 10, Lesson 4.
Exercise 5 gives a list of still more jobs and allows students to choose which they think they would be good (or awful) at and to give reasons. It is a development of the brief oral activity in Exercise 6 of the Student's Book.

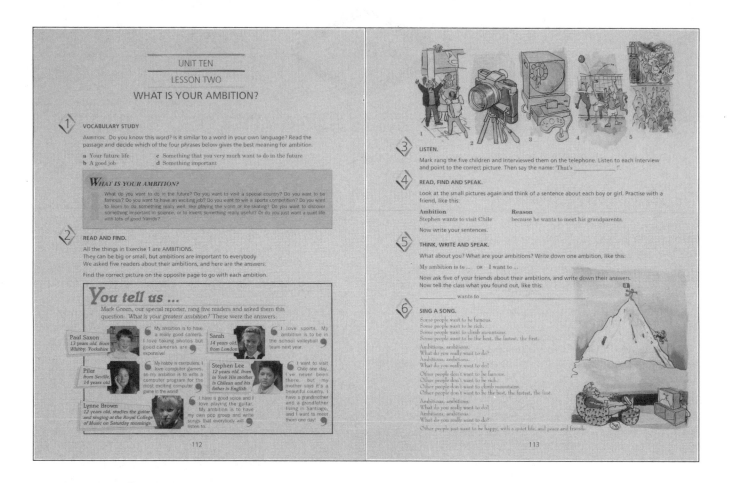

KEY VOCABULARY	ambition, college, pop group
KEY GRAMMAR POINTS	*My ambition is to ....;* *I want to ......* (**revised**)
SKILLS	Finding the best definition for a particular word (ambition) by choosing from very similar possibilities; Interviewing friends and taking notes about their answers (on ambitions); Reporting what other people say

UNIT 10

LESSON 2   WHAT IS YOUR AMBITION?

1 VOCABULARY STUDY

The aim of this section is to get students to make fine distinctions as regards the meaning of a word (*ambition*). All the alternatives have something to do with the meaning, but only (**c**) gives the full picture. Students should read the passage to help them decide.

2 READ AND FIND.

Let the students read the '**You tell us**' feature. Then they look at the five pictures on page 113 and decide which picture illustrates each ambition the best. They can write the name of each child and the number of the picture they choose in their exercise books. Elicit answers orally.

3 ▭ LISTEN.

Make sure that students understand that the cassette contains interviews with the five children from Exercise 2. Play it, with pauses and ask students to say the name of the child speaking and/or to point to the pictures.

4 READ, FIND AND SPEAK.

The cassette gave reasons for each ambition. Give the students time to think about reasons and prepare sentences. They can compare ideas with a friend. If necessary, play the cassette again to help them. They write their sentences. Check the sentences by moving round the class as students work, then collect answers orally.

5 THINK, WRITE AND SPEAK.

Ask students to think of one ambition they have. (It need not be for a job. It can be for something very simple and immediate.) They can use the language models in the Student's Book to help them form their sentences. Move round the class and help. Then ask students to ask each other questions like,*What's your ambition?* and take notes. (It is better if they do not simply look at each other's work, but ask and answer questions.) When they have finished, ask each student round the class to say something about another student's ambition.

6 ▭ SING A SONG.

The words of the song are very simple and should be immediately understood by most students. Allow them to read them through. Then play the cassette for them to listen to the tune. Play the cassette again for them to join in singing the song.
At the end of the song, find out how many students want to be like the people in the first verse and how many want to have a quiet life like the people in the second verse. Ask, *Who wants to be famous? (Hands up!), Who wants a quiet life? (Hands up!).*

WORKBOOK

Exercises 1, 2 and 5 are best done in class, so that students can hear the recordings again if they wish and discuss their answers in pairs or groups. Exercises 3 and 4 can be done out of class, but will benefit from some class discussion of results. Exercise 1 allows students who want to 'hear all the words' on a cassette to listen again and complete the exact words of each speaker in the Student's Book, Exercise 3, but then they must complete a sentence summarising each child's ambition. Exercise 2 can be used at first as a 'memory challenge' to see how many of the words of the song the students can remember. Later, you can play the song again to help them. They can check their answers by looking back at page 113 of the Student's Book. Exercise 3 is a matching activity. Some of the pictures are deliberately unusual or 'silly' to encourage imagination and appreciation of humour. Exercise 4 summarises the student's own ambitions and this has been prepared for in the Student's Book, Exercise 5. Exercise 5 is a suggestion for the class magazine which you may or may not decide (take a vote!) to use.

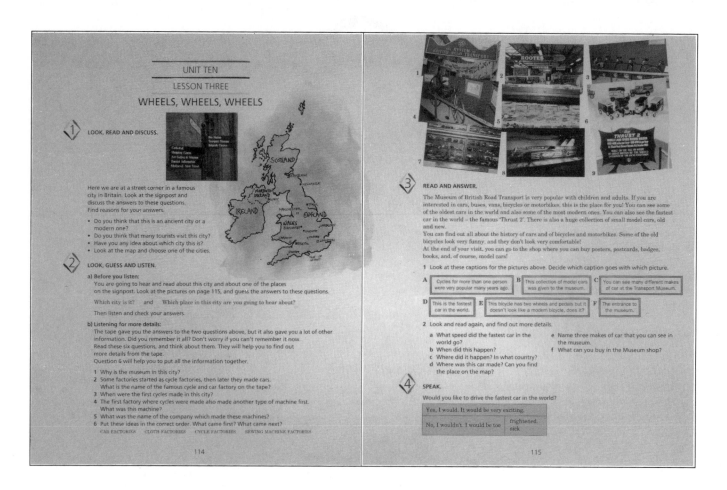

KEY VOCABULARY	businessman, cloth, drive (*verb*), entrance, exit, factory, fast, handlebars, make (*noun*) of car, Midlands, motor, motorbike, pedal, saddle, sewing machine, signpost, transport, tyre, van, wool
KEY GRAMMAR POINTS	Present Simple (**revised**) in description of a place; Past tense (**revised**) in history narrative; Words connected with time sequence and cause and effect: *at first, because, later, so, then*, etc. (**revised**); *Would you like to ....? Yes, I would/No, I wouldn't* (**revised**)
SKILLS	Tracing the sequence of events in an historical narrative; Matching pictures to their descriptions

LESSON 3   WHEELS, WHEELS, WHEELS

1 LOOK, READ AND GUESS.

Let the students look at the signpost and read the place names shown. They can deduce the answers to the first two questions by looking at, e.g. *Medieval Spon Street* and *Tourist Information*. Ask them to guess the identity of the place, but do not confirm the right answer (Coventry) yet.

2 ⊙⊙ LOOK, GUESS AND LISTEN.

The listening cassette is deliberately quite challenging, and the students need to be helped to arrive at the answers step by step. Do not let them panic if they do not understand everything the first or second time.

a) This encourages them to guess further and use their general knowledge. The word 'Coventry' does not appear on any of the museum notices, but some students may know that it is a famous car-producing city. All students should guess that they are going to hear about a motor museum. Play the cassette once through, with no task, except to find or confirm the name of the city. This will also help them to gain a general idea of what information is on the cassette.

b) Now the students are ready to listen again for detail. Read the questions (**1**) to (**6**) with them, and see if anyone remembers any information from the first hearing. (It does not matter if they don't, but you should let them try. It will lessen the 'listening load' if they already have some ideas.) Play the cassette once more. Let them compare answers with a friend. Then play the cassette once more, and collect answers orally. Play the cassette once more with pauses at the places where answers may be found.

3 READ AND ANSWER.

Let the students read the passage at their own pace, but set a time limit, e.g. three minutes should be sufficient, even for slower readers. Ask some oral questions, e.g. *What is 'Thrust 2'? What can you see at the museum?*
Let the students read the captions in the yellow boxes and decide which one goes with which picture. They answer by writing the letters of the pictures and the numbers of the captions in their exercise books. Collect answers orally.
Then read questions (**a**) to (**f**). Send the students back to the passage to scan and collect the detailed information as quickly as they can (*Hands up!*).

4 SPEAK.

This is a brief oral round-up to the lesson. Collect votes on who would or would not like to drive 'Thrust 2' and why.

WORKBOOK

Exercise 1 reinforces the knowledge about English geography which is one of the cultural aims of this book. Exercise 2 allows students who like to 'hear every word' to do some more listening to identify and 'collect' all the words of the first part of the cassette. This can be done as homework, but is better done in class with a replaying of the cassette to allow students to match sounds to words. In Exercise 3, the first activity encourages students to work out an exact definition of the word *transport*. This exactness in word use will be a major focus of Levels 5 and 6 of this course. The categorisation activity also encourages fine distinctions in word meaning. It can be done wholly in class, or the diagram-completion can be done for homework, and the answers discussed in class, followed by the oral guessing game. Exercise 4 gives interesting information about the history of the bicycle and supplies some basic 'bicycle' vocabulary.

CULTURAL NOTES

Coventry is also famous for the Legend of Lady Godiva. It is summarised here to remind you, in case you wish to extend the lesson by telling the story. In the 11th century, Coventry was ruled by Earl Leofric, a very greedy man. He wanted to tax the citizens very heavily. His wife, Lady Godiva, thought this was unjust and asked him to change his mind. He refused. She insisted, saying she would do **anything** to persuade him. So Leofric thought of a clever plan. He said that he would reduce the taxes if she would ride through the streets of the city with no clothes on. To his horror she agreed, and he had to keep his promise. She was safe because (**a**) she had very long hair, which covered her body and (**b**) all the citizens promised to shut their doors and windows and not to look. All except 'Peeping Tom' who looked (and, according to the story, became blind). Godiva is still a famous name in Coventry. There is a statue of her in the main square, and many businesses have the name 'Godiva', 'Godiva carpets, taxis', etc.

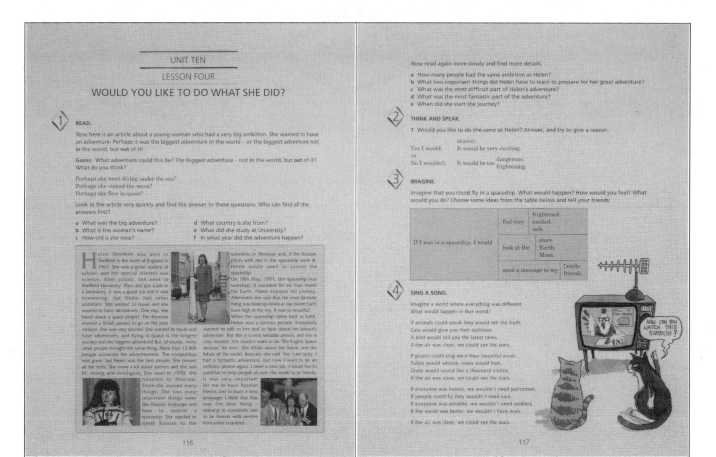

KEY VOCABULARY	adventure, ambition, astronaut, control (*verb*), cooperate, fit, laboratory, launch (*verb*), mission, modest, pass (*verb*), planet, sensible, space, spaceship
KEY GRAMMAR POINTS	Past tenses (**revised**) for narrative; Second conditional: *If I was in a spaceship, I would send a message to my friends;* Word play: *the biggest adventure in/out of the world.*
SKILLS	Scanning a passage for required information, slower reading for detailed information; Imagination/projection – thinking about how they would feel if on a space-journey

LESSON 4   WOULD YOU LIKE TO DO WHAT SHE DID?

1 READ.

Read the introduction with students. See if they can get the word play of *The biggest adventure in the world* (normal superlative) which is then modified to use *out of* with a literal meaning (since Helen Sharman went to space). The three alternative answers all support this meaning.
1 Read questions (**a**) to (**f**) with students and then ask them to scan the passage very quickly to find the answers, with the usual *Hands up!* when they have finished. The questions are deliberately in a different order from the information given in the passage.
2 Let students read the passage again to find the answers to questions (**a**) to (**e**) on page 117.

2 THINK AND SPEAK.

Practise short answers to second conditional questions by asking round the class, *Would you like to do what Helen Sharman did?* and at first accepting simple *Yes, I would, No, I wouldn't* answers. Then ask students to find a reason for their answers and prepare it, using the language model in the book to give them ideas. Say, *Hands up all the people who would like to fly in space?* Then ask, *Why?* and Let individuals give their reasons. Do the same for the people who would not like to fly in space.

3 IMAGINE.

This activity expands the use of the second conditional structure to making full sentences. Let the students study the blue table and prepare some sentences. They can practise these in pairs. Then ask individuals round the class. The table can also be used as a guide for writing sentences.

4 ⌑ SING A SONG.

The song concerns deliberately strange or fantastic situations to emphasise the hypothetical or improbable nature of most second conditional sentences. The refrain, *If the air was clean......* assumes that in most places the atmosphere is too polluted for all the stars to be seen. Let the students read it first. Then play the cassette for them to listen. Play it again for them to sing.

WORKBOOK

Exercise 1 can be done in class or for homework. Discuss the student's opinions in class. Exercise 2 is more fun to do in class since you can discuss musical tastes in (**a**) with the students and perhaps take a vote on their favourite type of music. For (**b**), let students use their imaginations and add ideas of their own to the list. The results for this would be fun to discuss, too. Exercise 3 can be done for homework. Exercise 4 is best done in class since you can then add to the explanation and guide students' choices.
Exercise 5 is a famous British joke (or perhaps it is an international joke?) which fits the theme. It reintroduces the *going to* structure for intentions, for receptive understanding.

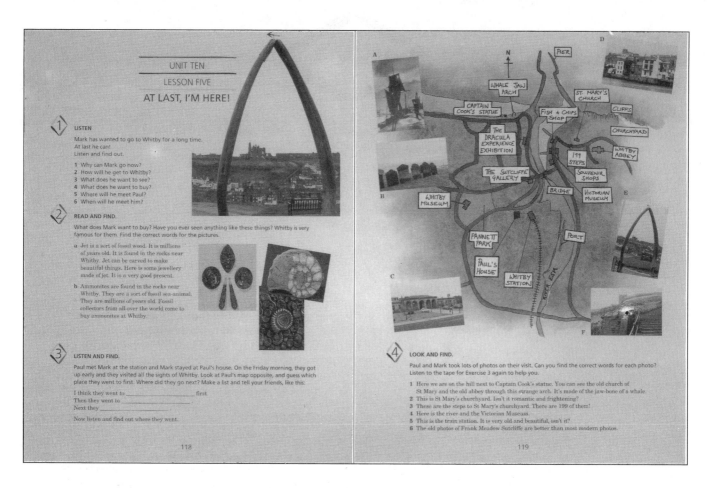

KEY VOCABULARY	ammonite, arch, bridge, churchyard, cliffs, dad, jaw, jet, jewellery, lunchtime, port, souvenir, statue, steps, view, whale
KEY GRAMMAR POINTS	Social language connected with hospitality and expressing thanks; Language for describing places and for guiding a friend around a place: *Here we are at ... Next, we're going to ...*
SKILLS	Listening for key words and phrases to re-construct the sequence of a tour round a town; Following a route on a map

LESSON 5   AT LAST, I'M HERE!

1 🔲 **LISTEN.**

The telephone conversation between Paul and Mark sets the scene for Mark's visit to Whitby. The language is friendly and not very demanding. Look at the questions before the students listen. Collect the answers orally. You do not need to spend very much time on this activity.

2 READ AND FIND.

The pictures and the captions are there to explain two possibly unfamiliar aspects of Paul's and Mark's conversation, and to show what it is that Mark buys during his tour in Exercise 3. Jet is a rather unusual material, but it is very typical of Whitby, where a huge industry was founded in the 19th century. Most of the jewellery made then was worn while people wore black for mourning a dead relative or friend, but it has no such sad connections these days.

3 🔲 **LISTEN AND FIND.**

The conversation between Paul and Mark as they tour Whitby should take most of the lesson to exploit.

Do it in small stages, like this:

1 Look at the map and the photos on page 119. This will orientate the students to the layout of the town, and show what some of the sights we will hear about really look like. If you wish, you can ask students what they think they can see in the photos. This is similar to the activity in Exercise 4, but do it in a quicker and more informal way, as a preparation for the listening.

2 Then follow the instructions on page 118. Let students find and put their fingers on Paul's house on the map and trace a good route for visiting the town. Of course, there are many different possibilities. Emphasise that this is not a 'test' and encourage the students to guess and write their answers, using the model language to help them.

3 Play the cassette once, and tell students to trace the route, pointing to the places as they hear them mentioned. Afterwards ask, *Did they go the same way as you suggested?* (The answer will probably be 'no' but this is not important.) Follow up by saying, *So where did they go first/next?* etc.

4 Play the cassette again for them to write a list of the places visited in the right order. (There is plenty of time just to write notes on the names, since Paul and Mark talk a lot at each place.) Let students compare their lists and find out any differences. Play the cassette again, pausing it at each 'place' for a final check.

4 LOOK AND FIND.

Students match the captions for the photos with the correct photos. All were taken by Mark and Paul according to the story except the black and white one which is one of Frank Meadow Sutcliffe's most famous. They write the number of the caption and the letter of each photo in their exercise books, e.g. 6.A. Then they can point to each photo and tell a friend what it is. They can listen to the cassette again, but this will probably not be necessary by this stage.

WORKBOOK

The Workbook concentrates on a realistic follow-up to such a visit. Two letters of thanks in Exercise 1. Students are guided to distinguish between the more formal language used to Paul's parents and the informal language used to Paul. They then reconstruct the two letters in Exercise 2. In Exercise 3, they write their own thank-you letters. This type of distinction between formal and informal language is introduced as a new concept here as an awareness-raiser and it will be developed further in Levels 5 and 6. It will become increasingly important to students in their early teens, especially if they are to have 'public' contact with young friends and adults from the English-speaking world.

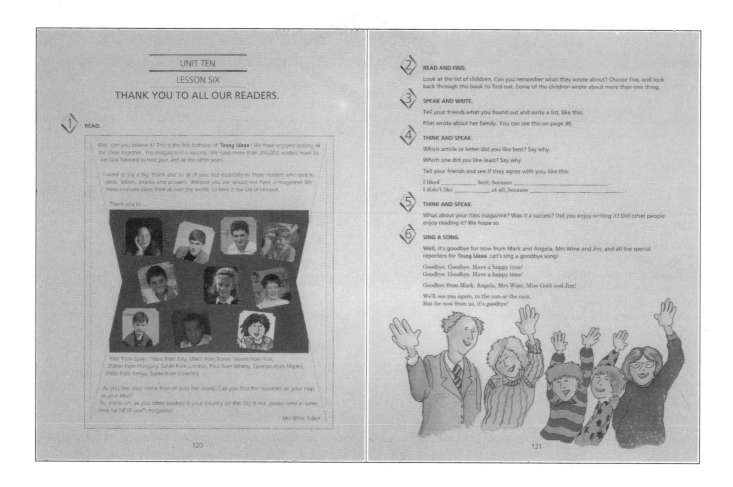

KEY VOCABULARY	All the vocabulary in this lesson is recycled
KEY GRAMMAR POINTS	All the grammar in this lesson is recycled
SKILLS	Finding countries in an atlas; Looking through a whole book (this textbook) using lesson headings to help to find particular information; Expressing and justifying personal preferences about its content; Thinking back about the success of their own class magazine

LESSON 6   THANK YOU TO ALL OUR READERS.

1 READ.

Students should read the very easy 'goodbye and thank-you article' and try to remember the names on the 'list of honour' that fit the faces in the pictures. Bring an atlas or a big map of the world to the classroom for students find the countries on.

2 READ AND FIND.

Students choose five of the people in the photos in Exercise 1, and try to find five things that they wrote in the book. They must say what they wrote and what pages they appeared on.

3 SPEAK AND WRITE.

Students tell their friends in pairs – or the whole class what they found. They listen to their friends and make a list of all the articles and contributions mentioned.

4 THINK AND SPEAK.

Now students give their opinions, using the language models suggested. They can turn back to the pages they have found to look more closely at them and justify an agreement or a disagreement with what their friends think.

5 THINK AND SPEAK.

I hope that the class magazine has been enjoyed, whether it 'came out' as a simple board display, or whether you were able to 'publish' it. Use this time to talk, probably in the native language about the successes and any problems they have had, and about what they learned from 'being editors' and cooperating to make a good 'product'.

6 ☐☐ SING A SONG.

The song is a reprise of the by now 'traditional' 'Goodbye' song from all the other levels of *Tiptop*. It is there as a relaxing finale to the book.

WORKBOOK

The Workbook, Exercise 1, contains a 'Whitby quiz' with the same idea of flicking through the book to find needed information, as in Student's Book, Exercises 2 and 3. Whitby was a 'unifying theme' for *Tiptop 4* because of its many connections with the worlds of fantasy, exploration, history and art, so it seemed appropriate to bring in the quiz here. If you wish, you can do it BEFORE the song in Exercise 6 above. Perhaps you could offer a small prize for the person who finishes first, gets the most answers correct, **and** includes the most correct page references!

Exercise 2 is included as an encouragement to the class to follow up one of the many possibilities for student exchange visits. See page 134 for a list of useful agencies.

PEN-FRIEND ORGANIZATIONS AND SCHOOL LINKING SCHEMES

Federation Internationale des Organisations de Correspondences et d'Echanges Scolaires (FIOCES),
29 rue d'Ulm,
75230 Paris,
Cedex 05,
France

Exists in thirty-six countries and on every continent. National member organizations, whose addresses can usually be supplied by the appropriate Ministry of Education, arrange individual (all ages) and group links.

Central Bureau for Educational Visits and Exchanges,
Seymour Mews House,
Seymour Mews,
London W1H 9PE.
Tel: 071-486 5101

Arranges school and class links with foreign countries. Individual pen-friend links for British school children aged 10-18 are arranged with those from many countries overseas.

Central Bureau for Educational Visits and Exchanges,
3 Bruntsfield Crescent,
Ediburgh EH10 4HD.
Tel: 031-447 8024

Arranges school and class links with foreign countries. Individual links with Scottish pen-friends are arranged directly only with applicants from schools in countries which are *not* members of FIOCES.

No charge is normally made for the above organisations' services.

World Correspondence Service (WCS),
'Charters',
Swannaton Road,
Dartmouth,
Devon TQ6 9RL

Issues lists of individuals between the ages of 6-19, 20-90 throughout the world requiring correspondents using the English language. A small subscription to cover costs of printing is charged. Enquirers must enclose a stamped addressed envelope (United Kingdom) or an international reply coupon (overseas). The WCS is affilated to FIOCES.

The Penpal List,
1 Burnwood Drive,
Wollaton,
Nottingham NG8 2DJ.
Tel: 0602-291383

Publishes every month a general list of about 100 people in the United Kingdom and overseas who are looking for pen-friends. Each list costs £1 for payment in sterling (£1.75 in other currencies) or three international reply coupons. Cheques should be made payable to 'The Penpal List'.
In addition there are three special interest lists.

GRAMMAR SUMMARY

THE ASSUMED STARTING POINT

Students who have followed *Tiptop* Levels 1 to 3 will have met the main aspects of English grammar listed below. Most of these items are recycled and deepened in *Tiptop 4*, but they are listed again when they come into particular prominence. Students who are new to the course are given a chance to 'catch up' or orientate themselves during the first three units.

LEVELS ONE TO THREE – MAJOR GRAMMAR AREAS

Verb groups

Be, have, can, must, as a group of verbs (modals and auxiliaries) with interrogatives formed by inversions of word order and negatives produced by insertion of NOT after the verb. The meanings of these verbs in particular contexts. Level 1 concentrated on this family because of its relative grammatical simplicity and high communicative value.

Main Verbs in **Present Simple** and **Past Simple**, with use of *do/did* as an operator to form interrogative and negatives. Extensive exposure to and use of common Irregular Verbs in the Past tense e.g. *came, went, thought,* as well as awareness of the rules for forming *-ed* endings to Regular Verbs. Levels 2 and 3 tried to introduce this very different 'system' of verbs in a gentle and communicative way.

Will as an auxiliary to signal Future Reference.

The **Present Perfect** to talk about life experiences as in, *Have you ever touched a snake?* The Present Perfect to talk about a very recent action as in, *I've finished.* Exposure to and use of Past Participle forms needed for the Present Perfect, both for Regular and Irregular verbs.

The **Present Continuous** to refer to actions occurring at the moment of speaking as in, *It's early morning. Everybody's starting the day.*

Present Continuous form of the verb to refer to Future Plans as in, *We're going away tomorrow.*

Going to to refer to intentions or imminent actions as in, Now I'm *going to* show you a new magic trick. I'm *going to* be sick!

Past Continuous for past actions interrupted by a single past action as in, *I was swimming in the sea when suddenly I saw a dolphin.*

First Conditionals *If* + Imperative as in, *If* you're happy clap your hands.
If + Future with *will* as in, *If* it is a nice day tomorrow we *will* go for a picnic.

Imperatives, positive and negative, in instructions, but also in offers and invitations, *Come in, have some lemonade,* and encouragement, *Don't worry. Be happy!*

Past Passive (as a formula only) as in, *The aeroplane was invented in 1911. Chewing gum was invented by a man from Mexico.*

Nouns

Use of *a* + noun for indefinite reference or 'first mention'.
Use of *the* + noun for unique reference as in, *the* sun, or for second and subsequent references.
Plural formations, regular *-s* and *-es* formations, spelling modifications such as, *story/stories, knife/knives*
Irregular plurals such as, *man/men, tooth/teeth*
Nouns used with adjectival meaning, *matchbox, table leg*

Adjectives

Attributive adjectives before the noun such as, *green leaves*
Predicative adjectives with **be** after the noun such as, His teeth *are yellow.*
Comparative and Superlative of adjectives with *-er, -est* + man, + in the (world)
Comparative and Superlative of adjectives with *more* and *most* + than + in the (world)

Adverbs and adverbial phrases

Adverbs with *-ly* such as, *quickly, suddenly.*
Irregular adjectives such as, *fast:* He runs *very fast.*
Adverbs of frequency, *once, twice, three times, sometimes, never, always, again, Have you ever...?*

Personal reference words

All Personal pronouns in subject, direct object and indirect object forms. All Possessive adjectives. *-self* words used for reflexive and emphatic meaning as shown below.

Pronouns		Possessive Adjectives	Possessive Pronouns	Reflexives/ Intensive Markers
I	me	my	mine	myself
You	you	your	yours	yourself
He	him	his	his	himself
She	her	her	hers	herself
It	it	its	–	itself
We	us	our	ours	ourselves
They	them	their	theirs	themselves

Each other for reciprocal actions.

Demonstratives and determiners

the, this, that, these, those a/an some any, no

*Someone/somebody/something, anyone/anybody/
anything, no-one/nobody/nothing, everyone/everybody/
everything*

Wh-question words
Who, what, why, where, how, how many, which

Sequence and logical link-words

before, after, if, why ... because, so, first, next, then, finally

Other items

Language of location and description, often using
prepositions, *at the top, opposite, in the middle, between,
diagonally* (from corner to corner).

TIPTOP FOUR

The Focus boxes in the lesson-by-lesson teaching
notes give detailed information to support the
teaching of each lesson, but it seemed useful to
supplement this with a summary of the main
grammar points of this part of the course, placed one
after the other to make it easier to trace how the
main new and old language is sequenced.

Unit 1, Lesson 1
(All revised from Levels 1 to 3)
Who...?
I like ... (best) because...
I'm interested in...

Unit 1, Lesson 2
Wh...? questions used for eliciting personal
information (revised from Levels 1 to 3)
be + good/bad at noun/verbal noun. *I'm good at
football/swimming.*

Unit 1, Lesson 3
Grammar terms: **adjective, noun**

Unit 1, Lesson 4
Each other to express reciprocal actions. Revision of
grammar terms: **adjective, verb**

Unit 1, Lesson 5
I hope
I'm worried } *(that) + will*
Adjectives derived from verbs with *-ing* and *-ed*
endings

Unit 1, Lesson 6
Will/won't for 'neutral' future reference,
     for promises
Use of the contraction *'ll*
Might for possibility (recognition only)

Unit 2, Lesson 1
Want to + verb (revised): I *want to* help Mrs Wine.
Want to + noun/pronoun object + verb: Mrs Wine
wants me *to* draw cartoons.

Unit 2, Lesson 2
Suggestions: (revised): *Let's..., How about ...ing?*
I think we must..., think we need..., Can we...?
Must + verb (revised): *They must think of a title.*
Will (revised): *Mark's class will do it.*

Unit 2, Lesson 3
Will for future reference (revised)
Would like to/want to... (revised)

Unit 2, Lesson 4
Shall for personal intentions: What *shall* I put in?
Expressions of location (revised): *at the top/bottom,
next to.* Indirect Speech in the Present: *I think that...*

Unit 2, Lesson 5
Expressions of location and position (revised): *at the
top/bottom, in the middle, diagonally* (from corner to
corner)
Let's... (revised)

Unit 2, Lesson 6
Do you like it? (revised)

Unit 3, Lesson 1
Present Simple (revised from Levels 2 and 3), for
daily routine and habits

Unit 3, Lesson 1
Must + verb (revised from Levels 2 and 3), to express
fashion imperative: They *must* be in bright colours.
**Indirect Speech with reporting verb in the Present
tense:** *Monica says (that) ...*
Present Simple and Past tense (revised from Levels 2
and 3) contrasted: *Once we liked yo-yos, but now we
don't.*

Unit 3, Lesson 3
Present Simple (revised) in general description.
Present Continuous (revised) for actions focused on
at the moment: *He's training to be a reporter.*
Superlative of adjectives (revised): *the youngest/the
oldest*

Unit 3, Lesson 4
Everybody; some + plural (both revised from Level 3)
Present Simple and Past tense combined: *The last
dinosaurs died about 65 million years ago. So everybody is
crazy about a sort of dead reptile!*
So (revised) as a logical connector. **So** (new) as an
intensifier of an adjective: Why are they *so* popular?
Indirect speech with the reporting verb in the
Present (revised): *Some scientists think that some
dinosaurs were clever.*
Indirect Speech in the Past (for recognition)

Unit 3, Lesson 5
Superlative of adjectives (revised): *the most frightening; too* (revised): *too frightening*
Present Simple (revised) used to summarise the plot of a story.
I like/hate/don't like... (revised)
Noun + *be* + *very* + adjective
        + *has* + adjective + noun
        + *looks like* + *a* + noun

Unit 3, Lesson 6
Might for possibility: I thought you *might* like to see...
Must for certainty: They *must* be mad.
Imperatives used in recommendations in advertisements: *Just put on these special slippers!*
too (revised): *too expensive*. Costs: *It costs £10.*
Indirect Speech with reporting verb in the Present and (that) omitted: *I think they must be very silly.*

Unit 4, Lesson 1
Present Simple (used for physical description of a place) integrated with Past tense (used to talk about its history).

Unit 4, Lesson 2
Superlatives (revised): *the nicest place is...*
Asking for and giving reasons: *Why...? because ...* (revised)

Unit 4, Lesson 3
I like/don't like (revised)
too + adjective (revised): *It's too crowded.*
Would in hypothetical sentences: In my ideal room the walls *would* be white.

Unit 4, Lesson 4
Would (revised) I *would* like... because...

Unit 4, Lesson 5
Revised grammar items only, because of main focus on vocabulary in this lesson.

Unit 4, Lesson 6
Want to + verb (revised)
Wh- questions (revised): *Where do you want to go? When do you want to go?*

Unit 5, Lesson 1   Too + adjective / Not + adjective + enough: *Too boring, not interesting enough*
Indirect Speech in the Past: *I thought that cover B was awful.*

Unit 5, Lesson 2
Indirect Speech (revised): *I think (that)...*

Unit 5, Lesson 3
Past tense (revised) in narrative
Language of description in the Past tense (revised): *It had a long horn on its head.*

Unit 5, Lesson 4
Present Passive (picked up from Level 3 but made focal here) in description of a process (stamp making): *The stamps are sent to the Post Office.*
Have to as equivalent to *must*, and as the negative of *must* when the meaning is *It's not obligatory.*

Unit 5, Lesson 5
Suggestions (revised): *How about ... ing?*
made of ... (revised from Levels 2 and 3): *The bottle is made of glass.*
Present Passive (revised): *The materials are sent to recycling centres.*
Negative comparisons: *not as ... as ...* : Britain is *not as* good *as* many other countries.

Unit 5, Lesson 6
Second Conditional *If* + Past tense + *would:* If I met a crocodile, I *would* be very frightened.
(This lesson builds on the familiarity of hypothetical *would* sentences, and adds the new feature of the *if* + Past tense form to make a 'full' Second Conditional sentence.)

Unit 6, Lesson 1
No new grammar points, since the lesson concentrates on punctuation terminology.

Unit 6, Lesson 2
Each other for reciprocal actions and feelings: We like *each other.*
Together: We play *together.*

Unit 6, Lesson 3
Present Simple and Past tense (revised) combined in narrative
Time sequence words: *then, next* (revised)

Unit 6, Lesson 4
Past tense (revised) in narrative
Use of the apostrophe + *s* (revised) for possession with singular and plural nouns: *Dogs' Home, Blackie's owner*

Unit 6, Lesson 5   Partitive expressions (revised): *none of them, some of them, all of them*
Time expressions: *during the first week, after one week*
Present Passive + *by* **to show the agent:** All of them are examined *by* a vet.

Unit 6, Lesson 6
Defining relative clauses: *A good friend is someone who...*
Present Simple (revised) for habitual or routine behaviour.

Unit 7, Lesson 1
Past tense and Present Simple combined
Apostrophe + *s* for possessive meaning (revised and consolidated)

Unit 7, Lesson 2
First Conditional (revised): *If + Present Simple + will*
Shouldn't (recognition only) for moral obligation

Unit 7, Lesson 3
Present Simple (revised) in descriptions of personal tendencies and habits
Indirect Speech (revised): *I think (that) ...; I am like that/not like that*

Unit 7, Lesson 4
Present Passive in question and statement forms:
How are they made? + by for agent: They are made *by* human beings. *+ by* for process: They are made *by* flattening the corn.
Expressions of shape and position (revised)
Expressions of probability (revised): *probably, certainly, possibly*

Unit 7, Lesson 5
Present Simple and Present Continuous (revised) combined in description of dreaming, to talk about habitual actions: (*Do you dream?*) and about the on-going events in a dream: (*You are flying.*)
Present Perfect (revised) to talk about life experiences: *Have you ever had a dream about...?*

Unit 7, Lesson 6
Present Simple (revised) for talking about general truths about oneself or about routines and habits: *I dream a lot; Some people wake up in the night and go to sleep again.*
Past tense (revised) to talk about the events of last night
Time Sequence words (revised): *first, next, then*

Unit 8, Lesson 1
Present Simple (revised) for general truths: *+ so do I/so does he* (revised from Level 3) Past tense (revised) in narrative
more ... than (in verb phrases): Often the children know *more* about computers *than* some teachers.

Unit 8, Lesson 2
Each other for reciprocal actions
Imperatives used in instructions (revised)
Will used for predictions about the future (revised)
Use of apostrophe in contracted forms of verbs (revised)
more ... than (revised)

Unit 8, Lesson 3
Could for potential choices: Mark *could* go by train or car.
Can't (revised) for impossibility: He *can't* get to Whitby by coach.
Must (revised) for necessity: He *must* change at Darlington.
Expressions of distance: **a long way, a long way away:** It's a *long way* from London to Whitby. He lives *a long way away.*

Unit 8, Lesson 4
Suggestions: *Why don't we ...? Let's* (both revised)
Imperatives in direct advice: *Write to the Town Council ...* **Should** for gentle advice or moral opinion: I think that you *should* talk to him honestly.

Unit 8, Lesson 5
Defining Relative Clauses: *Animals that/which are free*
Each other used for reciprocal actions (revised): Can they help *each other*?
If (revised) for conditions: It's alright to keep animals in captivity, *if* they have enough space.

Unit 8, Lesson 6   I
would like to.../I'd like to... (revised)

Unit 9, Lesson 1
Too many (revised), **too few**

Unit 9, Lesson 2
260 people *out of* 520
It depends on ...
If + Present Simple to express real conditions (First Conditional): *How many ...?* (revised)
Relative clauses: *people who ...* (revised)

Unit 9, Lesson 3
Present Simple and Past tenses (combined) in description of a place
Expressing similarities and differences over time: *Thirty years ago it was* + adjective *now, it is ...* + adjective

Unit 9, Lesson 4
Past tense (revised) about habits and characteristics in the past

Unit 9, Lesson 5
Should/shouldn't for moral obligation
Indirect Speech with the reporting verb in the Past tense: *Would they learn to catch fish?* (for recognition only)
Pronouns (revised)

Unit 9, Lesson 6
Can/Can't (revised) in rules of a game: You *can* say any word beginning with the correct letter.
a/an + adjective (revised)

Unit 10, Lesson 1
Defining Relative Clauses: *A vet is **a person who** looks after sick animals.*
Who...? (revised) as a question word
I want to be a ... (revised)

Unit 10, Lesson 2
I want to + verb (revised)
My ambition is to...

Unit 10, Lesson 3
Present Simple (revised) in a description of a place

Past tense (revised) in narrative of the history of a place
Time Sequence words (revised): *at, first, later, then*
Cause and effect and consequence words (revised): *so, because*
Would (revised): *Would* you like to ...? Yes I *would/* No I *wouldn't*

Unit 10, Lesson 4

Past tense (revised) for narrative
Second Conditional Sentences (revised): *If I was in a spaceship, I would feel very sick. If plants could sing, we'd hear beautiful music.*

Unit 10, Lesson 5

Language associated with hospitality and thanks: *Welcome to ... Here we are at ...*
-ing forms of the verb to express plans (revised): *First we're going to ... Next, we're going to ...*
Distinguishing formal from informal language (to be developed in Levels 5 and 6).

Unit 10, Lesson 6

No new grammar. All revision and consolidation.

WORDLIST

Many of the words on this list are new in *TipTop* 4 but many of them are
reactivations of previously used words from Levels 1 to 3. The numbers
on the list tell you the lesson in which the word comes for the first time,
or the lesson in which the word is most important. For example,
5.6 means Unit Five, Lesson Six.

A

abandoned (6.4)
abbey (4.1)
actually (5.2)
adjective (1.4)
adverb (9.1)
advice (8.4)
agriculture (4.5)
alien (3.4)
alphabetical order (2.3)
ambition (10.2)
ambulance (6.5)
ammonite (10.5)
analyse (9.2)
ancient (4.5)
appearance (3.4)
approximately (4.5)
arch (10.2)
archer (7.3)
argument (8.4)
article (2.3)
artistic (7.3)
astrologer (7.1)
astronaut (10.4)
astronomer (10.1)
atlas (4.5)
attack (7.3)
attractive (2.5)
author (4.6)
autograph (5.2)

B

beach (4.4)
beads (3.2)
beige (4.3)
biro (5.6)
blow (*v*) (5.3)
bone (5.3)
bossy (6.6)
bowl (6.5)
brave (7.1)
bright (4.3) CASS.
broadcast (*v*) (6.5)
bull (7.1)

C

cage (6.1)
calendar (7.4)

canary (8.4)
capital letter (6.1)
captain (4.1)
captivity (8.4)
cardboard (5.5)
carpet (4.3)
carry (5.5)
cartoon (2.1)
carve (10.5)
case (5.6)
cassette player (4.3)
casual (5.2)
cathedral (5.6)
century (4.1)
character [*in a story*] (7.5)
character [*personality*] (6.5)
cheerful (2.6)
churchyard (10.5)
circus (8.4)
clear (2.5)
cloth (10.3) CASS.
clothes peg (5.5) CASS.
coast (9.5) CASS.
coin (5.4)
collection (4.2)
college (10.2)
colourful (2.5)
come out (2.3)
comedy (3.1)
comment (3.1)
common (7.5)
compare (1.2)
complain (2.3)
complicated (5.1)
computer mail (6.1)
confident (6.6)
confusing (2.5)
connected (4.1)
constitution (4.5)
contact (*v*) (2.3)
container (5.5)
contents page (2.4)
control (10.4)
co-operate (10.4)
copy (*n*) (2.3)
corn (7.4)
corner (4.3)

corridor (7.5)
countryside (4.2)
craze (3.2)
crazy (3.4)
cream [*colour*] (4.3)
crowd (9.3)
crowded (4.3)
cruel (8.4)
currency (4.5)
curtains (4.3)
cushions (4.3)
cyan (5.4)
cycle (10.4)

D

dad (3.3)
daily (3.1)
daughter (3.3)
defeat (*v*) (9.1)
democratic (2.2)
department (4.3)
depend (*v*) (9.2)
description (3.6)
design (*v*) (2.5)
detail (4.3)
dictate (4.4)
dictation (6.1)
difficulty (8.4)
direction (8.3) CASS.
directly (8.3)
disappear (6.3) CASS.
disaster (6.3)
disc-jockey (10.1)
discover (4.1)
disk (8.2)
disk-drive (8.2)
doll (5.5) CASS.
domesticated (8.4)
don't mention it! (6.1) CASS.
dream (*n*) (7.5)
dream (*v*) (7.5)
drive (*v*) (10.3)
dummy (3.2)
dungeon (8.6)
during (8.3) CASS.

E

earthquake (6.3)
editor (2.3)

U

university (6.1)
unlucky (7.2)

V

valuable (9.3)
van (10.3)
vase (9.3)
verb (1.6)
version (6.1)
vet (3.3)
view (10.5)
violent (9.6)

visitor (6.3)
voice (6.4)
volcano (4.6)
vote (*n*) (2.2)
vote (*v*) (2.2)

W

walk (*n*) (1.3)
wall (4.3)
washbasin (4.3)
waste (3.6)
waves (4.2)
What on earth ...? (3.6)

wind (7.4)
wine (4.4)
won't (1.6)
woof (6.4)
word processing (8.2)

Y

Yeti (7.4)
yo-yo (3.2)

Z

zip-fastener (5.6)
zodiac (7.1)

TAPESCRIPT

Unit 1, Lesson 1

2 LISTEN.

1 Jim I'm a secretary. I love my work. It's very interesting, but one day I want to be a photographer.

2 Angela I love singing and music and stories. One day I want to be a writer or a musician.

3 Mrs Wine I love my work. I'm the Director of a charity.

4 Miss Gold I love my work. I like all the children in my class.

5 Mark I enjoy school. My teacher is very nice. One day I want to be an artist.

Unit 1, Lesson 2

3 SING A SONG.

Hello again, hello again. It's nice to see you here again.
It's always nice to see good friends.
It's nice to see you here again.
Each year some things are different, but some things are the same.
It's always nice to see good friends. It's nice to see you here again.

Unit 1, Lesson 3

1 LISTEN.

Mark Oh hello, Angela. How are you? Did you have a good holiday?

Angela Yes, thank you. It was fantastic. Did you?

Mark Yes, I did. It was very nice. Do you want to see my photos?

Angela Ooh, yes! Wow, they are lovely! Do you want to see mine?

Mark Yes. They are great too!.

3 LOOK AND LISTEN.

Angela Do you like this one, Mark? We stayed in an old hotel by the sea in Scotland.

Mark Mmm, it looks great. How about this one of *my* holiday? This is the Children's Summer School in Italy. We stayed in a house by a lake in the mountains.

Angela What did you do there?

Mark Well, we did lots of sports like riding, and we visited some exciting places. Look at this photo of a castle.

Angela I swam in the sea every day. Here is a picture of the beach.

Mark Did you meet any dolphins this year?

Angela Of course. I met my old friend again. Look! Here he is in this photo.

Mark Fantastic. We had some Italian lessons, and I did a computer course, too! I'm an expert now!

Angela My parents and I had a great time. Sometimes we went for long walks.

Mark So did we, but I preferred riding. So, I suppose now we must put our photos in our albums.

Unit 1, Lesson 4

4 SAY A RHYME.

What can you do if you don't know a word?

Ask your friends?
Ask your teacher?
Use a dictionary?
Try to guess?

Yes, yes, all these ideas are good ideas.
Ask, ask, look it up, or guess!

Unit 1, Lesson 5

2 LISTEN.

Angela So you had a nice holiday. I'm very glad. But are you happy to be back at school?

Mark Well ... yes, but last year at school was very exciting. The World Help Charity project was very interesting and fun. It was so exciting to help them to write that book! But now I'm worried ...

Angela Oh? Why?

Mark Well ...

4 LISTEN AND CHECK.

Mark Well... last year was very exciting for me. As I said, that project with the World Help Charity was interesting and it was fun. I loved it. So what can we do this year? I don't want to do boring things at school.

Angela Well, I don't see any problems. I'm not worried. I'm sure that we can find exciting things to do this year.

Mark Yes, but what?

Angela I don't know at the moment, but I'm sure we will find something.

Mark Hmm. I hope you're right!

Unit 1, Lesson 6

1 LISTEN.

Mark Hello, Mark Green speaking.

Mrs Wine Hello, Mark! It's me – Mrs Wine from the World Help Charity. Do you remember me?

Mark Of course, I remember you! How are you?

Mrs Wine Very well, thank you. Listen Mark, I have something very important to say. I have a suggestion to make, and I think it's a very exciting suggestion.

Mark Oh good! I want to hear something exciting. Please tell me.

Mrs Wine Well. You remember our book 'Children for Charity'?

Mark Of course, I do! That was great fun!

Mrs Wine Well, the book is very successful. Everybody loves it.
And now I have a new idea. I want to publish a magazine for children from all over the world. Will you help, Mark?

Mark Of course I will. How can I help?

Mrs Wine Will you write stories and draw pictures for the magazine, please? You are a very clever boy. I need your help!

Mark Wow! Of course, I will! How exciting!

Mrs Wine And will you ask your friends and teachers at school to help, too?

Mark Of course, I will! I'm sure they will all be very happy! Wow! I was worried that this year at school might be boring, but now I know it won't be! Oh, thank you, Mrs Wine.

Mrs Wine Oh Mark! Thank you so much for saying 'Yes'. I'll write to you with more information. Oh, I'm so happy!

Mark So am I! Wow. Thanks for the suggestion. Write soon!

Mrs Wine I will. Goodbye for now, Mark.

Mark Goodbye, Mrs Wine, and thanks.

5 SAY A RHYME.

Hello. Hello, I'm ill.
I'm in bed, I feel sick. I'm ill.
Will you come and see me and make me feel better?
I will. I promise I will.

But please don't bring your noisy little brother
He'll just make me feel much worse!
I won't, I promise I won't.

I'll come and see you, and I won't bring my brother.
I promise I will, and I promise I won't.
I won't bring my brother but I'll come and see you.
I will. I promise I will.

Unit 2, Lesson 1

2 LISTEN AND WRITE.

Mark: Listen everybody. I've had a very exciting letter from Mrs Wine. Do you remember her? Yes, the lady from the World Help Charity. She wants to publish a magazine for children all over the world, and she wants us to help her. She wants stories, interviews, news items, puzzles and quizzes. She wants pictures and photos. She wants me to draw cartoons. She wants to sell the magazine, and make money for her charity. Do you think it's a good idea?

Please say 'yes'! I want you to say 'yes'! I want to do it! It will be so exciting!

3 THINK AND LISTEN.

Mark Do you think it's a good idea? Please say 'yes'! I want you to say 'yes'! I want to do it! It will be so exciting! What do you think?

Class Wow! Yeees!
Let's have something about hobbies.
How about a section on Pets?
We need something on Pop Music.
I'd like to read a horror story!
I think we must have a Penfriend section – you know names and addresses of people who want to write to each other.

Mark And I think we need a section on what children think about different things – you know who their best friend is – what their favourite sandwich is – things like that. Let's call it **'You tell us'**.
What about Famous Places and Travel?
Space travel is very exciting. Can we have a section on that sometimes?
And a Sports Section?
Yeess. Let's do it. Let's write to Mrs Wine and say 'Yes'!!!

Unit 2, Lesson 2

3 LISTEN.

Mark Hello.

Mrs Wine Hello? Is that Mark?

Mark Yes, Mark Green speaking.

Mrs Wine Oh good. Hello, Mark. This is Sally Wine. How are you?

Mark Fine thanks, and you?

Mrs Wine Fine thanks. Listen Mark, thank you for your letter. I'm so happy that you will all help me. So now we need to make some plans.

Mark Yes. What must we do now?

Mrs Wine Well, first we must find a good name for the magazine.

Mark Yes. That's very important.

Mrs Wine Then we must write an advert for the magazine.

Mark Yes, of course. People must know what will be in it!

Mrs Wine Then we need to contact schools and children all over the world, and ask them to buy it!

Mark Yes. People must buy the magazine. We can't have a magazine without readers!

Mrs Wine Exactly. So Mark, will your school help me with some ideas for a title, and will you write a good advertisement for me?

Mark Of course, we will. How exciting!

Mrs Wine Then I will send the letters. I have a good list of names and addresses.

Mark   Oh good. I'll tell my class tomorrow, and we will send you our ideas.

Mrs Wine Thank you so much, Mark. I look forward to hearing from you. Bye.

Mark   Goodbye, Mrs Wine.

4 LISTEN.

Mark OK. You know that I asked you for some good ideas for a title for our magazine. I collected all your ideas and I asked you to vote for the best one. Thank you for voting. I've counted all the votes and these are the results:

GREEN HELP	5 votes
YOUNG IDEAS	11 votes
GREEN WORLD	6 votes
WORLD IN DANGER	2 votes
POOR WORLD	1 vote
GREEN KIDS	2 votes
KIDS FOR CHARITY	3 votes
LET'S HELP	4 votes

So the winner is... **Young Ideas**. 34 people voted, and 11 people preferred **Young Ideas**. That's nearly one third of the class. So is that all right? Can we choose **Young Ideas**?

Class Yes!

Mark OK. Now, let's write an advert for our new magazine **Young Ideas**. Then we can send it to Mrs Wine!

Unit 2, Lesson 3

3 LISTEN.

Mark   Hello. Mark Green speaking.

Mrs Wine Hello Mark. It's me – Sally Wine! Congratulations! Your title and your advert were just perfect! Please thank your class from me!

Mark   Oh, great.

Mrs Wine So, last Monday I sent 5000 letters.

Mark   Wow! That's fantastic! Who did you contact?

Mrs Wine Well, the letters went to more than 20 countries. Do you want to know which ones?

Mark   Yes. Then I can tell my friends.

Mrs Wine OK. I'll give them to you in alphabetical order. That's the easiest way, isn't it?

Mark   Sure. Go ahead. I'll take notes.

Mrs Wine OK. I wrote to people in:

Argentina	France
Australia	Greece
Austria	Hungary
Brazil	India
Bulgaria	Italy
Canada	Japan
Chile	Latvia
The Czech Republic	Lithuania
Estonia	Mexico
Poland	Switzerland
Portugal	Turkey
Slovakia	USA
Spain	Venezuela

Mark   Didn't you write to anybody in the UK?

Mrs Wine Oh yes, of course. Sorry. I wrote to people and I rang schools all over the UK. In England, Scotland, Wales, and Northern Ireland.

Mark   Fantastic! You must be very tired.

Mrs Wine Well, I am, a bit, but Jim helped me. So let's wait and see what they all say!

Unit 2, Lesson 4

2 LISTEN

Mrs Wine Well Jim, how is the new magazine?

Jim   Well, I've got lots of ideas. In fact, I've got too many for one magazine! Will you help me to choose some good ones for the first one?

Mrs Wine Of course. Hmmm, let's see. Well, we must have a Contents page!

Jim   Of course. What do you think about the Poem page?

Mrs Wine How many poems have you got?

Jim   Well, only one. And I wrote it!

Mrs Wine Well, I think it's better to wait. Let's wait until our readers send us their poems.

Jim   Yes, we can start our Poetry page in the second magazine.

Mrs Wine The Komodo Dragon story looks interesting. What a fantastic photo! Let's put that in.

Jim   Fine. And I think the tangram puzzle is a good idea for the first magazine.

Mrs Wine Certainly, then we can have tangram puzzles in all the later magazines.

Jim   We can have a Letter page in this magazine. I have got lots of 'Good Luck' letters from new readers.

Mrs Wine Great.

Jim   And Mark has an idea for a **'You tell us'** page. He asks readers a question about their lives and then they send their answers for the next magazine.

Mrs Wine So we must put that in. I don't think we want Pet Photos or My Holiday Photos this time. Let's wait for readers to send us their photos.

Jim   Good idea. So, I think that's all for now. Wow!

Mrs Wine It looks very interesting, Jim.

Jim   Thanks, Mrs Wine.

Unit 2, Lesson 5

3 LISTEN.

Jim   Well, I've got five ideas for the cover. What do you think?

Mrs Wine Hmm. Well, the one with the title in the middle is very colourful and interesting, but it isn't very clear. I think a magazine cover must be clear as well as interesting. I like the one with the title at the top best.

Jim Yes, I agree with you.

Mrs Wine So let's have that one.

Jim Fine. Well, that was a quick decision!

Unit 2, Lesson 6

2 LISTEN.

Miss Gold Well, class, we've all got out copies of **Young Ideas!** I wonder what will be in it! I can't wait to read it! Do you think Mrs Wine has used any of our ideas this month?

Class Let's have a look inside.

Mark Hurrah!

Miss Gold Yes, Mark. Is your idea in there?

Mark Yes, it's here on page 10. I sent an idea called **'You tell us'**.

Miss Gold What about you, Angela?

Angela Yes, I sent a photo of my holiday. But it isn't here.

Miss Gold Oh dear. What about you, Tom?

Tom No, I can't see it. I sent an idea for a tangram puzzle. Yes, it's here.

Miss Gold And you, Patrick?

Patrick I sent a letter to say, good luck, to the new magazine. I can't see it. No ... Oh yes! It's here on the Letters page.

Miss Gold Oh, great! Now what about my idea? I sent a mathematics quiz. No, it's not here. Oh well, perhaps they'll print it sometime later on.

Unit 3, Lesson 1

2 LISTEN.

Susan Hello.

Mrs Wine Hello. Is that Susan?

Susan Yes. Speaking.

Mrs Wine Oh Susan, it's Sally Wine here. Listen Susan, could you help me, please? I want to send a questionnaire to all the people who wrote to me about **Young Ideas.** I'm not sure if it is good or not. Can I read the questions and get some answers from you? Then you can tell me if you think the questionnaire is OK.

Susan Of course. I'm happy to help.

Mrs Wine Thanks. OK, well it starts with questions about name, age, sex, country and city or town.

Susan Of course! Well, that's easy. My full name is Susan Jacobs – that's J-A-C-0-B-S......, I'm 12 years old, I'm a girl of course, so I should write Female and I come from Coventry in England.

Mrs Wine So here are the main questions: The next section is called Your Daily Life.

Number one: What days do you go to school or work?

Susan I go to school from Monday to Friday, of course. Doesn't everyone?

Mrs Wine Well no, actually, Susan. In some countries people go to school on Saturdays.

Susan Do they really? Ugh!

Mrs Wine Number two: Is it easy for you to get up in the mornings, or do you hate the mornings?

Susan Oh, I hate the mornings. It's very difficult for me to get up!

Mrs Wine Number three: How do you travel to work or to school?

Susan Usually I walk, but if I'm late or the weather is bad, I go by bus.

Mrs Wine What's your favourite way of travelling?

Susan By train. I love travelling by train.

Mrs Wine What is your favourite meal of the day? (Please say why.)

Susan Dinner, because my mother or my father always cooks something nice, and we all eat together, and we talk.

Mrs Wine What do you like to do in the evenings?

Susan I like to watch TV, or sometimes I paint or organise my collection of models.

Mrs Wine Models? That's interesting. What sort of models?

Susan Model animals. I have got hundreds, all sorts, but lots of model cats and dinosaurs. I'll send you some photos of them for the magazine if you like.

Mrs Wine Super. Please do! But now for the next question:

Number seven: What is your favourite time of the week? (Please say why.)

Susan Oh, that's Sunday mornings, because I can stay in bed late, and then perhaps go for a walk or to see my friends. I love Sundays.

Mrs Wine OK thanks, that's that part. Now the next part is called 'Your opinions and interests'. The first question is:

Do you like watching TV? What sort of programmes do you like? What sort of programmes do you hate?

Susan Well yes, I like watching TV. My favourite programmes are nature programmes and comedy programmes. I love animals and I like to laugh. I like music programmes too, and the news. But I hate quiz programmes. They are usually very silly. And I don't like Soap Operas! I know that many children do, but I don't! And I think that Sports programmes are really boring!

Mrs Wine Now listen carefully to this list of subjects and tell me your answers. Which three of these subjects do you think are the most interesting? Is there one subject that you think is really boring? Are you ready for the list?

Susan Yes, go on.

Mrs Wine Animals and nature   Science and technology   Family life in other countries   Food   Fashion and clothes   Famous people in history   Famous people of today   Art   Films   Music   Sport   Famous places   Monsters and strange animals

Well, what do you think?

Susan Hmmm. Well, the one really boring subject for me is Sport. Ugh! But the three subjects I think are really interesting are animals and nature, art and fashion and clothes. All the others are OK, but I am not interested in sport.

Mrs Wine Well, thank you Susan. What do you think of my questionnaire. Is it too long?

Susan No, not really. And I think it will give you some good information about your readers. So, yes you can use it! You don't need to change it!

Mrs Wine Thanks Susan. I'll sent it out now.

Unit 3, Lesson 2

4 SING A SONG.

Is it in or is it out?
Fashions come and fashions go.
What's the reason?
I don't know.

Last year, this year, next year, never.
What's the reason?
I don't know.

Unit 3, Lesson 4

3 READ, LISTEN AND FIND.

Narrator Mark rang four readers and asked them this question:

Mark Why are dinosaurs so popular?

He took notes and he summarised the answers in a short way. Here is what the four readers said:

Peter Well, as you know I'm from Kenya, and my country is very famous for dinosaurs. People have found many skeletons here. I think it's very interesting to think about the past and about a very different world. I like to imagine life many millions of years ago. It's fascinating!

Ken Well, my part of the USA is very famous for dinosaurs, of course, but everybody in the USA likes them! I think it's because of all the films and stories.

People here are not really interested in the real dinosaurs, just in the idea of fantastic, dangerous monsters. There have always been stories about dragons and other fantastic animals, even before people found any dinosaur skeletons.

Pilar Hmmmm, that's an interesting question. Let me think. Yes, well, I think that people like them because they looked so strange and interesting! Some of them had horns on their heads. Some of them had very long necks. Some of them had funny faces. I don't think they were beautiful or intelligent, but they looked fascinating.

Sarah Well, I'm not sure about other people, but I know what I think. I like dinosaurs because they were so big. Some of them were really enormous. People like really big things. Well I do, anyway.

Unit 3, Lesson 5

2 LISTEN AND CHECK.

1   King Kong – the giant gorilla. He arrived in New York from Africa and he frightened everybody. He even climbed the famous Empire State Building!

2   The Wolf Man – every month, when the moon was full, this poor man turned into a wolf. His teeth were long and white and his body was covered in hair.

3   Frankenstein's Monster – this monster was made by a scientist called Frankenstein. He looked like a human being, but he was very ugly, and everyone was frightened of him.

4   Count Dracula – the famous vampire from Transylvania. He was a tall, handsome man and very clever, but his face was white and his eyes were red and he had terrible long, white teeth. He attacked people and drank their blood.

5   Godzilla – the dinosaur monster. He was a very big reptile. He came from another world and he frightened everybody. In some films, he had a big fight with King Kong.

6   The Alien – a monster from space. He looked terrible and he was terrible. Have you seen the 'Alien' films? They are very frightening.

All these monsters are very popular. Why? Do people like being frightened? Perhaps the most popular monster in the world is Count Dracula! Did you know that more than 500 films have been made about him? There are American films, French films, British films, Mexican films, Japanese films about him, and films from many other countries

Unit 3, Lesson 6

3 LISTEN.

Presenter Hello, boys and girls! Welcome to our 'Things to buy' programme on WONDER RADIO.

Is it difficult for you to get up in the mornings? Yes? Well, I've got a great idea for you! Buy this fantastic dinosaur clock. Its tail moves and it shines in the dark. When it's time for you to get up, it gives a great roar like this. If that doesn't wake you up in the mornings, nothing will! It costs only ten pounds ninety-five pence. Ring this number for more details: 66666666.

The next thing is 'Sticky fingers'. It's really horrible, but it's useful. It's made of plastic and it's sticky. Just throw it and the arm will stretch and the hand will stick to anything it touches. Then just pull and it will bring the things back to you. It's very useful if you are too tired to pick up your book or your newspaper. Please do not throw it at your dog or cat! It costs two pounds, and you can buy it in most toyshops in your town.

The last thing for today is a pair of slippers. A pair of slippers? How boring! But these slippers aren't boring. They look like cars and they have headlamps on the front. The headlights shine when you put them on. So if you get up at night to go to the bathroom, just find your special slippers, and you don't need to switch on the light or find your torch! They are quite expensive. They cost fifteen pounds, fifty pence, but they are warm and comfortable and very useful. You can find them in most shoe shops.

Well, that's all for now. Happy shopping!

Unit 4, Lesson 1

1 LISTEN.

Mark Hello. Mark Green speaking.
Mrs Wine Hello, Mark. It's me, Sally Wine! Listen, I have some very exciting news!
Mark Oh yes.
Mrs Wine Yes! Everybody loves the new magazine. I have 8000 readers now, from 22 countries!
Mark Wow! That's fantastic!
Mrs Wine Yes, and I must tell you that the reactions to your **'You tell us'** idea were very positive. It's the most popular section in the magazine. So, well done, Mark!
Mark Great.
Mrs Wine Yes. It is the most popular part of the magazine. But listen, Mark, about your question for the next magazine. You know, 'What is your favourite place?'
Mark Ye-es?
Mrs Wine Well, we have had more than 50 answers! I had one very good answer from a reader who lives in Whitby. Whitby is his favourite place, and he wrote us a long letter with some very interesting things in it. His name is Paul Saxon. He's 13 years old and he has sent us some lovely old photos and a history of his home town. You know that Whitby is important in the story of Dracula, and he tells us all about

it. I thought you'd be interested, because you like vampire stories! His letter is too long for the **'You tell us'** section, so I'm going to print his letter and his photos on a different page. Do you think that is a good idea?
Mark Well, that's great! What a good idea! I can't wait to see it!
Mrs Wine Thanks, Mark, and goodbye!

Unit 4, Lesson 2

4 LISTEN.

Paul's father Hello...
Mark Oh, hello, Is that Paul Saxon?
Paul's father No, it's his father. I'll call him for you. Paul! There's somebody on the phone for you.
Paul Hello. Paul speaking.
Mark Hello, Paul. My name's Mark Green. I am the special reporter for the **Young Ideas** magazine.
Paul Oh yes! I sent you a letter about Whitby.
Mark Well, we thought it was very interesting. Whitby seems a fascinating place.
Paul Yes, it is.
Mark You wrote about lots of different places in Whitby. What are your favourite places?
Paul Well, first the abbey. It's so wild and romantic. I always think of the story of Dracula when I go there. Then I like to visit the gallery of Frank Meadow Sutcliffe photos. That's because my hobby is photography. I want to be a photographer when I grow up! Then, I really like the 'Dracula Experience' exhibition. It's very interesting. You can find out all about the story of Dracula and it's frightening too!
Mark Hmm. Listen, Paul. Will you write some more things for the magazine and send us some more photos? We think you have a lot of talent!
Paul Of course, I will. Wow! It's very exciting to see my name in a magazine, and I am very proud of my town. I want more people to know about it.
Mark Well, it was very nice to talk to you. And Paul, I wonder ...
Paul Yes.
Mark Well, I'd really like to visit Whitby one day. Will you show me all the sights, when I come?
Paul Of course! I'd really like that! Why don't we keep in touch? Perhaps we could write to each other. I'd really like to have a penfriend.
Mark What a good idea! Yes. I'll write to you soon, and one day I hope to come and meet you.
Paul Super. Well, thanks very much for calling, and I look forward to a letter soon.
Mark Yes. I'll write soon. That's a promise! And, thanks again for your super article. Bye.

Unit 4, Lesson 3

2 LISTEN.

Mark   So, this is Susan's picture of her room. We're going to put it in the magazine.

Angela   Ugh! Mark! What an awful room! I hate it!

Mark   Oh, do you think so? I think it's all right. I quite like it.

Angela   Oh no. It's horrible! Look at those colours, green walls, purple curtains and a purple bed. It's awful! The only nice thing is the collection of animal models.

Mark   Well, I don't agree. I think it's nice and bright, and I really like the dinosaur clock. It's fun, and I like her collection of animals too. But ....perhaps you're right about the curtains. Yes, they are a horrible colour! OK. So I like the room, generally, but I hate the curtains.

Angela   Well. I'm glad you agree about the curtains. I hate the whole room and you like most of it. But, then, people never agree about personal things like rooms!

Unit 4, Lesson 4

4 LISTEN.

Mark   Hello, Mark Green here.

Martin   Oh Mark, this is Martin here – you know – I promised you an article about San Marino.

Mark   Oh yes. Is there a problem?

Martin   No, not really, except I'm very late. I know that you want it tomorrow.

Mark   Well, yes I do really.

Martin   Well, I've just finished it and it's too late to post it. I wonder ...... could I dictate it to you now? It isn't very long.

Mark   OK. You read it to me, and I'll listen and take notes. Oh, I can record it with my cassette recorder as you speak. Don't worry about the punctuation. I'm sure I can put that in, but perhaps you can help me with the spelling of any unusual words.

Martin   OK. Here goes ....

Dear **Young Ideas**. I was very interested in the article about historic Whitby. I'd like to write about another historic and beautiful place. It's not a town, like Whitby. It's a country, but it isn't much bigger than Whitby! It is called San Marino.

Last year, I was very lucky. My parents took us on holiday to Italy. Our hotel was in Rimini, (that's R-I-M-I-N-I) at the seaside. We had a lovely time swimming and sitting on the beach, but one day we visited San Marino. Here are some facts about this interesting place.

Did you know that San Marino is one of the smallest, independent countries in the world? It is 'inside' Italy, but it is not part of Italy. You can use Italian money and everybody speaks Italian, but the people

there are **not** Italian. They are proud to be different. They are friends with Italian people, and they like them, but they are not Italian. It is a very small place, so how do people make money to live? The answer is 'Tourism': hotels, restaurants, gift shops. Many people come to San Marino just to buy gifts and souvenirs – especially stamps and coins. Stamps from San Marino are famous all over the world. I hope you like the picture of my stamps! San Marino also has very good wine, and olive oil, and you can buy delicious cakes and sweets, but tourism is the most important industry these days.

San Marino is a very ancient place. It was founded in 301 AD by a saint. Marinus (that's M-A-R-I-N-U-S) was a stone-cutter from Dalmatia (D-A-L-M-A-T-I-A) – across the sea from Italy. He came to Italy with his friends to escape from the Roman emperor, Diocletian (D-I-O-C-L-E-T-I-A-N). The name 'San Marino' is Italian for 'Saint Marinus' of course. San Marino is an independent country, and it is a Republic. That means that it does not have a King or a Queen.

Mark   That's great Martin. I'll type it into my computer now.

Martin   Well, I'm sorry to be so late.

Mark   Never mind. Better late than never!

Unit 4, Lesson 6

2 LISTEN AND FIND.

Narrator   Hello, all you listeners to WONDER RADIO. This is 'Our Wonderful World' programme. Are you ready for our quiz? Look at the 11 pictures, and see if you can recognise these exciting places from my words. Put the numbers of my descriptions next to the correct photos. If you get them all right, perhaps you will win a visit to one of the places! First, I'm going to give you an example.

No.1 Can you see all the dinosaurs in the picture? We are in one of the most famous museums in the world. Yes! It's the Natural History Museum in London. So write the number 'one' next to that picture. That was easy, wasn't it, because I said the name. The next descriptions will be more difficult, because I won't say the names! Ready? OK.

No.2 This ancient castle is in one of the smallest countries in the world.

No.3 This building is nearly 2000 years old. The Romans used it for very cruel games and sports. Christians and lions fought there. Ugh! Horrible! But it is very popular with tourists, today.

No.4 This is one of the most beautiful buildings in the world. Once it was a Christian Church. Now it is a Moslem Mosque.

No.5 This is a very new place. It is in France. If you go there for a visit, you can meet Mickey Mouse and all his friends.

No.6 This is a fantastic place, and it's a natural place. Nobody built it. The rocks here are millions of years old. There is a river at the bottom. You can travel from the top down to the bottom on a donkey, or very active people can walk!

No.7 This is the highest mountain in the world. The first people to arrive at the top were Edmund Hillary and Sherpa Tenzing Norgay, in 1953. Since then many other people have climbed it.

No.8 This is the only building that you can see from a spaceship! It is nearly 2400 km long.

No.9 This is another mountain, but don't try to climb it! It's very dangerous, because it is a volcano! In 79 AD, it erupted and destroyed the cities of Pompeii and Herculaneum, in Italy.

No.10 This is a photo of a park in a famous city. The man who designed the lovely building was the famous architect, Gaudi.

No.11 This is another natural place. It is full of green leaves, huge trees and wonderful animals, birds and insects.

Unit 5, Lesson 1

2 LISTEN AND CHECK.

Mrs Wine OK, Jim. Let's see your ideas for the cover for **Young Ideas**.

Jim Well, I've got five here. I've called them A,B,C,D and E.

Mrs Wine Hmmm, A is OK. It's quite pretty. I like all the flowers, but they are all yellow. There's too much yellow on it. No, I don't think I like it very much, really.

Jim Yes, you're right. I agree. So let's look at B. What do you think?

Mrs Wine Well, there is a lot of information on the cover. That's very useful, but really I think there are too many words, and not enough pictures. It's very complicated and confusing. Covers need to be simple and attractive.

Jim Yes, I agree. It is a bit confusing.

Mrs Wine A bit? It's very confusing. In fact, I think it's awful. Sorry, Jim. What about C?

Jim Well, that is simple, and I think it's clear, but what about the colours? I used just black and white and a bit of red and green.

Mrs Wine Yes, that is a good design. Well done, Jim, but....

Jim But?

Mrs Wine But I think it needs more colours. It's good, but it isn't colourful enough.

Jim Well, then I am sure you won't like D! I used only black and white for this one!

Mrs Wine Hmmm. It is a good design. It's very elegant, but it's not good for our readers. I'm sure they prefer colourful, exciting covers. They'll think that this one is too boring.

Jim Oh dear! Well, I hope you will like the last one – E. It's my favourite.

Mrs Wine Yes! That's just fine! It's clear and it's colourful, and I really like the picture of the dinosaur. That's an interesting cover. Well done, Jim! We'll use E for this month's magazine!

Jim Oh, good. I like E best, too.

Mrs Wine So we agree. You know, Jim, I think you have a lot of talent. I am very happy to work with you. I'm sure our magazine will be a great success.

Jim Thanks, Mrs Wine.

Mrs Wine Not at all. I always say what I think.

Unit 5, Lesson 2

3 THINK AND LISTEN.

Narrator Mark telephoned some readers of **Young Ideas** to find out about what they collected. He asked them all the same question:

'Do you like collecting things? If so, what do you collect, and can you tell me why?'

Listen first to his conversation with Pedro.

Pedro ¡Hola!

Mark Oh, hello. Do you speak English?

Pedro Yes, I do.

Mark Can I speak to Pedro Marquez, please?

Pedro Speaking.

Mark Oh, Pedro. This is Mark Green from the **Young Ideas** magazine. Can I ask you a question, please? We want to print your answer in the next magazine.

Pedro Of course. I'm happy to help.

Mark Well, the question is, 'Do you like collecting things? If so, what do you collect, and can you tell me why?'

Pedro Hmm. Well, I collect badges.

Mark Badges? What sort of badges?

Pedro Well, if I visit a nice place or join a club, I buy a badge.

Mark Why?

Pedro Well, it helps me to remember interesting places, and they are not expensive, **and** I like to wear something colourful or attractive on my jacket or T-shirt.

Mark How many badges have you got?

Pedro Oh, about a hundred, I think. I change my badges every day! My favourites are from the Battersea Dogs' Home, and from the Dinosaur Exhibition in London.

Mark Well, thanks very much for your help. Can I print your answers in the magazine?

Pedro Of course. I will look forward to seeing it. I really like **Young Ideas**.

Mark Thanks. And thanks again for your help.

Pedro Not at all.

Mark Bye.

Pedro Bye.

Narrator Now listen to the answers the other readers gave. Paula said:
'Well, I collect T-shirts.'

Mark Wow! what sort of T-shirts?

Paula All sorts, but I like ones with words and pictures on them. My favourite is a red and black one from Whitby with the words 'I love Dracula' on it. I've also got a blue one from Battersea Dogs' Home, Battersea.'

Mark Why do you like T-shirts?

Paula Well, I like to wear casual clothes and they are cheap and practical and fun.

Narrator Chris said:
'Well. I collect stamps.'

Mark What sort of stamps?

Chris Well, only beautiful ones. The country isn't important, if the stamps are beautiful.

Mark Why do you like stamps?

Chris Well, collecting stamps is quite cheap, and I don't have a lot of money. I like beautiful and interesting pictures and stamps have often got lovely pictures on them. They are small, but they are beautiful. It's a good way of making friends, too, because you can swap stamps with other people.

Narrator Susannah said:
'Well, I collect autographs.'

Mark Oh, What sort of autographs?

Susannah Well, of famous people of course – but people from all over the world. I write letters to them, and they usually send me a photograph with a signature. Sometimes they send me a letter, too.

Mark Why do you do it?

Susannah Well, I like to practise my English, and most famous people know some English. I enjoy reading the answers to my letters.

Mark Who have you written to?

Susannah Oh, hundreds of people, but my best autographs are from: Michael Jackson (he sent me a photo), Margaret Thatcher (she sent me a short letter, too) and Mr Havel from the Czech Republic. Oh, and I got a very kind letter and a photo from Luciano Pavarotti, you know, the great Italian tenor. I got a letter from Helen Sharman, the British astronaut, too. It was really interesting.

Unit 5, Lesson 3

2 LISTEN AND REPEAT.

Narrator The Triceratops had three horns on its head. It looked terrible but it ate leaves.
The Diplodocus had a very long neck and a very long tail. It ate meat.
The Parasaurolophus had a long horn on its head. The horn had a hole through the middle. It blew through it and it made a loud noise.

5 LISTEN.

Girl Wow! Look at that one! Isn't it strange?

Boy Which one?

Girl The one with the long horn on its head. I wonder what it needed that for?

Boy Let's have a look at the label. Hmmm.

Girl Oh yes, it says it blew through its horn and made a loud noise. I suppose that was useful for calling its friends.

Boy Like elephants do, you know ...

Girl And look at this other one – with three horns. It looks very dangerous.

Boy Yes, but it says here that it ate only leaves. It didn't eat other dinosaurs.

Girl But I expect it used its horns to fight dinosaurs which wanted to eat it! Like that Tyranosaurus Rex over there.

Boy Yes. I'm sure you're right!

Unit 5, Lesson 4

5 LISTEN.

Narrator How are stamps made? Well, first the Post Office decides about a good subject – like animals or ships or birds or famous people. Then an artist paints a big picture. This picture is then photographed on to film. The picture on the film is much smaller, of course. A different film is made for each of the main colours. These colours are called CYAN – a sort of blue, MAGENTA – a sort of red, YELLOW and BLACK. Each colour is then copied on to a different metal plate. The metal plates are used in a printing machine. The four colours are printed on top of one another, the four colours mix on the paper, and they make all the colours of the original painting. Of course, many stamps are printed at the same time on big sheets of paper.
Then another machine makes the holes between the stamps. Another machine puts the glue on the back of the stamps. Then the stamps are ready to go to the Post Office.

Unit 5, Lesson 5

4 LISTEN.

Angela What a strange idea – an exhibition of rubbish!

Mark But it's a clever idea, too. It really shows us how people in some countries **use** things that we throw away. I think it teaches us a good lesson. Britain is a rich country compared to many of the countries we can see here – but we waste a lot of things.

Angela Hmmm. I suppose that's why the exhibition is called 'New from old'. I don't think I would like to have many of these things in my house, but ....

Mark But we are lucky. We have enough money to buy new things. I think some of the ideas are really clever, and some of the things are quite attractive.

Angela	Yes, the toys are clever. I like the doll made from a wooden clothes peg, and the horse made from metal wire is quite pretty.
Mark	Yes, and you know – dolls like that were very popular in Britain a hundred years ago.
Angela	Were they?
Mark	Oh yes. I've seen them in a Toy Museum.
Angela	The chair made from old rubber tyres isn't very beautiful, but it's a practical idea.
Mark	So is the case made of old cardboard drink containers.
Angela	It wouldn't be very strong, but I suppose it would be useful to carry light things.
Mark	I think the best idea is the oil lamp, made from an old glass light bulb.
Angela	Yes, and it's quite attractive, too.
Mark	The shelves made from old wooden fruit boxes are a good idea.
Angela	Yes. Actually, my cousin had some shelves like that in his room when he was a student, and he didn't have much money. I remember them now. They looked quite nice.
Mark	What's this thing made from an old metal drinks can?
Angela	Oh, that's a cheese-grater. You know, in the kitchen, for breaking up cheese to put on your spaghetti. Ugh! I hope it's clean!
Mark	Oh Angela, don't be so fussy!
Angela	The flower pot made from an old metal oil can is a good idea. I've seen those in many countries, but usually people paint them white!
Mark	What about the tray?
Angela	Where?
Mark	The tray over there. It's made of small pieces of newspaper mixed with glue.
Angela	Oh yes, I know how to do that! It's called papier maché. We made some papier maché models in our art classes last year. It's better if you paint it afterwards.
Mark	So you do recycle things, then!
Angela	Of course I do. It's just that this exhibition makes me a bit sad.
Mark	Well, it makes me happy to think how clever people in poorer countries are. They make the things they need.
Angela	Yes 'New from old'.
Mark	What do you like best?
Angela	Hmmm, well, the tray.
Mark	I like the oil lamp best.
Angela	Good. So can we go home now?

Unit 5, Lesson 6

4 SING A SONG.

If I was a great collector,
I could choose from all the things in the world,
These are the things I would put in my garden,
Or have in my room for me to enjoy.

I'd have a pyramid in my garden,
And a big tall statue of Julius Caesar.
I'd have a basketball pitch in my garden,
And a great big lake full of crocodiles.
I'd have a Big Wheel in my garden,
And a telescope to look at the stars.

I'd have a TV in my bedroom,
With all my favourite programmes and films.
I'd have a telephone in my bedroom,
And I'd talk to Julius Caesar every night.
I'd have a picture by Salvador Dali on my wall,
And a robot to do my homework of course.

I'd have tall trees in my garden,
And cats and bats and birds all around.
I'd have an elephant in my garden,
Waiting ready to take me to school.
I'd have Tower Bridge in my garden,
And a boat to take me across the lake.

I'd have my favourite books in my bedroom,
Dracula, Frankenstein and Treasure Island.
I'd have photos of all my friends in my bedroom,
Angela, Count Horror, and Boris the cat!
And a dinosaur in the corner,
A friendly, small, one. He could sleep on my bed!

Mmmmmmm ...

Unit 6, Lesson 1

3 THINK, LISTEN AND WRITE.

Giorgio	Pronto?
Mrs Wine	Oh! Posso parlare con Giorgio Rossi?
Giorgio	Sono io.
Mrs Wine	Oh good! Giorgio? Can we speak English, please! My Italian isn't very good! This is Sally Wine from **Young Ideas**.
Giorgio	Oh! Mrs Wine! Hello! Did you get my article? I sent it by computer mail.
Mrs Wine	Yes, I got it and it's very good! I want to publish it. But there is a problem.
Giorgio	A problem?
Mrs Wine	Yes. Something went wrong with the computer, and there is no punctuation!
Giorgio	Oh no!
Mrs Wine	Well, I have corrected the first paragraph, but I just want to check the punctuation of the second paragraph. Can you dictate it to me, please?
Giorgio	Of course. Just let me find my copy... Here it is. Yes. Are you ready?
Mrs Wine	Yes. I think the second paragraph begins with these words 'My favourite unusual pet ...'
Giorgio	Yes, that's right. Do you want me to begin from there?
Mrs Wine	Yes, please.
Giorgio	OK. New sentence, capital letter. 'My favourite unusual pet from history is the pet that Lord Byron (that's capital L, capital B, of course, then comma) the

153

famous poet (comma) kept when he was studying at the University of Cambridge (Full stop after Cambridge, and capital U for University and for Cambridge.) New sentence. The University (capital U for University, of course) rules said that nobody could keep a cat or a dog (comma after dog) so Lord Byron (capital L and B again!) kept a pet bear instead (Exclamation mark after instead ... new sentence.) I hope you like my cartoon about this (full stop)'

And that's the end of the paragraph and the end of the article. So, did you like it? I have sent the photo of my pet gecko and the cartoon of Lord Byron's bear by express post, so I hope they will arrive soon.

Mrs Wine They have already arrived. So your article is ready for the magazine.

Giorgio That's great! I'm very sorry about the problem with the computer! So, did you like my article, really?

Mrs Wine I loved it. I think your name for your pet lizard is very clever, and the story about Lord Byron is very funny.

Giorgio Great. My English teacher at school told us that story. We study literature, but she also tries to tell us interesting things about the writers. It's much more fun that way!

Mrs Wine Yes. I agree, Well, Giorgio, please write to us again.

Giorgio Of course, I will. I really enjoy **Young Ideas**!

Mrs Wine I'm happy to hear it. So goodbye, Giorgio, and thank you for your help.

Giorgio Don't mention it. I can't wait to see my article in the magazine. Goodbye!

Unit 6, Lesson 2

2 SING A SONG.

I like you and you like me,
We are friends.
We are friends, we are friends,
It's good to have a friend.

5 SAY A RHYME.

My best friend is a dolphin,
I met him in the sea.
He was beautiful, friendly and clever,
And I know that he really liked me.

We played and we swam together,
Happy in the sea.
I thought he was wonderful, friendly and clever,
I was proud that he really liked me.

So this is my holiday photo,
My friend the dolphin and me.
I will go back and find him next year,
I know that he'll remember me!

Unit 6, Lesson 3

2 LISTEN AND FIND OUT.

Presenter Well, hello listeners! Today I'm talking to a very brave little girl, Maureen Smith. All her friends call her 'Maury'. At the moment she is in the Children's Ward of the local hospital. She has a broken arm and cuts on her face and legs, but we hope that she can go home tomorrow. She has some visitors – her mother and brother and father, but she also has two unusual visitors – two dogs (the hospital gave special permission for the dogs to visit!) One dog is her pet Rory, the other is a dog with no name yet. And then there is me – your 'Tell us your story' special reporter, Bernard Glory. So, Maureen what happened to you, and why are these dogs here?

Maureen Well, it's a strange story. My dog Rory is only small – he's a dachshund. I always take him for a walk in the evenings. We were in a street near my house and suddenly I heard another dog barking. Bark, bark, bark. It sounded like a big dog. I was a bit afraid, but we went to see what was happening. There is an empty house in this street. Nobody lives there. I looked through the window. In the kitchen there was this big alsatian dog. He was all alone, and he was very frightened, and he was very thin. I decided to try to rescue him, so I broke the window with my shoe and climbed through it into the house.

Presenter That was a bit silly, wasn't it? The dog could have been dangerous! Why didn't you just go home and tell your parents? They could have telephoned the police or a Dogs' Home.

Maureen Of course, you're right, but I was so worried about the dog that I didn't think properly! I wanted to give him some water. Anyway, he wasn't dangerous. He was just frightened and hungry and thirsty. He wasn't friendly, but he didn't attack me. He was too weak.

Presenter So, what happened then?

Maureen Well, I got into the kitchen and I gave the dog some water. Then I tried to open the front door of the house, but it was locked. Then I tried to get back out of the kitchen window, and then I fell and broke my arm and I cut myself on the glass of the window.

Presenter Ooh. Where was Rory?

Maureen He was waiting for me in the street.

Presenter What happened then?

Maureen Well, the alsatian was barking and Rory was barking. Then suddenly Rory disappeared. He just ran away! I was very frightened.

Presenter But what happened then?

Maureen Ten minutes later, my mother and father arrived with Rory! He ran home and barked and barked, and my parents followed him back to the empty house! They found me in the garden with my broken arm.

Presenter Wow. Rory is a clever dog!

Maureen Yes, he is. Then my parents rang for an ambulance for me, and here I am in hospital. And then they rang the Battersea Dogs' Home for our new friend!

Presenter What about the alsatian? I see (and hear) that he is here to visit you with Rory?

Maureen Well, he is now a guest of the Battersea Dogs' Home – the famous home for lost dogs. But Rory seems to like him. He's huge and Rory is very small, but they are good friends, already.

Presenter Well, Rory saved you and he saved the alsatian too. What will happen to the alsatian?

Maureen Well, I hope my family will adopt him! Rory likes him and he likes Rory. Rory saved him and me and they are good friends already! He has no home of his own. Come on, Mummy and Daddy! He's lovely! He isn't dangerous! He just needs a proper home!

Parents We...ell ...

Presenter Oh, go on! It would be a happy ending! Maury tried to rescue him, and Rory rescued him and Maury! And Bernard Glory is here to report the story. It's a good rhyme, isn't it?

Maureen Yes! They are smiling! They will adopt him! Oh thanks, Mummy and Daddy! I know I was silly! He could have been dangerous, but he wasn't. Can I call him 'FLOORY' because I found him on a kitchen floor? So, then we'll have Rory and Floory. Let's ask the Battersea Home if we can have him!

Presenter Well, I think that silly, brave, Maureen will have a new pet, soon. But my question is: Who abandoned 'Floory'? It was very cruel. What sort of person could have left a dog alone in an empty house with no food or water? Remember listeners, if you find a lost or abandoned animal, it's much better to phone the police or an animal home. Don't break windows like Maureen did, or try to catch the animal or you might find yourself in hospital, too! Well, I hope we'll have a happy ending to the story of Rory and Floory and Maury – and Glory.

Maureen OK. You're all right! I was silly, but it's hard to be careful if you love animals!

Unit 6, Lesson 5

4 LISTEN AND FIND.

Narrator Some stray and abandoned dogs are collected from police stations and brought to the Home in the special, red 'Battersea Dogs' ambulances.
Others are brought in by people who find them.
First they are examined by a vet, and they are given medical treatment if they need it.
All of the dogs are given a bath!
All the time, each dog is watched and looked after by the staff.
Dogs are sold to people who want a new pet.

Unit 6, Lesson 6

2 LISTEN.

Mark What's this, Angela?

Angela It's my board game for the **Young Ideas** magazine. It's called 'The Good Friends Game'.

Mark Hmmm. How do you play it?

Angela Well, here are the rules. I'll read them to you.
1. Everybody starts on Square One. You read the *question* and choose your answer.

Mark Uh-huh. I see.

Angela 2. After Square One you must go to Square Three or Square Seven according to your answer.

Mark OK.

Angela 3. Answer the question on your new square and go to the next square.

Mark Yes, I understand.

Angela 4. Find the next square, read the question and choose another answer.
5. When you get to the end, read the description of you in one of the green boxes A to N.

Mark I see. I could arrive in box **a** or **b** or **c** or **d** or **e** or **f** or **g** or **h** or **i** or **j** or **k** or **l** or **m** or **n**! Then I look at the description in my box and I find out what sort of friend I am! Hmm. Sounds interesting. Is it scientific?

Angela Of course not! But I hope it's fun! Let's try it!

Mark OK, let's try.

Unit 7, Lesson 1

3 LISTEN.

Narrator Here are the star signs and their dates. Which star sign is yours?

ARIES - the RAM - born on or between 21st March and 19th April
TAURUS - the BULL - born on or between 20th April and 20th May

GEMINI - the TWINS - born on or between 21st May and 21st June

CANCER - the CRAB - born on or between 22nd June and 22nd July

LEO - the LION - born on or between 23rd July and 22nd August

VIRGO - the YOUNG GIRL - born on or between 23rd August and 22nd September

LIBRA - the SCALES - born on or between 23rd September and 23rd October

SCORPIO - the SCORPION - born on or between 24th October and 21st November

SAGITTARIUS - ARCHER - born on or between 22nd November and 21st December

CAPRICORN - the GOAT - born on or between 22nd December and 19th January

AQUARIUS - the WATER CARRIER - born on or between 20th January and 18th February

PISCES - the FISHES - born on or between 19th February and 20th March

Unit 7, Lesson 2

3 LISTEN AND FIND.

Mrs Wine Oh, Jim. Can you help me, please? I need some more ideas about superstitions for the magazine.

Jim Certainly, Mrs Wine. I'm an expert on superstitions. Just listen to this!

It's unlucky to open an umbrella inside the house.
It's very unlucky to break a mirror.
It's unlucky to look at the full moon through glass.

If you find a pin and pick it up, that's very lucky.
If you spill the salt, that's very unlucky, but if you pick up some of it and throw it over your left shoulder, everything will be all right.

It's lucky to have a horseshoe in your house.
Many people think that the colour green is unlucky.

Mrs Wine Wow, Jim. What a long list! You don't believe all that, do you?

Jim Of course, I don't. I'm not superstitious, but it's very interesting.

Unit 7, Lesson 3

1 LISTEN AND FIND.

Narrator Welcome to WONDER RADIO again. This programme is about star signs and personalities. Do you believe that your personality is influenced by the date of your birthday? Some people do and some people don't! Just listen and find your star sign! Then decide for yourself!

ARIES – the RAM – born on or between 21st March and 19th April
You have a very strong personality. Your ideas are *your* ideas. Sometimes you are not very polite! But you help people, if you can.

TAURUS – the BULL – born on or between 20th April and 20th May
You have a very strong personality. You love your family, but you often quarrel with your friends. However, you also protect your friends.

GEMINI – the TWINS – born on or between 21st May and 21st June
You are very imaginative and you love to talk and to communicate. You have many friends and you are artistic, but sometimes you change your ideas suddenly. You often surprise people!

CANCER – the CRAB – born on or between 22nd June and 22nd July
You love your home and your family. You are kind, but if someone attacks you, you can be very dangerous! You are a very strong person.

LEO – the LION – born on or between 23rd July and 22nd August
You are brave and strong. You love your family and your friends, and if anyone attacks them you can be very dangerous.

VIRGO – the YOUNG GIRL – born on or between 23rd August and 22nd September
You are sweet and kind. You believe in everybody. You like beautiful things, and you are very tidy and clean.

LIBRA – the SCALES – born on or between 23rd September and 23rd October
You like to make friends. You are very tidy. If people quarrel, you like to help them to be friends again.

SCORPIO – THE SCORPION – born on or between 24th October and 21st November
You are clever and imaginative, but if someone attacks you, you can be very dangerous.

SAGITTARIUS – the ARCHER – born on or between 22nd November and 21st December.
You are often dangerous. You attack people before they attack you! But you are also clever and kind, if you like someone. Your friends are happy when they are with you.

CAPRICORN – the GOAT – born on or between 22nd December and 19th January
You are strong and brave, and you are good to your friends. You can organise things very well, but sometimes you are dangerous!

AQUARIUS – the water CARRIER – born on or between 20th January and 18th February
You like peace. You have many friends. You enjoy discussions. You try to help people. You are kind.

PISCES – the FISHES – born on or between 19th February and 20th March
You are clever, and you think a lot. You use your intelligence. Sometimes you are not very friendly. But you are very nice to your real friends.

Unit 7, Lesson 4

4 LISTEN AND FIND.

Narrator Hello, listeners to WONDER RADIO! This programme is about 'Mysteries and magic'. Do you like mysteries? Many people do. Last week I talked about corn circles in England, but this week I'm going to talk about three more big mysteries that are interesting to many people.

The first is about a huge animal. Some people believe in it and some people don't. If you believe in it, its name is 'Nessie', and it lives in a big lake in Scotland. Many people say that they have seen strange things in that lake, and some people say that they have found footprints on the land. The lake is Loch Ness and the 'official' name of the animal is 'The Loch Ness Monster', but people who believe in it call it 'Nessie' for short. Many people say that they have seen SOMETHING huge swimming in the lake. It has a long neck and a small head, they say. Many people believe in the Lock Ness Monster, but my question is 'Why has nobody ever seen a baby monster or a dead monster?' If there is SOMETHING strange in that lake, surely there is a family of monsters, not just one!

The next mystery is an international one, and not just a British one. It is 'Strange Rain'. Many people, in many countries, all over the world say that they have seen strange things falling from the sky – frogs, fish, nuts, peas, snakes. Well, perhaps the wind picked up frogs or fish from lakes, but how can we explain the other things? It's very strange, isn't it?

Back to Britain. One of the most famous places in Britain is Stonehenge. Thousands of tourists visit it every year. You can see a circle of huge stones. Scientists think that it is thousands of years old. The stone circle is in the middle of England, on Salisbury Plain, but the stones came from hundreds of kilometres away – from the mountains of Wales. Two big questions are: How did our ancestors carry these heavy stones? and WHY? Why did they work so hard to move huge stones to this place? What was the purpose of Stonehenge? We know, that on Midsummer's Day, the light of the sun strikes one of the rocks directly. Was Stonehenge a sort of calendar? Most people don't care. They think it is a beautiful place to visit, but on Midsummer's Day the traffic is terrible. Many people want to see this place. Why?

Well, that's three mysteries. There are many more mysteries in 'Our wonderful world'. Next week I'm going to talk about The Bermuda Triangle. (Why do many ships and aeroplanes disappear there?), the Yeti (Is there a **huge** monkey living in the mountains near Nepal and Mount Everest?) and the reasons why dinosaurs became extinct. They were big and strong, so why are there no dinosaurs in the world today?

Unit 7, Lesson 5

3 LISTEN.

Narrator Many very imaginative people get their best ideas in dreams. Here are the stories of how two famous writers got their ideas for their books. The two books are 'Frankenstein' by Mary Shelley, and 'Dracula' by Bram Stoker.

Frankenstein
Do you remember Frankenstein's monster in the films? Well, the story for these films comes from a famous book. One dark night in 1816, three famous people decided to write horror stories. The people were the poet, Lord Byron, another famous English poet, Shelley, and his wife, Mary. They were on holiday in Switzerland and they were bored. That night, there was a storm and Mary had a dream. The next day she started to write her famous book. It was published two years later in 1818.

Dracula
You all know about Bram Stoker, the author of 'Dracula'. Where did he get the idea? Well, he got it from a dream, a very bad dream, and he had the dream because he had crab for supper! He had indigestion! Not very romantic! He was on holiday in Whitby, when he had the dream, and he decided that Whitby was a good place for part of the story. It's wild and romantic, and it was a perfect place for his story.
Of course, he didn't write the whole story immediately. He spent years reading history books and books of folklore. He wanted all the details to be correct. The book was published in 1897.

Unit 7, Lesson 6

6 SING A SONG.

It's late and I'm sleepy,
It's time to go to bed.
It's a long long time until morning,
But it's time to go to bed.

Dark night, dark night,
I wonder what dreams will come to me?
Nice dreams, funny dreams, bad dreams or
NIGHTMARES?
I wonder what dreams will come to me?

Unit 8, Lesson 2

2 LISTEN.

Mark Oh, Miss Gold. Will you help me, please?

Miss Gold Of course I will, if I can. What's the problem?

Mark Well, I want to write something about exhibitions and museums.

Miss Gold Yes. What's the problem?

Mark Well, my article has a lot of difficult words in it. Can you help me with my

	spelling, please? I want my article to be perfect, but you know I am very bad at spelling!
Miss Gold	Of course. Let me see your article, then.
Mark	Well, I'm writing it on the computer, so let's go to the computer room.
Miss Gold	OK. But I don't know much about computers.
Mark	That's no problem. I am an expert! Ah, Miss Gold, perhaps I can teach **you** something, then. I can teach you about word processing on the computer.
Miss Gold	Fantastic. So I can help you, and you can help me. We can help each other!
Mark	Great. So, let's have a lesson together. First I will show you how to use the word-processing program, then you can help me with my spelling.
Miss Gold	Great. So let's start!

4 LISTEN AND FIND.

Mark	OK. It's very easy. First you switch the computer on, like this:
Miss Gold	OK. What do I do now?
Mark	Now, put your disk into the disk-drive.
Miss Gold	Yes, OK. What now?
Mark	Type the name of the program you need.
Miss Gold	OK, so that's write 'W-R-I-T-E'.
Mark	Good. Now you can see your program is on the screen.
Miss Gold	Yes.
Mark	Now you are ready to start work.
Miss Gold	Great, so next time, I'll know what to do. OK. So now let's look at your article on the screen.
Mark	Right. So I'll just type in its name – MUSEUMS.

6 LISTEN.

Mark	OK, Miss Gold. Here's my article on the screen now. Please help me with my spelling.
Miss Gold	Hmmm .... OK, there are six mistakes. Can you find them?
Mark	No! Help! I know it's not perfect, but I can't find the mistakes!
Miss Gold	OK, let me help you. There are four mistakes with nouns. Look carefully ...
Mark	Ah! Are they 'question', 'answers', 'letters' and 'museums' ...?
Miss Gold	Yes. Now, you need to change those words. Tell me what you think.
Mark	Ah! I know! 'Question' needs a 'u', 'letters' needs two 't's', 'answers' needs a 'w' and I should put the 'e' before the 'u' in 'museum' but I got museum right at the end!
Miss Gold	That's right! Then one of your adjectives is wrong.

Mark	Ah yes! I left out a 't' in 'fantastic'.
Miss Gold	Good, now the other word is a verb.
Mark	Yes, of course. I left out the 'u' in counted. Well thank you very much. I can spell quite well, really, but I am not very good at typing. I hope you liked your computer lesson.
Miss Gold	Yes, I did. But Mark, why didn't you ask the computer to check your spelling? I don't know much about computers, but I know that they can help you with spelling.
Mark	I usually do, but human beings are more fun, and I can learn more from you!

7 LISTEN AND WRITE (DICTATION).

Hello readers (exclamation mark) Time for your **'You tell us'** section again (full stop) Do you remember the question I asked you last time (question mark) Yes (exclamation mark) (quotation marks) What do you think about museums (question mark, end quotation marks) Well (comma) I got a fantastic response (full stop) More than 500 letters (full stop) I got so many answers that I decided to analyse the results (comma) scientifically (full stop) I counted the people who **really like** them (comma) the people who **really hate** them and another important group (comma) the people who said **it depends on the museum** (full stop)

Unit 8, Lesson 3

2 LISTEN AND CHECK.

Mark	Hello.
Paul	Hello? Is that Mark? It's Paul Saxon here!
Mark	Well, hello Paul. How are you?
Paul	I'm fine. And you?
Mark	Great! Listen, Mark, I'd love to meet you. I want to invite you to come and see me. Why don't you come to stay with me and my family in Whitby for a few days?
Mark	That would be super. I'd love to. But we need to think carefully about it. We need to make plans. When and how?
Paul	Yes, when is a problem. It's a very long journey from London, so you will need one day for travelling in each direction. And I want you to spend a weekend, at least. That means travelling on a Friday and perhaps going home on a Monday or a Tuesday.
Mark	So I can't come during the school term. We must wait until the holidays.
Paul	Yes, now how can you get here? It's a complicated journey. You can come by train, but it's very complicated from London, or you could come by train and bus, but that's quite complicated, too.
Mark	Yes, and I don't think my parents will want me to travel alone! I know! My father sometimes goes to York by car for his work.

Perhaps I can ask him if he will bring me there sometime?

Paul Yes, that's a good idea! I'm sure you can find a way to get from York to Whitby. But let's find out more about all the possible ways of getting from London to Whitby. Then we can talk again and make plans.

Mark Great! Thank you very much for the invitation Paul – and thank your parents, too. So let's find out more and then we can talk again, soon.

Paul Fine. So I look forward to hearing from you! Bye.

Mark Great! Bye, Paul. Speak to you soon!

3 LISTEN AND FIND OUT.

A: Hello. This is the 'Can we help you?' Tourist Service in London. How can I help you?

Mark Well, I need to travel from London to Whitby. Have you any suggestions?

A: Hmm. That's a complicated journey. Let me try the computer ... Hmm. Well, you could go by train, but you must change trains twice. You can go from London (King's Cross) to Darlington. Then you must change trains and go to Middlesborough. There, you can get a train to Whitby. It takes about five hours.

Mark Hmm. That sounds complicated. What about going by coach?

A: Let me see ... no. Sorry, you can't go directly there by coach.

Mark How about by train and bus?

A: Hmmm. Yes. That's possible. Go by train to York, and take a bus directly to Whitby. But there is a problem. There are only about three buses from York to Whitby each day! And the bus journey takes about two hours. A better way is to go to York by train, change trains at York and go to Scarborough by train. At Scarborough, you can get a bus from outside the railway station. The buses go every hour. The journey by bus is about one hour.

Mark Phew! It's very complicated, isn't it?

A: Yes. The easiest way is by car. You can go on the motorway from London to York, then there is a lovely drive on an ordinary road over the famous Yorkshire moors. The journey will take you about five or six hours.

Mark Well, thank you. I'm 12 years old, so I can't drive there myself, but I think I will ask my father to take me to York in his car! The other ways sound very complicated and difficult!

6 LISTEN AND FIND.

Susan Hello. Is that Mark Green? It's Susan Jacobs here.

Mark Well, hello Susan! How are you?

Susan I'm fine. And you?

Mark Fine, thanks.

Susan Listen, Mark. I want to invite you to come to Coventry. Why don't you come for a day, and we can see the Transport Museum together?

Mark That would be super. I'd love to.

Susan When can you come?

Mark What about next Tuesday?

Susan Perfect. Take the train from London at 9.10. It arrives at about 11.35. I'll meet you at the station.

Mark Well, see you then.

Susan Great. I look forward to it. Bye.

Mark Bye.

Unit 8, Lesson 4

1 READ, LISTEN AND ANSWER.

Jim Look at all these letters! Some are happy letters, about nice or interesting things, but some are about problems – about things that worry people or make them sad or angry. You know, Mrs Wine, that gives me an idea. Why don't we have a Problem page in the magazine?

Mrs Wine Good idea. What can we call it?

Jim What about 'Problems, problems, problems'?

Mrs Wine No. That's too negative. We need a more positive name.

Jim OK. What about 'Can I help you?'

Mrs Wine Yes, that's perfect. Right, now Jim, you need to write something to explain the new section, and you need to choose some letters for this month.

Jim Yes, well I've got lots of letters about personal problems, but that's a bit negative for the first time. How about these three letters? They are all asking for advice about things to do in readers' towns and cities.

Mrs Wine Yes. Good idea.

Unit 8, Lesson 5

2 THINK AND LISTEN.

Pilar Hello, I'm Pilar from Spain. I think that it's all right to keep some wild animals in captivity, if they have enough space and a good home.

Sarah I'm Sarah from England. My opinion is that it's always cruel to keep wild animals in captivity.

Peter Hello. This is Peter from Hungary. If people see wild animals in a zoo, they learn to love them and then they try to help animals all over the world.

Steven I'm Steven from Scotland. Animals like pandas are in danger. It's a good idea to keep some in captivity, because then we can look after them.

Georgio Hello. This is Georgio from Naples. It's OK to keep animals in captivity, but we mustn't make them do tricks. That's cruel.

Unit 8, Lesson 6

1 LOOK AND LISTEN.

Hello, listeners! We've got some fantastic suggestions for you today about 'things to see and do in Britain'.

Number one: Do you want to be frightened? Well, the London Dungeon is the perfect place. You can see monsters, ghosts, skeletons, all sorts of horrible things. The only problem is, perhaps it's too frightening for your parents! Tell them to wait outside!

Number two: Would you like to walk under the sea and see fantastic sea monsters like sharks and octopuses? Well you can, if you visit the Sea Life Centre in Scarborough.

Number three: Do you think that science is boring? Well, it isn't! Come to the Eureka Museum in Halifax, and do experiments, watch videos and find out more about the wonderful world of science.

Number four: Do you want to have fun! Come and spend a day with us, in our fantastic Theme Park. Alton Towers is the perfect place for an exciting day.

Unit 9, Lesson 1

2 READ AND LISTEN.

Angela Oh Mark. Come and help me with my mini saga.
Mark What's the problem?
Angela Well, I have 57 words instead of 50.
Mark OK, so you need to get rid of seven words. Let me read it. Hmmmm. I know. You could take out this phrase here. You don't need all those adjectives. So take out 'clever and playful'. That's three words.
Angela Yes, and aha! Instead of saying 'friends who are human', I could say 'human friends' so that's another two words. I need to take out two more.
Mark Ah! I know! Look! In the third sentence you could take out the words 'that' and 'really'.
Angela Yes, I'll take out 'that' but I want to keep 'really'. It's an important word.
Mark OK. So one more word to go. Ah! I know! Take out 'that' in the last sentence.
Angela Yes. Great, so that's exactly 50 words. Let's read it through in the new version then.

My best friend is a dolphin. I met him in the sea. He was beautiful and friendly, and I know he really liked me. Of course, I have human friends. Dudley isn't my only friend, but it's wonderful to look into the eyes of an animal and know it understands.

Unit 9, Lesson 2

3 LISTEN AND REPEAT.

Listen to Mark talking about his results. Then listen again, and say each sentence after him.

Mark Well, these are my results. I have 520 answers. 260 people say they like museums. Hmm ... that's exactly half. That's exactly 50 percent. 130 people say IT DEPENDS. That's exactly 25 percent or one quarter. 78 people HATE museums. That's exactly 15 percent. And 10 percent of people gave 'other answers'.

Unit 9, Lesson 3

2 LOOK, SPEAK AND LISTEN.

Narrator Well, did you guess the secret? The two pictures are of the same museum – the Natural History Museum in London, but there is 30 years' difference. The old dinosaur exhibition was very quiet and rather boring, but the modern exhibition is very exciting. It's full of models, pictures, videos, computers, quizzes, and things to do. The children who visit the exhibition these days aren't quiet. In fact, it's a very noisy place, full of laughs and shouts.

4 LISTEN.

Dinosaur footprints are sometimes found. If we look carefully at them, we can find out all sorts of things. For example, how many types of dinosaur made the footprints. We can count the toes and see if they had big claws or not. We can also see if they moved on two legs or four. We can see how fast they were moving. Big deep footprints with long distances between them tell us that the animal was moving fast. Sometimes footprints tell a story, for example, big footprints following small footprints suggest that a meat-eating dinosaur was chasing a smaller one.

The strange dinosaur in picture G is called a Parasaurolophus. The big horn on its head was probably useful, for signalling to its friends. We think that Parasaurolophus lived in big groups, and needed to communicate to others in the group. The horn has a hole down the middle and the hole is connected to the mouth and nose on the inside of its head. We think that Parasaurolophus could blow through this horn and make a sound like a trumpet – like this. That would be very useful for saying 'danger' or 'come here!'

Unit 9, Lesson 5

2 READ AND LISTEN.

This is the true story of three dolphins from England. Their names are Rocky, Missy and Silver. Rocky once lived in a dolphinarium in Morecambe, a seaside town in the North West of England, Missy and Silver lived in a dolphinarium in Brighton, another seaside town, but on the south coast of England.

For nearly 20 years, Rocky did his tricks for the children in Morecambe, and for many years Missy and Silver did the same in Brighton. Then people began to think about the situation. The dolphins weren't happy. There were many problems. So, what happened next?

Rocky became ill. He had problems with his skin, and he stopped eating. Missy and Silver weren't happy either, they didn't want any food either. People realised that it was cruel to keep them in captivity. A big campaign started: 'THESE DOLPHINS MUST GO FREE'. People wrote to the newspapers and protested outside the dolphinaria. They also collected a lot of money to help the dolphins. Finally the two towns decided to close their dolphinaria and to let the dolphins go free. But there were two problems:

The first one was 'Where could they go?'
A solution was found very quickly. There is a wonderful dolphin sanctuary in the Caribbean Sea, where old or ill dolphins are looked after by kind people. The three dolphins could go there.
The second problem was, 'How could the dolphins feed themselves?' After 20 years in captivity, perhaps they would not remember how to catch fish! A solution was found to that problem, too. People at the sanctuary would teach them how to look after themselves in the sea. They were very good teachers, and we know that dolphins are very intelligent. They would soon remember!
So, it was decided that the dolphins could go, but there was another problem:
How could they get there? It is thousands of kilometres from England to the Caribbean. They couldn't swim there. How would they know where to go? Dolphins are very intelligent, yes, but they can't read maps! Their new human friends worried about this problem. Then they found a solution. The dolphins could travel by air!
They were given some medicine to make them sleepy, then very carefully each dolphin was put into a special box full of water, and the boxes were put on to an aeroplane. It was a long flight – many hours – and perhaps the dolphins were frightened in the dark, but when they got there, there were no problems! When Rocky was let out of his box into the warm blue waters of the Caribbean Sea, he gave a loud, happy squeak and started swimming around excitedly, jumping and splashing. In fact, he had no problems learning how to catch his own fish again, and his skin problem got better very soon. Missy and Silver were the same. So now they are free in the sea. They still are friendly to people and sometimes they come back to the shore to say 'hello'. Sometimes they do their old tricks, but the difference is – they are free, and they want to do them. No problems!

4 SPEAK.

Many years a prisoner,
Lots of food but a tiny pool.
Children laughing at my tricks,
I smiled, but I was sad and lonely.
Then one day they put me in a box,
I was frightened in the dark.
We travelled.
Then, splash!

Free in the sea.
Thank you – somebody.

Unit 9, Lesson 6

2 LISTEN.

Miss Gold OK, class, shall we play 'My cat's a clever cat'?
Class Ooh, yes, Miss.
Miss Gold OK. I'll start. My cat's an artistic cat.

My cat's a big cat.
My cat's a clever cat.
My cat's a democratic cat.
My cat's an exciting cat.
My cat's a friendly cat.
My cat's a grey cat.
My cat's a happy cat.
My cat's an interesting cat.
My cat's a jolly cat.
My cat's a kind cat.
My cat's a lovely cat.
My cat's a musical cat.
My cat's a noisy cat.
My cat's an ordinary cat.
My cat's a purple cat.
My cat's a quiet cat.
My cat's a red cat.
My cat's a silly cat.
My cat's a thin cat.
My cat's an unusual cat.
My cat's a violent cat.
My cat's a white cat.
My cat's a xenophobic cat.
My cat's a young cat.
My cat's a Zambian cat.

Voices What?

Yes, you know – a cat from Zambia in Africa.

Unit 10, Lesson 1

5 LISTEN AND ANSWER.

Keith I am a postman. My job is OK, but it isn't perfect. The pay is terrible. Every day I bring letters and parcels to people in my village. I know everybody and I enjoy that. We say 'hello' every day. In the early morning, I work indoors in the Post Office, sorting letters, but for most of the day I am in the street. I like working in the open air. Sometimes the weather is bad, but I have a nice warm uniform. The thing I hate about my job is fierce DOGS!

Frank Well, I think that my job is the nicest in the world. I work in a hospital. I'm not a doctor. I work for the hospital radio. I am a disc-jockey. The pay is terrible, but I love the job! Every day I speak to the patients on the hospital radio. I play records for them and I sing 'Happy Birthday' to people who have a birthday. Everybody knows me. The only thing I don't like is being indoors all day. I like the open air!

Bill For me, the nicest job is to be a newspaper reporter. I hate my job. I am a shop assistant. I sell computers and typewriters. It's a useful job, but it isn't exciting. I like meeting people, but I hate working indoors. The pay is very good, but I want to be a famous reporter – not a bored and useful shop assistant!

Unit 10, Lesson 2

3 LISTEN.

Narrator Mark Green, our special reporter, rang five readers and asked them this question:
'What is your greatest ambition?'
These were the answers:

Paul	My ambition is to have a really good camera. I love taking photos but good cameras are expensive!
Lynne	I have a good voice and I love playing the guitar. My ambition is to have my own pop group and write songs that everybody will listen to.
Stephen	I want to visit Chile one day. I've never been there, but my mother says it's a beautiful country. I have a grandmother and a grandfather living in Santiago, and I want to meet them one day!
Pilar	My hobby is computers. I love computer games, so my ambition is to write a computer program for the most exciting computer game in the world!
Susan	I love sports. My ambition is to be in the school volleyball team next year.

6 SING A SONG.

Some people want to be famous.
Some people want to be rich.
Some people want to climb mountains.
Some people want to be the best, the fastest, the first.

Ambitions, ambitions.
What do you really want to do?
Ambitions, ambitions.
What do you really want to do?

Other people don't want to be famous.
Other people don't want to be rich.
Other people don't want to climb mountains.
Other people don't want to be the best, the fastest, the first.

Ambitions, ambitions.
What do you really want to do?
Ambitions, ambitions.
What do you really want to do?

Other people just want to be happy, with a quiet life, and peace and friends.

Unit 10, Lesson 3

2 LOOK, GUESS AND LISTEN.

Radio presenter Hello. Here we are in the famous Museum of British Road Transport. It is one of the places that thousands of tourists come to see every year in Coventry. Coventry is a very ancient city, and it still has many beautiful old buildings, but a lot of Coventry is modern. There are many factories here, and the Shopping Centre is very modern, and not very beautiful. Many tourists come here every year. One of the things they come to see is the Museum of British Road Transport. Coventry is a good place for this museum, because Coventry is a very important place in the history of cycles and motor vehicles like cars, vans, and buses. There are still many car factories in and around the city.
The story started in the early 19th century. Coventry was already famous then for its industry and its factories. Coventry working people were very clever with their hands. The Midlands of England are very green. The grass is good, and there are many sheep farms. Farmers sent the wool to factories to make cloth. There were many factories in Coventry that made cloth. Then the sewing machine became important, and Coventry had some factories that made sewing machines, because, of course, there is a connection between cloth and sewing! The Singer sewing machine factory was the most famous. It's still a very famous name! But how did transport become important in Coventry? Well, sewing machines have wheels, don't they? And wheels are very important if you want to make cycles or cars! In the 19th century, everybody wanted a cycle. Cycles were a big craze! The first big cycle factories were in France, but cycles were so popular that the French factories could not make enough cycles for everybody. The businessmen in Coventry were very clever. The Singer factory in Coventry changed some of its machines. Now it could make cycles, too, and it could sell cycles. Then other businessmen copied the idea. The Rover cycle factory opened. When cars became important, both the Singer and the Rover factories started to make cars, too. You can't buy a new Singer car now, but there is still a Rover factory in Coventry.

So, if anybody asks you why the car industry started in Coventry, just say 'It's because the sheep in the Midlands of England have very good wool'!

Unit 10, Lesson 4

4 SING A SONG

Imagine a world where everything was different,
What would happen in that world?

If animals could speak they would tell the truth,
Cats would give you their opinions.
A bird would tell you the latest news.
If the air was clean, we could see the stars.

If plants could sing we'd hear beautiful music,
Tulips would whistle, roses would hum.
Grass would sound like a thousand violins,
If the air was clean, we could see the stars.

If everyone was honest, we wouldn't need policemen,
If people could fly they wouldn't need cars.
If everyone was sensible, we wouldn't need soldiers,
If the world was better, we wouldn't have wars.
If the air was clean, we could see the stars.

Unit 10, Lesson 5

1 LISTEN.

Paul Hello, Paul Saxon speaking.

Mark Paul! It's Mark Green, here!

Paul Hello. Have you any news about your visit?

Mark Yes. It's good news. It's the school holidays next week, so I am free. Are you?

Paul Yes, I am.

Mark My Dad has an appointment for business in Middlesborough next week, and he says I can come with him in the car, next Thursday. I can take a train from Middlesborough in the afternoon and get to Whitby on Thursday evening. We can spend Friday visiting Whitby, and then my dad will pick me up in Whitby on Saturday morning.

Paul That's perfect. You can stay at my house, of course. What train will you get on Thursday?

Mark Well, I think I can get the 5 o'clock train from Middlesborough. That arrives in Whitby at about 5.45.

Paul Perfect. I will be there at the station. Ring me up if there is any problem. Wear some good shoes because you will have to walk a lot, but I am sure we will have a good time. Tell me what you want to see.

Mark Everything.

Paul Fine. I will work out a good route. I am very proud of my town and I want you to enjoy it!

Mark Oh Paul, I want to buy some things, too. Can you find out about the right shops?

Paul Of course. What do you want to buy?

Mark Well, I know Whitby is famous for fossils and for jet. Can you suggest some good shops for that?

Paul Of course. Fossils are very cheap in our shops, but jet is a bit expensive.

Mark That's OK. I want to buy some jet jewellery for my mother. It's for her birthday.

Paul Well, I'm sure we can find something nice.

Mark Great. I look forward to meeting you then.

Paul OK. See you next Thursday evening! Bye.

Mark Bye.

3 LISTEN AND FIND.

Paul Well, Mark, I hope you are ready for our long walk!

Mark Absolutely!

Paul Great! Well, I've planned the day, so let's get going! We'd better start now.
Well, you remember the station. It's very old

and quite beautiful. In the Dracula story, Count Dracula travelled to London from this station, in a big box of earth from Transylvania.

Mark Ugh!

Paul Of course, you can't travel directly from Whitby to London these days!

Mark Yes, I know. What a pity!

Paul Now, here we are at the port.

Mark What super boats!

Paul Yes, Whitby is still very famous for boat building and for fishing ...
Now, this is the bridge across the River Esk. It opens when a big boat needs to go from the river to the sea. We'll go across it later, but not now.
This is the famous Dracula Experience exhibition. I'm sorry, but it is closed at the moment. It's only open in the summer, but it's very interesting and frightening!
Now we must go up the hill. Here is the statue of Captain Cook, the famous explorer.

Mark And what is this arch?

Paul It's made of the jaws of a whale. Whitby was very famous in the last century for whale-hunting.

Mark Ugh! I don't like whale hunting. It's very cruel.

Paul I know, but we don't hunt whales these days. Look at the view through the arch. You can see St Mary's church and the churchyard, and near it the ruins of the Abbey. They are very important in the Dracula story. Dracula loved the old churchyard!

Mark Can we go there?

Paul Of course, but first we must go down the hill again, across the bridge and into the old town. Come on ...
Here we are on the bridge, now we can visit the Victorian Museum and some of the shops.

Mark The Victorian museum was very interesting.

Paul Yes. It gives you a good idea of the life here 100 years ago. Most people lived by fishing.

Mark People were very poor, weren't they?

Paul Yes. Life was difficult. Now we have tourists to help our economy.

Mark That was a great shop!

Paul Yes, it was very interesting. I'm sure your mother will love the jet bracelet you bought.

Mark And my ammonite will look very good in my fossil collection.

Paul How about some lunch? This fish and chip shop is one of the best in town.

Mark Great! I love fish and chips. People say that British food is terrible, but I don't agree. Fish and chips is simple, but it's cheap and delicious! Yes ... let's go ...

Paul Now are you ready for some exercise, after lunch?

Mark Yes.

Paul Good because now we are going to see the old church and the abbey. We have to go up 199 steps to get there.

Mark 197, 198 ... wow 199 steps!

Paul Here we are. Count Dracula loved this place.

Mark Yes, I can see why.

Paul Now down the steps and across the bridge again to see my two favourite places. The first is the Frank Meadow Sutcliffe photo gallery... And here we are.

Mark Yes. I remember. You are very interested in photography.

Paul Yes. Look at all these wonderful photos. Many of them are more than 100 years old, but they are fantastic! When I grow up, I want to be a photographer, like Sutcliffe.

Mark Well, that's a big ambition. He was brilliant!

Paul The last place on our tour is the museum. It's not a very modern museum, but it has some fantastic things in it.

Mark Wow. Look at those fossils!

Paul Yes, it's full of fossils, and jet, and information about our fishing history.

Mark I prefer old-fashioned museums. This is super!

Paul And now our last stop. Home for dinner! Come on!

Mark Paul, that was a fantastic day. Thank you so much. I've wanted to see Whitby for a long time and now I have!

Paul Don't mention it. I love showing people my town. It's small, but it has so many important connections with art and history. I'm very proud of it.

Unit 10, Lesson 6

6 SING A SONG.

Well, it's goodbye for now from Mark and Angela, Mrs Wine and Jim and all the special reporters for **Young Ideas**. Let's sing a goodbye song!

Goodbye, goodbye, have a happy time!
Goodbye, goodbye, have a happy time!

Goodbye from Mark, Angela, Mrs Wine, Miss Gold and Jim!

We'll see you again in the sun or the rain,
But for now from us, it's goodbye!